The Everett Massacre

A Da Capo Press Reprint Series

CIVIL LIBERTIES IN AMERICAN HISTORY

GENERAL EDITOR: LEONARD W. LEVY

Claremont Graduate School

The Everett Massacre

A History of the Class Struggle in the Lumber Industry

By Walker C. Smith

DA CAPO PRESS • NEW YORK • 1971

A Da Capo Press Reprint Edition

This Da Capo Press edition of
The Everett Massacre
is an unabridged republication of the
first edition published in Chicago *c.* 1920.

Library of Congress Catalog Card Number 72-151619
SBN 306-70150-2

Published by Da Capo Press, Inc.
A Subsidiary of Plenum Publishing Corporation
227 West 17th Street, New York, N.Y. 10011

Manufactured in the United States of America

The Everett Massacre

The Everett Massacre

By Walker C. Smith

A History of the Class Struggle in the Lumber Industry

I. W. W. Publishing Bureau
Chicago, Ill.

THIS book is dedicated to those loyal soldiers of the great class war who were murdered on the steamer Verona at Everett, Washington, in the struggle for free speech and free assembly and the right to organize:

FELIX BARAN,
HUGO GERLOT,
GUSTAV JOHNSON,
JOHN LOONEY,
ABRAHAM RABINOWITZ,

and those unknown martyrs whose bodies were swept out to unmarked ocean graves on Sunday, November Fifth, 1916.

PRINTED BY THE
MEMBERS OF THE
GENERAL RECRUITING
UNION I. W. W.

PREFACE

In ten minutes of seething, roaring hell at the Everett dock on the afternoon of Sunday, November 5, 1916, there was more of the age-old superstition regarding the indentity of interests between capital and labor torn from the minds of the working people of the Pacific Northwest than could have been cleared away by a thousand lecturers in a year. It is with regret that we view the untimely passing of the seven or more Fellow Workers who were foully murdered on that fateful day, but if the working class of the world can view beyond their mangled forms the hideous brutality that was the cause of their deaths, they will not have died in vain.

This book is published with the hope that the tragedy at Everett may serve to set before the working class so clear a view of capitalism in all its ruthless greed that another such affair will be impossible.

C. E. PAYNE.

With grateful acknowledgments to C. E. Payne for valuable
assistance in preparing the subject matter, to Harry
Feinberg in consultation, to Marie B. Smith
in revising manuscript, and to J. J.
Kneisle for photographs.

EVERETT, NOVEMBER FIFTH

By Charles Ashleigh

["* * * and then the Fellow Worker died, singing 'Hold the Fort' * * *"—From the report of a witness.]

Song on his lips, he came;
  Song on his lips, he went;—
This be the token we bear of him,—
  Soldier of Discontent!

Out of the dark they came; out of the night
  Of poverty and injury and woe,—
With flaming hope, their vision thrilled to light,—
  Song on their lips, and every heart aglow;

They came, that none should trample Labor's right
  To speak, and voice her centuries of pain.
Bare hands against the master's armored might!—
  A dream to match the tools of sordid gain!

And then the decks went red; and the grey sea
  Was written crimsonly with ebbing life.
The barricade spewed shots and mockery
  And curses, and the drunken lust of strife.

Yet, the mad chorus from that devil's host,—
  Yea, all the tumult of that butcher throng,—
Compound of bullets, booze and coward boast,—
  Could not out-shriek one dying worker's song!

Song on his lips, he came;
  Song on his lips, he went;—
This be the token we bear of him,—
  Soldier of Discontent!

Released Free Speech prisoners who visited the graves of their murdered Fellow Workers at Mount Pleasant Cemetery, May 12, 1917.

The Everett Massacre

CHAPTER I.

THE LUMBER KINGDOM

Perhaps the real history of the rise of the lumber industry in the Pacific Northwest will never be written. It will not be set down in these pages. A fragment—vividly illustrative of the whole, yet only a fragment—is all that is reproduced herein. But if that true history be written, it will tell no tales of "self-made men" who toiled in the woods and mills amid poverty and privation and finally rose to fame and affluence by their own unaided effort. No Abraham Lincoln will be there to brighten its tarnished pages. The story is a more sordid one and it has to do with the theft of public lands; with the bribery and corruption of public officials; with the destruction and "sabotage," if the term may be so misused, of the property of competitors; with base treachery and double-dealing among associated employers; and with extortion and coercion of the actual workers in the lumber industry by any and every means from the "robbersary" company stores to the commission of deliberate murder.

No sooner had the larger battles among the lumber barons ended in the birth of the lumber trust than there arose a still greater contest for control of the industry. Lumberjack engaged lumber baron in a struggle for industrial supremacy; on the part of the former a semi-blind groping toward the light of freedom and for the latter a conscious striving to retain a seat of privilege. Nor can the full history of that struggle be written here, for the end is not yet, but no one who has read the past rightly can doubt the ultimate outcome. That history, when finally written, will recite tales of heroism and deeds of daring and unassuming acts of bravery on the part of obscure toilers beside which the vaunted prowess of famous men will seem tawdry by comparison. Today the perspective is lacking. Time alone will vindicate the rebellious workers in their fight for freedom. From all this travail and pain is to be born an Industrial Democracy.

The lumber industry dominated the whole life of the Northwest. The lumber trust had absolute sway in entire sections of the country and held the balance of power in many other places. It controlled Governors, Legislatures and Courts; directed Mayors and City Councils; completely owned Sheriffs and Deputies; and thru threats of foreclosure, blackmail, the blacklist and the use of armed force it dominated the press and pulpit and terrorized many other elements in each community. The sworn testimony in the greatest case in labor history bears out these statements. Out of their own mouths were the lumber barons and their tools condemned. For, let it be known, the great trial in Seattle, Wash., in the year 1917, was not a trial of Thomas H. Tracy and his co-defendants. It was a trial of the lumber trust, a trial of so-called "law and order," a trial of the existing method of production and exchange and the social relations that spring from it,—and the verdict was that Capitalism is guilty of Murder in the First Degree.

To get even a glimpse into the deeper meaning of the case that developed from the conflict at Everett, Wash., it is necessary to know something of the lives of the migratory workers, something of the vital necessity of free speech to the working class and to all society for that matter, and also something about the basis of the lumber industry and the foundation of the city of Everett. The first two items very completely reveal themselves thru the medium of the testimony given by the witnesses for the defense, while the other matters are covered briefly here.

The plundering of public lands was a part of the policy of the lumber trust. Large holdings were gathered together thru colonization schemes, whereby tracts of 160 acres were homesteaded by individuals with money furnished by the lumber operators. Often this meant the mere loaning of the individual's name, and in many instances the building of a home was nothing more than the nailing together of three planks. Other rich timber lands were taken up as mineral claims altho no trace of valuable ore existed within their confines. All this timber fell into the hands of the lumber trust. In addition to this there were large companies who logged for years on forty acre strips. This theft of timber on either side of a small holding is the basis of many a fortune and the possessors of this stolen wealth can be distinguished today by their extra loud cries for "law and order" when their employes in the woods and mills go on strike to add a few more pennies a day to their beggarly pittance.

Altho cheaper than outright purchase from actual settlers, these methods of timber theft proved themselves quite costly and the public outcry they occasioned was not to the liking of the lumber barons. To facilitate the work of the lumber trust and at the same time placate the public, nothing better than the Forest Reserve could possibly have been devised. The establishment of the National Forest Reserves was one of the long steps taken in the United States in monopolizing both the land and the timber of the country.

The first forest reserves were established February 22, 1898, when 22,000,000 acres were set aside as National Forests. Within the next eight years practically all the public forest lands in the United States that were of any considerable extent had been set off into these reserves, and by 1913 there had been over 291,000 square miles included within their confines. (*) This immense tract of country was withdrawn from the possibility of homestead entry at approximately the time that the Mississippi Valley and the eastern slope of the Rocky Mountains had been settled and brought under private ownership. Whether the purpose was to put the small sawmills out of business can not be definitely stated, but the lumber trust has profited largely from the establishment of the forest reserves.

So long as there was in the United States a large and open frontier to be had for the taking there could be no very prolonged struggle against an owning class. It has been easier for those having nothing to go but a little further and acquire property for themselves. But on coming to what had been the frontier and finding a forest reserve with range riders and guards on its boundaries to prevent trespassing; on looking back and seeing all land and opportunities taken; on turning again to the forest reserve and finding a foreman of the lumber trust within its borders offering wages in lieu of a home, it was inevitable that a conflict should occur.

With the capitalistic system of industry in operation, the conflict between the landless homeseekers and the owners of the vast accumulations of capital would inevitably have taken place, but this clash has come at least a generation earlier because of the establishment of the National Forests than it otherwise would. The land now in reserves would furnish homes and comfortable livings for ten million people, and have absorbed the surplus population for another generation. It is also true that the establishment of the National Forests has been one of the

---

(*) Data on Forest Reserve taken from 1911 Encyclopedia Britannica articles by Gifford Pinchot.

vital factors that made the continued existence of the lumber trust possible.

Prior to 1895 the shipments of lumber to the prairie states from west of the Rocky Mountains were very small, and of no effect on the domination of the lumber industry by the trust. Also, prior to that date but a small part of the valuable timber west of the Rocky Mountains had been brought under private ownership. But about this time the pioneer settlers began swarming over the Pacific Slope and taking the free government land as homesteads. As the timber land was taken up, floods of lumber from the Pacific Coast met the lumber of the trust on the great prairies. The lumber trust had looted the government land and the Indian reservations in the middle states of their timber, and had almost full control of the prairie markets until the lumber of the Pacific Slope began to arrive. In 1896 lumber from the Puget Sound was sold in Dakota for $16.00 per thousand feet, and it kept coming in a constantly increasing volume and of a better quality than the trust was shipping from the East. It was but natural that the trust should seek a means to stifle the constantly increasing competition from the homesteads of the West, and the means was found in the establishment of the National Forest Reserves.

While the greater portion of North America was yet a wilderness, the giving of vast tracts of valuable land on the remote frontier to private individuals and companies could be accomplished. But at this time such a procedure would have been impossible, tho it was imperative for the life of the trust that the timber of the Pacific Slope should be withdrawn from the possibility of homestead entry. In order to carry out this scheme it was necessary to raise a cry of "Benefit to the Public" and make it appear that this new public policy was in the interest of future generations. The cry was raised that the public domain was being used for private gain, that the timber was being wastefully handled, that unnecessary amounts were being cut, that the future generations would find themselves without timber, that the watersheds were being denuded and that drought and floods would be the certain result, that the nation should receive a return for the timber that was taken, together with many other specious pleas.

That the public domain was being used for private gain was in some instances true, but the vast majority of the timber land was being taken as homesteads, and thus taking the timber outside the control of the trust. That the timber was being wastefully handled was to some extent true, but this was inevitable in the development of a new industry in a new country, and so far as the Pacific Slope is concerned there is but little change from the methods of twenty years ago. That unnecessary amounts were being cut was sometimes true, but this served only to keep prices down, and from the standpoint of the trust was unpardonable on that account alone. The market is being supplied now as formerly, and with as much as it will take. The only means that has been used to restrict the amount cut has been to raise the price to about double what it was in 1896. The denuding of the watersheds of the continent goes on today the same as it did twenty-five years ago, the only consideration being whether there is a market for the timber. Some reforesting has been done, and some protection has been established for the prevention of fires, but these things have been much in the nature of an advertisement since the government has taken charge of the forests, and was done automatically by the homesteaders before the Reserves were established. There has never been any restriction in the amount of timber that any company could buy, and the more it wanted, the better chance it had of getting it. The nation is receiving some return from the sale of timber from the government land, but it is in the nature of a division of the spoils from a raid on the homes of the landless.

When the Reserve were established, the Secretary of the Interior was empowered to "make rules and regulations for the occupancy and the use of the forests and preserve them from destruction." No attempt was made in the General Land Office to develop a technical forestry service. The purpose of the administration was mainly protection against trespass and fire. The methods of the administration were to see to it first that there were no trespassers. Fire protection came later. When the Reserves were established, people who were at the time living within their boundaries were compelled to submit the titles of their homesteads to the most rigid scrutiny, and many people who had complied with the spirit of the law were dispossessed on mere technicalities, while before the establishment of the Reserve system the spirit of the compliance with the homestead law was mainly considered, and very seldom the technicality. And while the Forestry Service was examining all titles to homesteads within the boundaries of the Reserve with the utmost care, the large lumbering companies were given the best of consideration, and were allowed all the timber they requested and a practically unlimited time to remove it.

The system of dealing with the lumber trust has been most liberal on the part of the government. A company wanting several million feet of timber makes a request to the district office to have the timber of a certain amount and on a certain tract offered for sale. The Forestry Service makes an estimate of the minimum value of the timber as it stands in the tree and the amount of timber requested within that tract is then offered for sale at a given time, the bids to be sent in by mail and accompanied by certified checks. The bids must be at least as large as the minimum price set by the Forestry Service, and highest bidder is awarded the timber, on condition that he satisfies the Forestry Service that he is responsible and will conduct the logging according to rules and regulations. The system seems fair, and open to all, until the conditions are known.

But among the large lumber companies there has never been any real competition for the possession of any certain tract of timber that was listed for sale by request. When one company has decided on asking for the allotment of any certain tract of timber, other companies operating within that forest seldom make bids on that tract. Any small company that is doing business in opposition to the trust companies, and may desire to bid on an advertised tract, even tho its bid may be greater than the bid of the trust company, will find its offer thrown out as being "not according to the Government specifications," or the company is "not financially responsible," or some other suave explanation for refusing to award the tract to the competing company. On the other hand, when a small company requests that some certain tract shall be listed for sale, it very frequently happens that one of the large companies that is commonly understood to be affiliated with the lumber trust will have a bid in for that tract that is slightly above that of the non-trust company, and the timber is solemnly awarded to "the highest bidder."

When a company is awarded a tract of timber, the payment that is required is ten per cent of the purchase price at the time of making the award, and the balance is to be paid when the logs are on the landing, or practically when they can be turned into ready cash, thus requiring but a comparatively small outlay of money to obtain the timber. When the award is made, it is the policy of the Forestry Service to be on friendly terms with the customers, and the men who scale the logs and supervise the cutting are the ones who come into direct contact with the companies, and it is inevitable that to be on good terms with the foreman the supervision and scaling must be "satisfactory." Forestry Service men who have not been congenial with the foremen of the logging companies have been transferred to other places, and it is almost axiomatic that three transfers is the same as a discharge. The little work that is required of the companies in preventing fires is much more than offset by the fact that no homesteaders have small holdings within the area of their operations, either to interfere with logging or to compete with their small mills for the control of the lumber market.

That the forest lands of the nation were being denuded, and that this would cause droughts and floods was a fact before the establishment of the Reserves, and the fact is still true. Where a logging company operates, the rule is that it shall take all the timber on the tract where it works, and then the forest guards are to burn the brush and refuse. A cleaner sweep of the timber could not have been made under the old methods. The only difference in methods is that where the forest guards now do the fire protecting for the lumber trust, the homesteaders formerly did it for their own protection. In January, 1914, the Forestry Service issued a statement that the policy of the Service for the Kaniksu Forest in Northern Idaho and Northeastern Washington would be to have all that particular reserve logged off and then have the land thrown open to settlement as homesteads. As the timber in that part of the country will but little more than pay for the work of clearing the land ready for the plow, but is very profitable where no clearing is required, it can be readily seen that the Forestry Service was being used as a means of dividing the fruit—the apples to the lumber trust, the cores to the landless homeseekers.

One particular manner in which the Government protects the large lumber companies is in the insurance against fire loss. When a tract has been awarded to a bidder it is understood that he shall have all the timber allotted to him, and that he shall stand no loss by fire. Should a tract of timber be burned before it can be logged, the government allots to the bidder another tract of timber "of equal value and of equal accessibility," or an adjustment is made according to the ease of logging and value of the timber. In this way the company has no expense for insurance to bear, which even now with the fire protection that is given by the Forestry Service is rated by insurance companies at about ten per cent. of the value of the timber for each year.

No taxes or interest are required on the timber

that is purchased from the government. Another feature that makes this timber cheaper than that of private holdings, is that to buy outright would entail the expense of the first cost of the land and timber, the protection from fire, the taxes and the interest on the investment. In addition to this there is always the possibility that some homesteader would refuse to sell some valuable tract that was in a vital situation, as holding the key to a large tract of timber that had no other outlet than across that tract. There has been as yet no dispute with the government about an outlet for any timber purchased on the Reserves; the contract for the timber always including the proviso that the logging company shall have the right to make and use such roads as are "necessary," and the company is the judge of what is necessary in that line.

The counties in which Reserves are situated receive no taxes from the government timber, or from the timber that is cut from the Reserves until it is cut into lumber, but in lieu of this they receive a sop in the form of "aid" in the construction of roads. In the aggregate this aid looks large, but when compared with the amount of road work that the people who could make their homes within what is now the Forest Reserves could do, it is pitifully small and very much in the nature of the "charity" that is handed out to the poor of the cities. It is the inevitable result of a system of government that finds itself compelled to keep watch and ward over its imbecile children.

So in devious ways of fraud, graft, coercion, and outright theft, the bulk of the timber of the Northwest has been acquired by the lumber trust at an average cost of less than twelve cents a thousand feet. In the states of Washington and Oregon alone, the Northern Pacific and the Southern Pacific railways, as allies of the Weyerhouser interests of St. Paul, own nearly nine million acres of timber; the Weyerhouser group by itself dominating altogether more than thirty million acres, or an area almost equal to that of the state of Wisconsin. The timber owned by a relatively small group of individuals is sufficient to yield enough lumber to build a six-room house for every one of the twenty million families in the United States.

Why then should conservation, or the threat of it, disturb the serenity of the lumber trust? If the government permits the cutting of public timber it increases the value of the trust holdings in multiplied ratio, and if the government withdraws from public entry any portion of the public lands, creating Forest Reserves, it adds marvelously to the value of the trust logs in the water booms. Even forest fires in one portion of these vast holdings serve but to send skyward the values in the remaining parts, and by some strange freak of nature the timber of trust competitors, like the "independent" and co-operative mills, seems to be more inflammable than that of the "law-abiding" lumber trust. And so it happens that the government's forest policy has added fabulous wealth and prestige and power to the rulers of the lumber kingdom.

But whether the timber lands were stolen illegally or acquired by methods entirely within the law of the land, the exploitation of labor was, and is, none the less severe. The withholding from Labor of any portion of its product in the form of profits—unpaid wages—and the private ownership by individuals or small groups of persons, of timber lands and other forms of property necessary to society as a whole, are principles utterly indefensible by any argument save that of force. Such legally ordained robbery can be upheld only by armies, navies, militia, sheriffs and deputies, police and detectives, private gunmen, and illegal mobs formed of, or created by, the propertied classes. Alike in the stolen timber, the legally acquired timber, and in the Government Forest Reserves, the propertyless lumberjacks are unmercifully exploited, and any difference in the degree of exploitation does not arise because of the "humanity" of any certain set of employers but simply because the cutting of timber in large quantities brings about a greater productivity from each worker, generally accompanied with a decrease in wages due to the displacement of men.

With the development of large scale logging operations there naturally came a development of machinery in the industry. The use of water power, the horse, and sometimes the ox, gave way to the use of the donkey engine. This grew from a crudc affair, resembling an over-sized coffee mill, to a machine with a hauling power equal to that of a small sized locomotive. Later on came "high lead" logging and the Flying Machine, besides which the wonderful exploits of "Paul Bunyan's old blue ox" are as nothing.

The overhead system was created as a result of the additional cost of hauling when the increased demand for a larger output of logs forced the erection of more and more camps, each new camp being further removed from the cities and towns. Today its use is almost universal as there remains no timber close to the large cities, even the stumps having been removed to make room for farming operations.

Roughly the method of operation is to leave a straight tall tree standing near the logging track in felling timber. The machine proper is set right at the base of this tree, and about ninety feet up its trunk a large chain is wrapped to allow the hanging of a block. From this spar tree a cable, two inches in diameter, is stretched to another tree some distance in the woods. On this cable is placed what is known as a bicycle or trolley. Various other lines run back and forth thru this trolley to the engine. At the end of one of these lines an enormous pair of hooks is suspended. These grasp the timber and convey it to the cars.

The Flying Machine as now used in Western logging.

Ten to twenty thousand feet of logs a day was the output of the old bull or horse teams. The donkey engine brought it to a point where from seventy-five to one hundred thousand could be turned out, and the steam skidder doubled the output of the donkey. Ordinarily the crew for one donkey engine consists of from thirteen to fifteen men, sometimes even as high as twenty-five, but this number is reduced to nine or even lower with the introduction of the steam skidder. Loggers claim that the high lead system kills and maims more men than the methods formerly in vogue, but be that as it may, the fact stands out quite plainly that as compared with a line horse donkey, operated with a crew of twenty-five men, the flying machine will produce enough lumber to mean the displacement of one hundred men.

At the same time the sawmills of the old type have disappeared with their rotary or circular saws, dead rollers, and obsolete methods of handling lumber, and in their place is the modern mill with its band saw, shot-gun feed, steam nigger, live rollers, and resaw. Nor do the mills longer turn out rough lumber to be re-handled by trained specialists and highly skilled carpenters with large and costly kits of intricate hand tools. Relatively unskilled workers send forth the finished products, window sashes, doors, siding, etc., carpenters armed only with square, hammer and saw, and classed with unskilled labor, put these in place, and a complete house can be ordered by parcel post.

As is usual with the introduction of new machinery and methods where the workers are not in control, the actual producers find that all these innovations force them to work at a higher rate of speed under more hazardous conditions for a lower rate of pay. It is true of all industry in the main, particularly true of the lumber industry, and the mills of Everett and camps of Snohomish county have no exceptions to test this rule.

The story of Everett has no hint of romance. Some time in the late seventies the representatives of John D. Rockefeller gained possession of a tract of land in Western Washington, on Puget Sound, about thirty miles north of Seattle. The land was heavily timbered and water facilities made it a perfect site for mill and shipping purposes. The Everett Land Company was organized, the tract was plotted, and the city of Everett laid out. The leading streets, Rockefeller, Colby, Hoyt, etc., were named for these early promoters. Hewitt Avenue was given the name of a man who is today recognized as the leading capitalist of the state of Washington. Even the building of those streets reflected no credit upon the city. The work was done by what amounted to convict labor. Unemployed workers, even tho they were plentifully supplied with money, were arrested and without being allowed the alternative of a fine were set to work clearing, grading, planking and, later on, paving the streets. Perhaps it is too much to expect freedom of speech to be allowed on slave-built streets.

In their articles of incorporation the promoters reserved to themselves all right to the ownership and control of public utilities, such as water, light and power and street railway systems. A mortgage of $1,500,000 was placed upon the property. After a time the company failed, the mortgage was foreclosed and the property purchased by Rucker Brothers. The Everett Improvement Company was then organized with J. T. McChesney as president. It held all rights to dispose of public utility franchises. The firm of Stone & Webster, the construction, light, heat, power and traction trust, secured franchises granting them the right to furnish light and power for the city of Everett and also to operate the street railway system for 99 years. The Everett Improvement Company owns a dock lying to the south of the municipally owned City Dock where the Everett tragedy was staged. Thru its alliances the shipping of Everett is in the hands of the same group of capitalists that control all other public utilities. The waterworks was sold to the city but has remained in the hands of the same officials who were in charge when its title was a private one. Everett operates under the commission form of government.

The American National Bank was organized with McChesney as president. The only other bank of importance in Everett was the First National. These two institutions consolidated with Wm. C. Butler as president and McChesney as one of the directors. The Everett Savings and Trust Company was later organized, with the same stockholders and under the same management as the First National Bank. The control of every public service corporation in Everett is directly in the hands of these two banks, and, indirectly, thru loans to industrial corporations, they control both the lumber and the shingle mills of Snohomish County in which Everett is situated.

Everett, the "City of Smokestacks," as its promoters have named it, is an industrial community of approximately 35,000 people. Its main activities are the production of lumber and shingles, and shipping. The practically undiversified nature of its economic life binds all those engaged in the employment of labor into a common body. The owners of the lumber and shingle mills, the owners and officials of the banks where the lumber men do business, the lawyers representing the mills and the banks, the employers engaged in shipping lumber and supplies for the lumber industry, their lawyers and their bank connections, the owners of hardware stores that supply equipment for the mills and allied industries, all are united by common ties and common interests and they all support one policy. Not only are they banded together against the wage workers but they also oppose the entrance of any kind of business that will in any way menace their rule. They arose almost as one in opposition to the entrance of the ship building industry into Everett, despite the fact that it would add measurably to the general prosperity of the city, and with a full knowledge that their harbor offered wonderful natural facilities for that line of endeavor. In the face of an action that threatened their autocratic power their alleged "patriotism" vanished.

In 1912 the Everett Commercial Club was organized. In the month of December, 1915, following a visit from a San Francisco representative of the Merchants and Manufacturers' Association, it was re-organized on the Bureau plan as a stock concern. Stock memberships were issued to employers and business houses and were subsequently distributed among the employers and their employes. Memberships were doled out to persons who would be subservient to the wishes of the small group of capitalists representing the great corporate interests. W. W. Blain, secretary of the Commercial Club, testified, under oath, that the Everett Improvement Company took 25 memberships, the First National Bank took 10, the Weyerhouser Lumber Company 10, the Clough-Hartley Mill Company 5, the Jamison Mill Company 5, and other mills and allied industries also purchased memberships in bulk. Organized labor, however, had no representation at the Commercial Club.

There is nothing in the history of Everett to suggest the usual spontaneous outgrowth of the honest endeavors of hardy pioneer settlers. From the first day the Rockefeller interests set foot in the virgin forests of Snohomish County up to the present time, the spirit of democracy has been crushed by the greed and cupidity of this small and powerful group.

The struggle at Everett was but one of the inevitable phases of the larger struggle that takes place when a class or group that has no property comes in contact with those who have monopolized the earth and its resources. It was no new, marvelous, isolated case of violence. It was the normal accompaniment of industry based upon the exploitation of wage workers, and was of one piece with the outbreak on the Mesaba Range, in Bayonne, Ludlow, Paint Creek, Paterson, Lawrence, San Diego, Fresno, Spokane, Homestead and in countless other places. All these apparently disconnected and sporadic uprisings of labor and the accompanying capitalist violence are joined together in a whole that spells wage slavery. As one of the manifestations of the class conflict, the Everett tragedy cannot be considered apart from that age-long and world-wide struggle between the takers of profits and the makers of values.

CHAPTER II.

CLASS WAR SKIRMISHES

"Shingle-weaving is not a trade; it is a battle. For ten hours a day the sawyer faces two teethed steel discs whirling around two hundred times a minute. To the one on the left he feeds heavy blocks of cedar, reaching over with his left hand to remove the rough shingles it rips off. He does not, he cannot stop to see what his left hand is doing. His eyes are too busy examining the shingles for knot holes to be cut out by the second saw whirling in front of him.

"The saw on his left sets the pace. If the singing blade rips fifty rough shingles off the block every minute, the sawyer must reach over to its teeth fifty times in sixty seconds; if the automatic carriage feeds the odorous wood sixty times into the hungry teeth, sixty times he must reach over, turn the shingle, trim its edge on the gleaming saw in front of him, cut out the narrow strip containing the knot hole with two quick movements of his right hand and toss the completed board down the chute to the packers, meanwhile keeping eyes and ears open for the sound that asks him to feed a new block into the untiring teeth. Hour after hour the shingle weaver's hands and arms, plain, unarmored flesh and blood, are staked against the screeching steel that cares not what it severs. Hour after hour the steel sings its crescendo note as it bites into the wood, the sawdust cloud thickens, the wet sponge under the sawyer's nose fills with fine particles. If 'cedar asthma,' the shingle weaver's occupational disease, does not get him, the steel will. Sooner or later he reaches over a little too far, the whirling blade tosses drops of deep red into the air, and a finger, a hand or part of an arm comes sliding down the slick chute."(*)

This description of shingle weaving was given by Walter V. Woehlke, managing editor of the Sunset Magazine, in an article which had as its purpose the justification of the murders committed by the Everett mob, and it contains no over-statement. Shingle weavers are set apart from the rest of the workers by their mutilated hands and the dead grey pallor of their cheeks.

"The nature of a man's occupation, his daily working environment, marks in a large degree the nature of the man himself, and cannot help but mold the early years, at least, of his economic organization. Men who flirt with death in their daily calling become inured to physical danger, they become contemptuous of the man whose calling fails to bring forth physical prowess. So do they in their organizations become irritated and contemptuous at the long-drawn-out process of bargaining, the duel of wits and brain power engaged in by the more conservative organizations to win working concessions. Their motto becomes 'Strike quick and strike hard,'* * *" So says E. P. Marsh, President of the Washington State Federation of Labor, in speaking of the shingle weavers.(*)

Logging, no less than shingle weaving, is a dangerous occupation. The countless articles of wood in every-day use have claimed their toll of human blood. A falling tree or limb, a mis-step on the river, a faulty cable, a weakened trestle; each may mean a still and mangled form. Time and again the loggers have organized to improve their working conditions only to find themselves beaten

(*) Sunset Magazine, February 1917. "The I. W. W. and the Golden Rule."

(*) Supplemental report on "Everett's Industrial Warfare," by President Ernest P. Marsh to State Federation of Labor convention held at Everett, Wash., from January 22 to 26, 1917.

or betrayed. Playing upon the natural desire of the woodsmen for organization, shrewd swindlers have formed unions which were nothing more than dues collection agencies. Politicians have fathered organizations for their own purposes. Unions built by the men themselves have fallen into the hands of officials who used them for selfish personal gain. Over and over the employers have crushed the embryonic unions only to see them rise again with added strength. Forced by the very necessities of their daily lives, the workers always returned to the fight with a new and better form of unionism.

Like the loggers, the shingle weavers were routed time and again, but their spirit never died. The Everett shingle weavers formed their union as a result of a successful strike in 1901. In 1905 they were strong enough to resist a proposed reduction of wages. In 1906 they struck in sympathy with the Ballard weavers, and lost. Within a year the defeated union was back as strong as before. By 1911 the International Shingle Weavers Union had attained a membership of nearly 2,000, the majority of whom were in accord with the Industrial Workers of the World. The question of affiliation with the I. W. W. was widely discussed and was only prevented from going to a referendum vote by the efforts of a few officials. Further discussion of the question was excluded from the columns of their official organ, "The Shingle Weaver," by the Ninth Annual Convention. (*)

Following this slap in the face, the progressive members quit the union in large numbers, leaving affairs in the hands of conservative and reactionary elements. Endeavors were made to negotiate contracts with the employers; and in 1913 the officials secured $30,000 from the American Federation of Labor and made a pretense at the organization of all workers in the woods and mills into one body. This was a move aimed at the Forest and Lumber

(*) Vol. 9, No. 2, The Shingle Weaver, Special Convention Number, February, 1911.

Workers of the I. W. W., which was feared alike by the employers and the craft union officials because of its new strength gained thru the affiliation of the Brotherhood of Timber Workers in the southern states. Instead of gaining ground by the move, the shingle weavers union lost in membership and subsequently claimed that industrial unionism was a failure in the lumber industry.

The industrial depression of 1914-15 found all unions in bad shape. Employers used the army of unemployed as an axe to cut wages. In the spring of 1915 notice of a wage reduction was posted in the Everett shingle mills. The weavers promptly struck. Scabs, gunmen, injunctions, and violence followed. The strike failed, the wage reduction was made, but the men returned to work relying upon a "gentlemen's agreement" that the employers would voluntarily raise the wages of the shingle weavers when shingles again sold for what they were bringing before the depression. Faith in agreements had gotten in its deadly work; the shingle weavers believed that the employers meant to keep their word.

In the spring of 1916 shingles soared to a price higher than had prevailed for years, but the promised raise failed to materialize. With but a skeleton of an organization to back them, a handful of determined delegates met in Seattle in April and decided to demand the restoration of the 1915 scale thruout the entire jurisdiction of the Shingle Weavers' Union, setting May 1st as the date when the raise should take effect.

At the time set, or shortly thereafter, most of the mills in the Northwest paid the scale. Everett, where the employers had given their "word of honor," refused the strikers' demand. The fight was on! The Seaside Shingle Company, which held no membership in the Commercial Club, soon granted the raise. Many of the other companies, notably the Jamison Mill, began the importation of scabs within the month. The cry of "outside agitators" was forgotten long enough to go outside in search of notorious gunmen and scab-herders. The slums, the hells of Capitalism, were raked with a fine-toothed comb for degenerates with a record for lawless deviltry. The strikers threw out their picket line and the ever-present class war began to show itself in other than peaceful ways.

During May, June and July the picket line had to be maintained in the face of strong opposition by the local authorities who were the pliant tools of the lumber trust. The ranks of the pickets were constantly being thinned by false arrest and imprisonment on every charge and no charge, until on August 19th there were but eighteen men on the picket line.

On that particular morning the Everett police searched the little handful of pickets in front of the Jamison Mill to make sure that they were unarmed, and when that fact was determined, they started the men across the narrow trestle bridge that extended over an arm of the bay. When the pickets were well out on the bridge, the imported thugs, some seventy in number, personally directed and urged on by their employer, Neil Jamison, poured in from either side, leaving no means of escape save that of making a thirty foot leap into the deep waters of the bay, and with brass knuckles and blackjacks made an attack upon the defenseless weavers. The pickets were unmercifully beaten. Robert H. Mills, business agent of the Shingle Weavers' Union, was knocked down by one of the openshop thugs and kicked in the ribs and face as he lay senseless in the roadway. From a vantage point, thoughtfully removed from the danger zone, the police calmly surveyed the scene.

When darkness fell that night, the pickets, aided by irate citizens, returned to the attack with clubs and fists. The tables were turned. The "moral heroes" had their heads cracked. Seeing that the scabs were thoroly whipped, the "guardians of the peace" rushed to the rescue with drawn revolvers. In the melee one union picket was shot thru the leg.

About ten nights later, Mr. Jamison herded his scabs into military formation and after a short parade thru the main streets led them to the Everett Theater; the party being in appreciation of their "efficiency." This arrogant display incensed the strikers and citizens, and when the scabs emerged from the show a near-riot occurred. Mills was present and altho too weak from his recent injuries to have taken any active part in the fray, he was arrested and thrown in jail in default of bail. The man who had murderously assaulted him at the mill swore out the complaint. Mills was subsequently tried and acquitted on a charge of inciting to riot. Nothing was done to his assailant. And in none of these acts of violence was the I. W. W. in any way a participant.

During this period there existed a strike of longshoremen on the entire Pacific Coast, including the port of Everett. The wrath of the employers fell heavily upon the Riggers and Stevedores because that body was not in sympathy with the idea of craft contracts or agreements, and because of the adoption by a large majority of a proposal to "amalgamate all the unions of the Maritime Transportation Industry, between the Warehouse at the Shipping Point and Warehouse at the Receiving Point into one big powerful organization, meeting, thinking, and acting together at all times."(*) The industrially united employers of the Pacific Coast did not relish the idea of the workers grouping themselves together along lines similar to those on which the owners were associated. The longshoremen's strike started on June 1st and was marked by more or less serious disorders at various points, most of the violence being precipitated by detectives placed in the unions by the employers. The tug boat men were also on strike in Everett, particularly against the American Tug Boat Company

(*) Proposition No. 5, submitted to referendum of membership of Pacific Coast District I. L. A., Riggers and Stevedores Local 38, at their annual election on Jan. 6, 1916.

One of the thousands who donated their fingers to the Lumber Trust. The Trust compensated all with poverty and some with bullets on November 5, 1916.

owned by Captain Harry Ramwell. All of the unions on strike in Everett were affiliated with the A. F. of L. Striking longshoremen from Seattle aided the shingle weavers on their picket line from time to time, and individual members of the I. W. W., holding duplicate cards in the A. F. of L. stood shoulder to shoulder with the strikers, but officially the I. W. W. had no part in any of the strikes.

Meanwhile in Seattle the I. W. W. had planned to organize the forest and lumber workers on a scale never before attempted. Calls for organizers had been coming in from the surrounding district and there were demands for a mass convention to discuss conditions in the industry. Yet, strange as it may seem to those who do not know of the ebb and flow of labor unions, there were at that time less than half a hundred paid-up members in the Seattle loggers branch, so great had been the depression from 1914 to 1916. The conference was set for July 4th and five hundred logger delegates responded, representing nearly as many camps in the district. Enthusiasm ran high! The assembled workers suggested the adoption of a plan of district organization along lines more in keeping with the modern trend of the lumber industry. The loggers' union, then known as Local 432, ratified the actions of the conference. As a preliminary move it was decided that an organizer be secured to make a survey of the lumber situation in the surrounding territory. General Headquarters in Chicago was communicated with, James Rowan was found to be available, and on July 31st he was sent to Everett to find out the sentiment for industrial unionism at that point.

That night Rowan spoke on Wetmore Avenue fifty feet back from Hewitt Avenue, in compliance with the street regulations. No mention was made of local conditions as Rowan had just come from another part of the country and was unaware that a shingle weavers strike was in progress. His speech consisted mainly of references to the Industrial Relations Commission Report, a pamphlet summarizing that report being the only literature offered for sale at the meeting. Toward the end of his speech Rowan declared:

"The A. F. of L. believes in signing agreements with the employers. The craft unions regard these contracts as sacred. When one craft goes on strike the others are forced to remain at work. This makes the craft unions scab on each other."

"You are a liar!" cried Jake Michel, an A. F. of L. representative, staunchly defending his organization.

From an automobile near the edge of the crowd, Donald McRae, Sheriff of Snohomish County, called to Michel:

"Jake, I will run that guy in if you say so."

"I don't see any need to run him in;" remonstrated Michel. "He hasn't said anything yet to run him in for."

Nevertheless McRae, usurping the powers of the local police department, made Rowan leave the platform and go with him to the county jail. McRae was drunk.

Rowan was held for an hour. Immediately upon his release he returned to the corner to resume his speech. Police Officer Fox thereupon arrested him and took him to the city jail. He was thrown into a dark cell for refusing to do jail work, was taken into court next morning and absurdly charged with peddling without a license, was denied a jury trial, refused a postponement, not allowed a chance to secure counsel, and was sentenced to thirty days imprisonment with an alternative of leaving town. No ordinance against street speaking at Wetmore and Hewitt then existed. Rowan chose to leave town. No time was set as to how long he was to remain away. He then left for Bellingham and from there went to Sedro-Woolley. Using an assumed name to avoid the blacklist he worked at the latter place for a short time to familiarize himself with job conditions, subsequently returning to Everett.

Levi Remick, a one-armed veteran of the industrial war, was next sent to Everett on August 4th to act as temporary delegate. He interviewed a number of people and sold some literature. Receiving orders to stop selling the pamphlets and papers, he inquired the price of a peddler's license and finding it prohibitive he returned to Seattle to secure funds to open an office. A small hall was found at 1219½ Hewitt Avenue, a month's rent was paid, and on August 9th Remick placed a sign in the window and started to sell literature and transact business for the I. W. W.

The little hall remained open until late in August. Migratory workers, strikers, and citizens generally, dropped in from time to time to ask about the organization or to purchase papers. Solidarity and the Industrial Worker were particularly in demand, the latter paper having commenced publication in Seattle on April 1st, 1916. A number of Everett citizens, desiring to hear a lecture by James P. Thompson, who had spoken in Everett without molestation in 1915 and in March and April of 1916, made donations to Remick sufficient to cover all expenses, and it was arranged that Thompson speak on August 22nd. Attempts to secure a hall met with failure; the halls of Everett were closed to the I. W. W. The conspiracy against free speech and free assembly was on in earnest! No other course was left but to hold the proposed meeting on the street, so Hewitt and Wetmore, the spot where the Salvation Army and various religious and political bodies spoke almost nightly, was selected and the meeting advertised.

Early in the morning on the day before the scheduled meeting, Sheriff McRae, commanding a body of police officers over whom he had no official control, stormed into the I. W. W. hall and tore from the wall all bills advertising Thompson's meeting, saying with an oath:

"That man won't be allowed to speak in Everett!"

Turning to Remick and throwing back his coat to display the badge, he yelled:

"I order you out of this town! Get out by afternoon or you go to jail!"

McRae was drunk. Stalking out as rapidly as his condition would permit he staggered down the street to a near-by pool hall where the order was repeated to the men assembled therein. These, with other workingmen, 25 in all were rounded up, seized, roughly questioned, searched, and all those who had no families or property in Everett were forcibly deported. That night ten more were taken from the shingle weaver's picket line and sent out of town without due process of law. Treatment of this kind became general.

"Not a man in overalls is safe!" declared the secretary of the Everett Building Trades Council. "Men just off the job with their pay checks in their pocket have been unceremoniously thrown out of town just because they were workingmen."(*)

Remick closed the little hall and left for Seattle the next morning to place the question of the Thompson meeting before the Seattle membership. Shortly before noon Rowan, who had just returned to Everett, went to the hall and finding it closed and locked he proceeded to open it up. Within a few minutes Sheriff McRae, in company with police officer Fox, entered the place and ordered Rowan to leave town by two o'clock. He then tore up the balance of the advertising matter for the Thompson meeting. McRae was drunk. Rowan went to Seattle, where the report of this occurrence made the members more determined than ever to hold the meeting that night.

With about twenty other members of the I. W. W., Thompson went to Everett. The Salvation Army was holding services on the corner. Placing his platform even further back from the street intersection Thompson waited until the Army had concluded and then commenced his lecture. Using the Industrial Relations Commission Report as the basis

(*) Dreamland Rink Meeting, Seattle, Nov. 19th, over 5,000 in attendance.

of his talk, he spoke for about twenty minutes without interruption. Then a body of fifteen policemen marched down the street and swung into the crowd. The officer in charge stepped up to Thompson and requested him to go to see the chief of police at the police station. After addressing a few remarks to the crowd Thompson withdrew from the platform. His place was taken at once by Rowan, who was immediately dragged from the stand and turned over to the same officer who had charge of Thompson and his wife. Mrs. Edith Frennette then spoke briefly and called for a song. The audience responded with "The Red Flag," but meanwhile Mrs. Frennette and Mrs. Lorna Mahler had been placed under arrest. In succession several others attempted to speak but were pulled or pushed off the stand. The police then formed a circle by holding hands around those who were close to the platform. One by one the citizens were allowed to slip outside the "ring-around-a-rosy" until only "desperadoes" were left. These made no effort to resist arrest, and were started toward the city jail. The officer entrusted with Thompson was so interested in his captive that Rowan was able to quietly remove himself from the scene, returning to the street corner where he spoke for more than half an hour before being rearrested.

Aroused by this invasion of liberty, Mrs. Letelsia Fye, an Everett citizen, arose to recite the Declaration of Independence, but even that proved too revolutionary for the tools of the lumber trust. A threatening move on the part of the police brought back the thought of her two unprotected children and caused her to cease her efforts to declare independence in Everett.

"Is there a red-blooded man in the audience who will take the stand?" called out the gallant little woman as she stepped from the platform. Jake Michel promptly accepted the challenge and was as promptly suppressed by the police at the first mention of free speech.

In the jail the arrested persons were searched one by one and thrown into the "receiving tank."

When Thompson's turn came, Commissioner of Public Safety, as Chief of Police Kelly was known under Everett's form or government, said to him:

"Mr. Thompson, I don't want to lock you up."

"That's interesting," replied Thompson. "Why have you got me down here?"

"We don't want you to speak on the street at this time."

"Have you any ordinance against it, that is, have I broken any law?" enquired Thompson.

"Oh no, no. That isn't the idea," rejoined Kelly. "We have strikes on, labor troubles here, and we don't want you to speak here at all. You are welcome at any other time, but not now."

"Well," said Thompson, "as a representative of labor, when labor is in trouble is the time I would like to speak, but I am not going to advocate anything that I think you could object to."

"Now, Thompson," said Kelly, "if you will agree to get right out of town I will let you go. I don't want to lock you up."

"Do you believe in free speech?" asked Thompson.

"Yes."

"And I am not arrested?"

"No, you are not arrested."

"Come up to the meeting then," Thompson said with a smile, "for I am going back and speak."

"Oh no, you are not!"—and Kelly kind of laughed. "No, you are not!"

"If you let me go I will go right up to the corner and speak, and if you send me out of town I will come back," said Thompson emphatically. "I don't know what you are going to do, but that's how I stand."

"Lock him up with the rest!" was the abrupt reply of the "Commissioner of Public Safety."

At this juncture James Rowan was brought in from the patrol wagon, and searched. As the officers were about to put him in the cell with the others, Sheriff McRae called out:

"Don't put him in there, he is instigator of the whole damn business. Turn him over to me." He then took Rowan in his automobile to the county jail and threw him in a cell, along with B. E. Peck, who had previously been given a "floater" out of town for having spoken on the street on or about August 15th. McRae was drunk.

More than half a thousand indignant citizens followed the twenty-one arrested persons to the jail, loudly condemning the outrage against their constitutional rights. Editor H. W. Watts, of the Northwest Worker, a union and socialist paper published in Everett, forcibly expressed his opinion of the suppression of free speech and was thereupon thrown into jail. Fearing a serious outbreak, Michel secured permission to address the people surrounding the jail. The crowd, upon receiving assurances from Michel that the men would be well treated and could be seen in the morning, quietly dispersed and returned to their homes.

The free speech prisoners were charged with vagrancy on the police blotter, but no formal charge was ever made, nor were they brought to trial. Next morning, Thompson and his wife, who had return tickets on the Interurban, were deported by rail, together with Herbert Mahler, secretary of the Seattle I. W. W. Mrs. Mahler, Mrs. Frennette and the balance of the prisoners were taken to the City Dock and deported by boat. At the instigation of McRae, and without a court order, the sum of $13. was seized from the personal funds of James Orr and turned over to the purser of the boat to pay the fares of the deportees to Seattle. Protests against this legalized robbery were of no avail; the amount of the fares was never repaid. Mayor Merrill of Everett, replying to a letter from Mahler, promised that this money would be refunded to Orr. His word proved to be as good as that of the Everett shingle mill owners. Prominent members of the Commercial Club lent civic dignity to the deportation by their profane threats to use physical force in the event that any of the deported prisoners dared to return.

Upon their arrival in Seattle the deported men conferred with other members of the union, telling of the beating some of them had received while in jail, and as a result there was organized a free speech committee composed of Sam Dixon, Dan Emmett and A. E. Soper. Telegrams were then sent to General Headquarters, to Solidarity and to various branches of the organization, notifying them of what had happened. At a street meeting that night, Mrs. Frennette, Mrs. Mahler and James P. Thompson, gave the workers the facts and collected over $50.00 for the committee to use in its work. In Everett the Labor Council passed a resolution stating that the unions there were back of the battle for free speech and condemning McRae and the authorities for their illegal actions. The Free Speech Fight was on!

Remick, in the meantime, had returned to Everett and found that all the literature had been confiscated from the hall. The day following his return, August 24th, Sheriff McRae blustered into the hall with a police officer in his train. Leering at Remick he exclaimed:

"You God damn son of a b—, are you back here again? Get on your coat and get into that auto!"

Seizing an I. W. W. stencil that was lying on the table he tore it to shreds.

"If anybody asks who tore that up,"—bombastically—"tell them Sheriff McRae tore it!"

Shoving Remick into the automobile with the remark that jail was too easy for him and they would therefore take him to the Interurban and deport him, the sheriff drove off to make good his threat. McRae was drunk.

On the corner that night, Harry Feinberg spoke to a large audience and was not molested. That this was due to no change of policy on the part of the lumber trust tools was shown when secretary Herbert Mahler went to Everett the following day in reference to the situation. He was met at the depot by Sheriff McRae who asked him what he had come to Everett for. "To see the Mayor," answered Mahler. "Anything you have to say to the Mayor, you can say to me," was McRae's rejoinder. After a brief conversation Mahler was deported to Seattle by the same car on which he had made the trip over. McRae was drunk.

F. W. Stead reopened the hall on the 26th and managed to hold it down for a couple of days. Three speakers appeared and spoke that night. J. A. MacDonald, editor of the Industrial Worker, opened the meeting. George Reese spoke next, but upon commencing to advocate the use of violence he was pulled from the platform by Harry Feinberg, who concluded the meeting. No arrests were made.

It was during this period that Secretary Herbert Mahler addressed a letter to Governor Ernest Lister, informing him of the state of lawlessness existing in Everett. A second letter was sent to Mayor Merrill and in it was enclosed a copy of the letter to Lister. No reply was received to the communication.

For a time following this there was no interference with street meetings. Feinberg spoke without molestation on Monday night and Dan Emmett opened up the hall once more. On Tuesday evening, the same night as the theater riot, Thompson addressed an audience of thousands of Everett citizens, giving them the facts of the arrests made the previous week, and advising the workers against the use of violence in any disputes with employers.

After having been held by McRae for eight days without any commitment papers, Rowan was turned over to the city police and released on September 1st. He returned to the street corner and spoke for several succeeding nights including "Labor Day" which fell on the 4th. Incidentally he paid a visit to the home of Jake Michel and, after industrial unionism was more fully explained, Michel agreed that the craft union contract system forced scabbery upon the workers. Rowan left shortly thereafter for Anacortes to find out the sentiment for organization in that section.

This period of comparative peace was due to the fact that the lumber barons realized that their actions reflected no credit upon themselves or their city and they wished to create a favorable impression upon Federal Mediator Blackman who was in Everett at the request of U. S. Commissioner of Labor Wilson. It was during this time, too, that the protagonists of the open shop were secretly marshalling their forces for a still more lawless and brutal campaign.

Affairs gradually slipped from the hands of the Everett authorities into the grasp of those Snohomish County officials who were more completely dominated by the lumber interests.

"Tom," remarked Jake Michel one day to Chief of Police Kelley, "it seems funny that you can't handle the situation."

"I can handle it all right," replied Kelley, bitterly, "but McRae has been drunk around here for the last two or three weeks and he has butted into my business."

It was on August 30th that the lumber trust definitely stripped the city officials of all power and turned affairs over to the sheriff. On this point a quotation from the Industrial Relations Commission Report is particularly illuminating in showing a common industrial condition:

"Free speech in informal and personal intercourse was denied the inhabitants of the coal camps. It was also denied public speakers. Union organizers would not be permitted to address meetings. Periodicals permitted in the camps were censored in the same fashion. The operators were able to use their power of summary discharge to deny free press, free speech, and free assembly, to prevent political activities for the suppression of popular government and the winning of political control. **I find that the head of the political machinery is the sheriff."**

In Everett the sheriff's office was controlled by the Commercial Club and the Commercial Club in turn was dominated, thru an inner circle, by the lumber trust. Acting for the trust a small committee meeting was held on the morning of the 30th with the editor of a trust-controlled newspaper, the secretary of the Commercial Club, two city officials, a banker and a lumber trust magnate in attendance. A larger meeting of those in control met in the afternoon and, pursuant to a call already published in the Everett Herald, several hundred scabs, gunmen, and other open shop advocates were brought together that night at the Commercial Club.

Commissioner of Finance, W. H. Clay, suggested that as Federal Mediator Blackman, an authority on labor questions, was in the city it might be well to confer with him regarding a settlement. Banker Moody said he did not think a conference would be advisable as Mr. Blackman might be inclined to lean toward the side of the laboring men, and at a remark by "Governor" Clough, formerly Governor of Minnesota and spokesman for the mill owners, to the effect that there was nothing to be settled the suggestion was not considered further.

H. D. Cooley, special counsel for a number of the mills, Governor Clough, a prominent mill owner, and others then addressed the meeting in furtherance of the plans already laid. Clough asked McRae if he could handle the situation. McRae said he did not have enough deputies.

"Swear in the members of the Commercial Club, then!" demanded Clough. This was done. Nearly two hundred of the men whose membership had been paid for by the mill owners "volunteered" their services. McRae swore in a few and then, for the first time in his life, found swearing a difficulty, so W. W. Blain, secretary of the Commercial Club, who was neither a city nor a county official, administered the remainder of such oaths as were taken by the deputies. The whole meeting was illegal.

From time to time the deputy force was added to until it ran way up in the hundreds. It was divided into sections A, B, C, etc. Each division was assigned to a special duty, one to watch incoming trains for free speech advocates, another to watch the boats for I. W. W. members, and others for various duties such as deporting and beating up workers.

This marked the beginning of a reign of terror during which no propertiless worker or union sympathizer was safe from attack.

About this same time the Commercial Club made a pretense of investigating the shingle weavers' strike. Not one of the strikers was called to give their side of the controversy, and J. G. Brown, international president of the Shingle Weavers' Union, was refused permission to testify. The committee claimed that the employers could not pay the wages asked. An adverse report was returned and was adopted by the club.

Attorneys E. C. Dailey, Robert Fassett, and George Loutitt, along with a number of other fair minded members who did not favor the open shop program, withdrew from membership on account of these various actions. Their names were placed on the bulletin board and a boycott advised. Feeling against the organization responsible for the chaotic conditions in Everett finally became so strong that practically all of the merchants whose places were not mortgaged or who were not otherwise dependent upon the whims of the lumber barons, posted notices in their windows,

"WE ARE NOT MEMBERS OF THE COMMERCIAL CLUB."

Their names, too, were placed on the bulletin board, and the boycott and other devices used in an endeavor to force them into bankruptcy.

Prior to these occurrences and for some time thereafter, the club was addressed by emmissaries of the open shop interests. A. L. Veitch, special counsel for the Merchants' and Manufacturers' Association, on one occasion addressed the deputies on labor troubles in San Francisco and the methods used to handle them. Veitch was later one of the attorneys in the case against Thomas H. Tracy, and he was employed by the state, it being stipulated that he receive no state compensation. H. D. Cooley, lumber mill lawyer and former prosecuting attorney, also spoke at different times on the open shop questions. Cooley was likewise an attorney for the prosecution in the Tracy case and he, like Veitch, was retained by "interested parties." Cooley was one of the anti-union speakers at a meeting of the deputies which was also addressed by F. C. Beach, of San Francisco, president of the M. & M., Robert Moody, president of the First National Bank of Everett, Governor Clough, mill magnate, F. K. Baker, president of the Commercial Club, and Col. Roland H. Hartley, open shop candidate for the nomination as governor of Washington at the pending election. Leigh Irvine, of Seattle, secretary of the Employers' Association, and Murray, president of the National Association of Manufacturers, were also active in directing the destinies of the Commercial Club.

A special open shop committee was formed, the nature of its operations being apparent when the following two quotations from its minutes, taken from among others of similar purport, are considered:

"Decided to go after advertisements in labor journals and the Northwestern Worker."

"Matter of how far to go on open shop propaganda at the deputies meeting this morning was discussed. Also the advisability of submitting pledges. Mr. Moody to take up matter of the legality of pledges with Mr. Coleman. Note: At deputies meeting all speakers touched quite strongly on the open shop, and as far as it was possible to see all in attendance seemed favorable."(**)

Just how far they finally did go is a matter of history. At the time, however, there were appropriations made for the purchase of blackjacks, leaded clubs, guns and ammunition, and for the employ-

---

Minutes of Open Shop Committee, Sept. 27th.
(**) Minutes of Open Shop Committee, October 29.

ment of detectives, labor spies, and "agents provocateur."(*)

(*) The incidents of the foregoing chapter are corroborated by the sworn testimony of prosecution witnesses Donald McRae, sheriff of Snohomish County; and D. D. Merrill, Mayor of Everett; and by witnesses called by the Defense, W. W. Blain, secretary of the Commercial Club: J. G. Brown, International president of the Shingle Weavers' Union; W. H. Clay, Commissioner of Finance in Everett; Robert Faussett, Everett attorney; Harry Feinberg, one of the defendants; Mrs. Letelsia Fye, Everett citizen; Jake Michel, Secretary Everett Building Trades Council; Herbert Mahler, Secretary Seattle I. W. W. and subsequently secretary of the Everett Prisoners' Defense Committee; Robert Mills, business agent Everett Shingle Weavers' Union; James Orr, and Levi Remick, I. W. W. members; James Rowan, I. W. W. organizer; and James P. Thompson, National Organizer for the I. W. W. and a speaker of international reputation.

J. T. (Red) Doran Capt. Jack Mitten
The Launch Wanderer.

CHAPTER III.

A REIGN OF TERROR

No sooner had Mediator Blackman left Everett than the "law and order" forces resumed their hostilities with a bitterness and brutality that seems almost incredible. On September 7th Mrs. Frennette, H. Shebeck, Bob Adams, J. Johnson, J. Fred, and Dan Emmett were dragged from the platform at Hewitt and Wetmore Avenues and were literally thrown into their cells. Next morning Mrs. Frenette was released but the men were "kangarood" for 30 days each. Petty abuses were heaped upon them and Johnson was cast into the "black hole" by the sheriff. Some of the men were severely beaten just before their release a few days afterward.

When Fred Reed and James Dwyer were arrested the next night for street speaking, the crowd of Everett citizens, in company with the few I. W. W. members present, followed the deputies to the county jail, demanding the release of Reed, Dwyer and Peck, and those who had been arrested the night before. In its surging to and from the crowd pushed over a post-rotted picket fence that had been erected in the early days of Everett. This violence, together with cries of "You've got the wrong bunch in jail! Let those men out and put the 'bulls' in!" was the basis from which the trust-owned press built up a story of a riot and attempted jail delivery. On the same flimsy basis a warrant was issued charging Mrs. Frennette with inciting a riot.

The free speech committee sent John Berg to Everett that same day to retain an attorney for the men held without warrants. He secured the services of E. C. Dailey, and, while waiting to learn the result of the lawyer's efforts, he went to the I. W. W. hall only to find it closed. A man was there waiting to get his blankets to go to work and Berg volunteered to get them for him. He then went to the county jail and asked for McRae. When McRae came in and learned that Berg wanted to see the secretary in order to get the keys to the hall, he yelled out:

"You are another I. W. W. Throw him in jail, the old son-of-a-b—!"

Without having any charges placed against him, Berg was held until the next morning, when McRae and a deputy took him out in a roadster to a lonely spot on the county road. Forcing him to dismount, McRae ordered Berg to walk to Seattle under threats of death if he returned, and then knocked Berg down and kicked him in the groin as he lay prostrate. McRae was drunk. Berg subsequently developed a severe rupture as a result of this treatment. He managed to make his way to Seattle and in spite of his condition returned to Everett that same night.

Undaunted by their previous deportations, and determined to circumvent the deputies who were seizing men from the railroad trains and regular boats, a body of free speech fighters, on September 9th, took the train to Mukilteo, a village about four miles from Everett, and there, by pre-arrangement, were taken aboard the launch "Wanderer."

The little boat would not hold the entire party and six men were towed behind in a large dory. There were 17 first class life preservers on board, the captain borrowing some to supplement his equipment.

When the "Wanderer" reached a point about a mile and a half from the Weyerhouser dock a boat was seen approaching. It was the scab tug "Edison," belonging to the American Tugboat Company. On board was Captain Harry Ramwell, Sheriff McRae and a body of about sixty deputies. When the "Edison" was about 200 feet away the sheriff commenced shooting—but let Captain Jack Mitten tell his own story.

"The first shot went over the bow. I don't know whether there was one or two shots fired, then there was a shot struck right over my head onto the big cast iron muffler. The next shot came on thru the boat,—I had my bunk strapped up against the wall, — and thru the blanket, — and the cotton in the blanket turned the bullet,—and it struck flat on the bottom of the bunk.

"I shut the engine down and went out to the stern door and just as I stepped out there was a shot went right by my head and at the same time McRae hollered out and says 'You son-of-a-b—, you come over here!' Says I, "If you want me, you come over here." With that they brought their boat and my boat up together. Six shots in all were fired.

"McRae commenced to take the people off the boat and when he had them all off he kicked the pilot house open and says, 'Oho, there is a woman here!' Mrs. Frennette was sitting in the pilot house. Anyhow, they took her and he says, 'You'll get a one piece suit on McNeil's island for this,' and then he says to Cap Ramwell—Cap Ramwell was sitting on the side—"This is Oscar Lindstrom, drag him along too.'

"Then they were going to make fast the line—they had made fast my stern line—and as I bent over with the line McRae struck me with his revolver on the back of the head, and when I straightened up he struck me in here, a revolver about that long. (Indicating.) I said something to him and then he ran the revolver right in here in my groin and he ruptured me at the same time. I told him 'It's a fine way of using a citizen.' He says, 'You're a hell of a citizen, bringing in a bunch like that,' he says, 'to cause a riot in this town.' I says, 'Well, they are all union men anyway.' He says, 'You shut your damn head or I will knock it clean off!' and I guess he would, because he had whiskey enough in him at the time to do it.

"There was a small man, I believe they call him Miller, he saw him standing there and he says, 'You here, too?' and he hauled off and struck him in the temple and the blood flowed way down over his face and shirt. He struck him again and staggered him. If he hadn't struck him so he would have gone inboard, he would have gone over the edge, close to the edge.

"Then there was a man by the name of Berg, it seemed he knowed John Berg. He said, 'You———, I will fix you so you will never come back!' and then he went at Berg, but Berg was foxy and kept ducking his head. He rapped him on the shoulders two or three different times, I wouldn't say how often, but he didn't draw blood on Berg. (An I. W. W. member named Kurgvel was also beaten on the head and shoulders.)

"They drove us all in alongside of the boiler between the decks, down on the main deck of the "Edison" and kept us there till they docked and got automobiles and the patrol wagon and filed us off into them and took us to jail."

The arrest of Captain Mitten and acting engineer Oscar Lindstrom made twenty-one prisoners in all, and these were jailed without any charge being placed against them. As Berg was taken into the jail, McRae cursed him roundly, ordering two deputies to hold him while a beating was administered over the shoulders and back with a leather strap loaded with lead on the tip.

The men were treated with great brutality within the jail. One young fellow was asked by the deputies, "Are you an I. W. W.?" and each time the lad answered "Yes!" he was thrown violently against the steel walls of the cell, until his body was a mass of bruises. Mitten was denied a chance to communicate with his Everett friends in order to get bail. The nights were cold and the prisoners had to sleep on the bare floor without blankets.

At the end of nine days all the men were offered their liberty except Mitten. They promptly refused the offer. "All or none!" was their indignant demand, and Peck and Mitten were set at liberty with the rest as a result of this show of solidarity.

Upon his release Captain Mitten found that the life preservers had been stolen from his boat, and the flattened bullet removed from his bunk. Scotty Fife, the Port Captain of the American Tugboat Company, told Captain Mitten that he had straightened up the things on the "Wanderer!"

Thus to the crimes of unlawful arrest, false imprisonment, theft, deportation, assault and physical injury, the lumber trust added that of piracy on the high seas. And all this was but a taste of what was yet to come!

Organizer James Rowan returned to Everett from Anacortes on the afternoon of September 11th and was met at the depot by three deputies who promptly took him to the county jail. There were at that time between thirty and forty other members of the I. W. W. being unlawfully held. Rowan learned that these men had been taken from their cells one at a time and beaten by the deputies, Thorne and Dunn having especially severe cuts on the face and head.

Rowan's story of the outrage that followed gives a glimpse of the methods employed by the lumber trust.

"As soon as I dropped off the train at Everett I was met by three deputies. One of them told me the sheriff wanted to see me and I asked if he was a deputy. He said, 'Yes,' and showed me a badge. Then I went up with two of the deputies to the county jail. In a minute or two Sheriff McRae came in and he was pretty drunk. He caught hold of me and gave me a yank forward, and he says, 'So you are back, eh?' and I says 'Yes.' And he says 'We are going to fix you so you won't come back any more.' There was some more abusive talk and then I was searched and put in a cell.

"Just after dark that night I was taken out of the cell, my stuff was given back, and McRae says, 'We are going to start you on the road to Seattle.' With a deputy he took me out to the automobile and McRae drove the automobile, and we had some conversation. McRae seemed to feel very sore because

I told the people on the street that the jail was lousy, and he says 'We wanted you to get out of here and you would not do it, and now,' he says, 'Now instead of dealing with officers you have to deal with a bunch of boob citizens, and there is no telling what these boobs will do.' There was more talk that is not worth repeating and most of it not fit to repeat anyhow.

"We went out in the country until we came to where the road crosses the interurban tracks about two miles from Silver Lake and McRae told me to get out. He then pointed down the track and says, 'There is the road to Seattle and you beat it!' so I started down the track.

"I hadn't gone far, maybe 50 or 75 yards, when I met a bunch of gunmen. They came at me with guns. They had clubs and they started to beat me up on the head with the butts of their guns and with the clubs. They all had handkerchiefs over their face except one. They threw a cloth over my head and beat me some more on the head with their gun butts and then they dragged me thru the fence at the right-of-way and went a little ways back into the woods. Then they held me down over a log about eighteen inches or two feet in diameter. There were about a dozen of them I would say. Two or three held each arm and two or three each leg and there were four or five of them holding guns around my ribs—they had the guns close around my ribs all the time, several of them—and they tore my clothes off, tore my shirt and coat off. Then one of them beat me on the back, on the bare back with some kind of a sap, I don't know just what kind it was, but I could hear him grunt every time he was going to strike a blow. I was struck fifty times or more.

"After he got thru beating me they went back to the fence toward the road and I picked up my scattered belongings and went down to Silver Lake, taking the first car to Seattle."

Rowan exhibited his badly lacerated and bruised back to several prominent Seattle citizens, and then

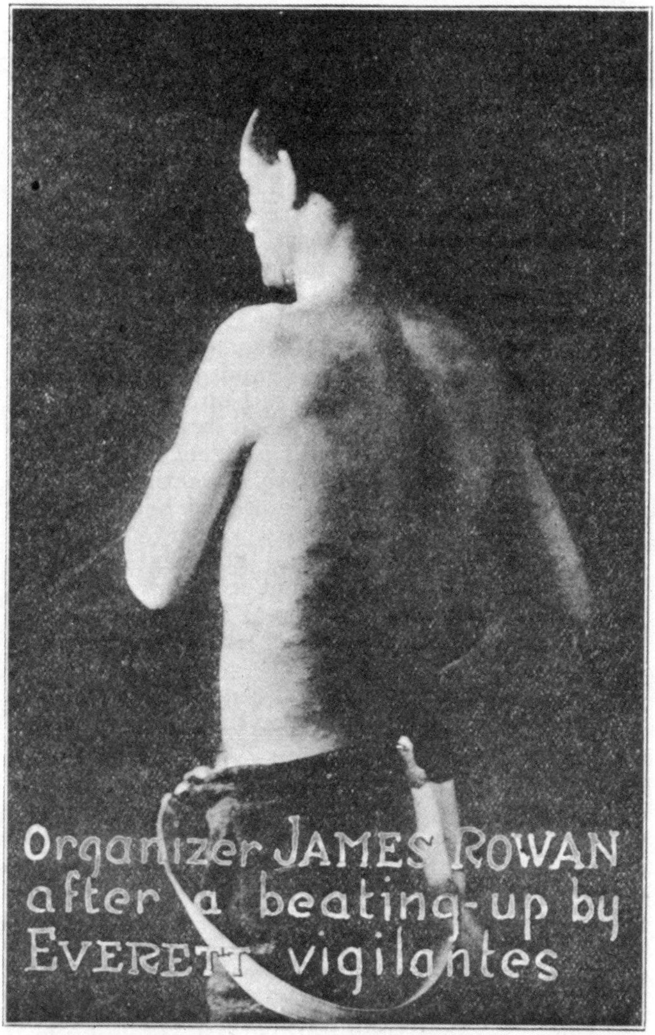

Organizer James Rowan;
Showing his back lacerated by Lumber Trust thugs.

had a photograph made, which was widely circulated. Contrary to the expectation of the lumber barons this treatment did not deter free speech fighters from carrying on the struggle. Instead, it brought fresh bodies of free speech enthusiasts to the scene within a short period.

The personnel of the free speech committee changed continually because of the arrest of its members. On Sunday, September 10th, at a mass meeting in Seattle Harry Feinberg and William Roberts were elected to serve. Roberts had just come down from Port Angeles and desired to investigate conditions at first hand, so in company with Feinberg he went to Everett on the 11th. They met Jake Michel, who telephoned to Chief of Police Kelley for permission to hold a street meeting.

"I have no objection to this meeting," replied Kelley, "but wait a minute, you had better call up McRae and find out."

Attempts to reach McRae at the Commercial Club and the sheriff's office met with failure. Meanwhile Feinberg had gone ahead with the meeting, the following being his sworn statement of what transpired:

"I went to Everett at 7:30 Monday night. I got a box and opened a meeting for the I. W. W. There must have been three thousand people on the corner, against buildings and looking out of the windows.

"I spoke about 35 minutes, with the crowd boisterous in their applause. Three companies of deputies and vigilantes, about one hundred and fifty thugs in all, marched down the street and divided up in three companies. One of the deputies came up and told me he wanted me and grabbed me off the box.

"They took me up to the jail, took my description, and my money and valuables, which were not returned. By that time Fellow Worker Roberts was brought in. A drunken deputy came in and grabbed me by the coat and dragged me out of the jail, with the evident permission of the officers. The vigilantes proceeded to beat me up on the jail steps. There were anyway fifty deputies waiting outside and all of them crowded to get a chance to hit me. They gave me a chance to get away finally and shot after me, or in the air, I could not tell which, but I was not hit by the bullets."

The sworn statement of William Roberts corroborated the foregoing:

"I took the box after Fellow Worker Feinberg had been arrested. The crowd were extreme in their hostility to the lawlessness of the officers. I told them to keep cool, that the I. W. W. would handle the situation, in their own time and way. They arrested me, and, right there, they clubbed me on the head. They brought me to the jail, where Feinberg was at the desk. They took me out of the jail and threw me into the bunch of vigilantes, with clubs. They started beating me around the body. One of them said: 'Do anything, but don't kill him!'

"Finally one of them hit me on the head and I came out of it and as I was getting away they shot in the air. A bunch of them then jumped into an automobile, came after me and again clubbed me. One of them knocked me out for ten minutes, according to one of the women who were watching.

"While we were in the jail, two men we did not know were brought into the jail with their heads cut open. The vigilantes were clubbing women right and left, and a young girl, about eight years of age, had her head cut open by one of Sheriff McRae's Commercial Club tools."

Roberts ran down the street to the interurban depot, where he hid behind a freight car until just before the car left for Seattle. Feinberg, with his face and clothing covered with blood, got on the same car about a mile and a half from Everett and the two returned to Seattle.

John Ovist, a resident of Mukilteo who had joined the I. W. W. in Everett on Labor Day, got on the box and said, "Fellow comrades——" but got no further. He was knocked from the box. Ovist states: "Mr. Henig was standing alongside of me when Sheriff McRae came up and cracked him over the forehead with a club. I don't know what else happened to him for just then Sheriff McRae came in front of me and pushed the fellow off the box. When the two fellows were arrested I started to speak and McRae took me and turned me over to one of them—I don't know what you call them—deputies, or whatever they are. He had a white handkerchief around his neck and he took me toward the county jail. There was a policeman standing in front of the jail. If I am not mistaken his name is Ryan, a short heavy-set fellow. I walked by him. Of course, I never thought he was going to hit me, but I felt something over behind. He hit me with a club behind the ear and cut my head until it was bleeding awful."

"When we came to the county jail, Henig, he was in there already. His face was red and he was full of blood. And they took us into the toilet to have us wash the blood off, and when I came back I heard screams and pounding.

"Then the sheriff recognized me, he had been down in Mukilteo before, and he says, 'What are you doing up here?' I said, 'Well, I didn't come up here, they brought me up here.' He says, 'You are a member of the I. W. W., too.' So I told him, I don't see why I should come and ask you what organization I should belong to!' So he opened the gate and says, 'Here is a fellow from Mukilteo,' he says. 'Beat it!' And I seen, I guess—a hundred and fifty or maybe two hundred, I didn't have time to count them, right out back of the jail lined up in lines on either side. And I had to run between them and come out the other end. They banged me on the head with clubs, and all over. I looked bad and I felt worse. I had blue marks on my shoulders and on my hips and under my knees.

"I got thru them and there was a couple ran after me, but I beat it ahead of them. I guess they intended to club me. I ran down to that depot where the electric car goes thru to Seattle and then I turned to look around because the car was at Hewitt and Colby, and as I went down the walk two men stopped me and asked me if I hadn't had enough. They told me to beat it, and as I turned around the same policeman, Ryan, I think his name is, hit me on the forehead and then pulled his gun and said, 'Beat it!' He was drunk and they were all swearing at me.

"After I got a block or so, there were two or three shots. I walked two more blocks and then was so dizzy I had to rest. Finally I walked further and an automobile came past me and I tried to holler but they didn't hear me. And then I walked a little further and the stage came along and they picked me up."

Eye witnesses declared that officer Daniels was one of those who fired shots at the fleeing men after they had been forced to run the gauntlet.

Frank Henig, an Everett citizen, tells what happened in these words:

"I will start from the time I left the house. My wife and I, and the little baby were going to the show. When we got on Wetmore there was a big crowd standing there. I had worked the night before in the mill and I had cedar asthma, so I said to my wife, 'I would like to stay out in the fresh air,' And she said, 'All right, I will meet you at nine o'clock at Wetmore and Hewitt.'

"There was quite a crowd and I got up pretty close in front so I could hear the speaker. I stood there a little while and finally the sheriff came along with a bunch of deputies, and the speaker said, 'Here they come, but now people, I will tell you, don't start anything, let them start it.'

"They took him off the box and arrested a couple of others with him, and then immediately after that the Commercial Club deputies came along in a row. They had white handkerchiefs around their necks. So I looked out there and the crowd commenced to yell and cheer like, and McRae got excited and started toward me, saying, 'We have been looking for you before.' When he said that I stopped—before that I had tried to get farther back—I stopped and he got hold of me. Meanwhile

Commissioner Kelley came up and took care of me and McRae walked away a little way. Kelley had hold of my right arm and he pinched me a little bit and I said 'Let go Kelley and I will go with you.'

"We stood there a few minutes longer and McRae came back. Kelley said 'Come along with me,' and just as I said 'All right,' McRae grabbed me by the coat and hit me on the head with a black club fastened to his strap with a leather thong. I was looking right at him and he knocked me unconscious. Then Kelley picked me up and shook me and I came to again, and I fell over the curb of the sidewalk.

"Kelley then turned me over to Daniels, a policeman in Everett, and he turned me over to a couple of Commercial Club deputies. Then Fred Luke came along and said, 'I will take care of him.' So we walked a little ways and he said, 'You better go to the doctor and have that dressed.' I said to him, 'Oh, I guess it ain't so bad,' and so he said, 'Come along with me and we will wash up at the jail.' I said, 'All right,' and while I was going up the steps to the jail, why a policeman by the name of Bryan or something like that,—a little short fellow, well anyhow he got canned off the force for being drunk, that is how I heard of him,—when I was kind of slow walking along because I was bleeding pretty bad. he said, 'Hurry up and get in there, you low-down, dirty son-of-a-b——!' And I answered, 'I guess I ain't arrested, I don't have to hurry in there.' So he cursed some more.

"I went into the jail and washed up and came back into the office of the county jail. The fellows that they had arrested were sitting in the chairs and McRae came in and grabbed one of the I. W. W.'s —I guess they were I. W. W.'s, anyway one of them that was arrested—and he says, 'What in hell are you doing up here, don't you know I told you to keep away from here?' and while he was going in the door into the back office I saw him haul off with his sap, but I don't see him hit him, but the little fellow cried like a baby.

"McRae came back and he looked at me and said, 'What in hell are you doing up here?' I didn't know what to say for a little while and then I said, 'I didn't do nothing, Mac, I don't see what you wanted to sap me for.' And he said, 'I didn't sap you,' he said, 'Kelley hit you.' Then I said to him, 'My wife says for me to meet her down at the corner of Wetmore and Hewitt at nine o'clock and I would like to go down there and meet her.' So he said, 'All right, you go; you hurry and go.' I was going out the front door and he said, 'No, don't go out there. If you go out there, they will kill you!' He led me to the back door of the jail, I don't know where it was, I never was in jail in my life before, and he said, 'Hurry and beat it, and pull your hat down over your head so they wont know you.' But when I got to town everybody knew, because there was blood still running all over my face after I washed up."

Henig endeavored to prosecute McRae for his illegal and unwarranted assault but all attempts to secure a warrant met with failure. Lumber trust law operates only in one direction.

In this raid upon the meeting McRae smashed citizens right and left, women as well as men. He was even seen to kick a small boy who happened to get in his path. Deputy Sam Walker beat up Harry Woods, an Everett music teacher; another deputy was seen smashing an elderly gentleman on the head; still another knocked Mrs. Louise McGuire, who was just recovering from a sprained knee, into the gutter; and Ed Morton, G. W. Carr and many other old-time residents of Everett were struck by the drunken Commercial Club thugs.

Mrs. Leota Carr called up Chief of Police Kelley next morning, the following being an account of the conversation that ensued:

"I said, 'What are you trying to kill my husband for?' and he kind of laughed and said he didn't believe it, and I said, 'Did you know they struck him over the head last night and he could hardly go to work today?' He said, 'My God, they didn't strike him, did they?' and I said, 'They surely did!' And he said 'Why there isn't a better man in town than he is,' and I said, 'I know it.' It surprised me to think that he thought I didn't know it myself. And then I said, 'These here deputies are making more I. W. W.'s in town than the I. W. W.'s would in fifty years.' And he said, 'I know it.' Then I said, 'Why do you allow them to do it? You are the head of the police department.' He replied, 'McRae has taken it out of my hands; the sheriff is ahead of me and it is his men who are doing it, and I am not to blame.' "

At the city park four nights after this outrage, only one arrest for street speaking having occurred in the meantime, the aroused citizens of Everett met to hear Attorney E. C. Dailey, T. Webber, and various local speakers deal with the situation, and to view at first hand the wounds of Ovist, Henig and other towns people who had been injured. Thousands attended the meeting, and disapproval of the actions of the Commercial Club and its tools was vehemently expressed.

This remonstrance from the people had some effect. The Commercial Club, knowing that all arrests so far had been unlawful, took steps to "legalize" any further seizing of street speakers at Hewitt and Wetmore Avenues. The lumber interests issued an ordinance preventing street speaking on that corner. The Mayor signed it without ever putting it to a reading, thus invalidating the proposed measure. This made no difference; henceforth it was a law of the city of Everett and as such was due to be enforced by the lumber trust.

During the whole controversy there had not been an arrest made on the charge of violation of any street speaking ordinance. With the new ordinance assumed to be a law, Mrs. Frennette went to Everett and interviewed Chief Kelley. After telling him that the I. W. W. members were being disturbed and mistreated by men who were not in uniform, she said:

"It seems that there is an ordinance here against street speaking and we feel that it is unjust. We feel that we have a right to speak here. We are not blocking traffic and we propose to make a test of the ordinance. Will you have one of your men arrest me or any other speaker who chooses to take the box, personally, and bring me to jail and put a charge against me, and protect me from the vigilantes who are beating the men on the street?"

Kelley replied that so far as he was concerned he would do the best he could but McRae had practically taken the authority out of his hands and that he really could not guarantee protection. So a legal test was practically denied.

Quiet again reigned in Everett following the brutalities cited. A few citizens were manhandled for too openly expressing their opinion of mob methods and several wearers of overalls were searched and deported, but the effects of bootleg whiskey seemed to have left the vigilantes.

On Wednesday ,Sept. 20th, a committee of 2000 citizens met at the Labor Temple and arranged for a mass meeting to be held in the public park on the following Friday. The meeting brought forth between ten and fifteen thousand citizens, one-third of the total population at least, who listened to speakers representing the I. W. W., Socialists, trades unions and citizens generally. Testimony was given by some of the citizens who had been clubbed by the vigilantes. Recognizing the hostile public opinion, Sheriff McRae promised that the office of the I. W. W. would not again be molested. As he had lied before he was not believed, but, as a test, Earl Osborne went from Seattle to open up the hall once more.

For a period thereafter the energies of the deputies were given to a course of action confined to the outskirts of the city. Migratory workers traveling to and from various jobs were taken from the trains, beaten, robbed and deported. As an example of McRae's methods and as depicting a phase of the life of the migratory worker the story of "Sergeant" John J. Keenan, sixty-five years old, and still actively at work, is of particular interest:

"I left Great Falls, Mont., about the 5th of September after I had been working on a machine in the harvest about nine miles from town. The boys gathered together—they were coming from North Dakota—and we all came thru together. We had an organization among ourselves. We carried our cards. There was a delegate with us, a field delegate, and I was spokesman, elected by the rank and file of the twenty-two. There was another division from North Dakota on the same train with us, going to Wenatchee to pick apples. We were going to Seattle. I winter in Seattle every year and work on the snow sheds.

"We carried our cooking utensils with us, and when we got off at a station we sent our committee of three and bought our provisions in the store, and two of the cooks cooked the food, and we ate it and took the next train and came on. This happened wherever we stopped.

"We arrived in Snohomish, Wash., on Sept. 23rd at about 8:45 in the morning. When the committee came down I sent out and they brought me back the bills—I was the treasurer as well—one man carried the funds, and they brought back $4.90 worth of food down, including two frying pans, and when I was about cooking, a freight train from Everett pulled in and a little boy, who was maybe about ten years old, he says, 'Dad, are you an I. W. W.?' I says, 'I am, son.' 'Well,' he says, 'there are a whole bunch of deputies coming out after you.' I laughed at the boy, I thought he was joshing me.

"About half an hour after the boy told me this the deputies appeared. In the first bunch were forty-two, and then Sheriff McRae came with more, making altogether, what I counted, sixty-four. The first bunch came around the bush alongside the railroad track where I was and the sheriff came in about twenty minutes later with his bunch from the opposite way.

"In the first bunch was a fat, stout fellow with two guns. He had a chief's badge—a chief of police's badge—on him. He was facing toward the fire and he says, 'If you move a step, I will fill you full of lead!' I laughed at him, says I, 'What does this outrage mean?' There was another old gentleman with a chin beard, fat, middling fat, probably my own age, and he picked up my coat which was lying alongside me and looked at my button. He says, 'Oh, undesirable citizen!' I says, 'What do you mean?' He says, 'Are you an I. W. W.?' I says, 'I am, and I am more than proud of it!' 'Well,' he says, 'we don't want you in this county.' I says, 'Sure?' He says, 'Yes.' I says, 'Well, I am not going to stay in this county, I am going to cook breakfast and go to Seattle.' He says, 'Do you understand what this means?' I says, 'No.' He says, 'The sheriff will be here in a few minutes and he will tell you what it means.' I heard afterward that this man was the mayor of Snohomish.

"I was sitting right opposite the fire wtih my coffee and bread and meat in my hand when Sheriff McRae came up and says, 'Who is this bunch?' So a tall, black deputy, a tall, dark complected fellow, says, 'They are a bunch of harvest hands coming from North Dakota.' McRae says, 'Did you search these men?' And he says, 'Yes.' 'Did you find any shooting arms on them?' He says, 'No.' They had searched us and we had no guns or clubs.

"McRae then asked, 'Who is their leader?' and this old gentleman that spoke to me first, he says, 'They have no leader, but that old man over there is the spokesman.' So he came over to me and says, 'Where are you going?' I says, 'I am going to Seattle.' Then he used an expression that I don't think is fit for ladies to hear. I says, 'My mother was a lady and she never raised any of us by the name you have mentioned, and,' I says, 'I don't think I have done anything that I will have to walk out of the county.' He says, 'Do you see that track?' I says, 'Yes.' He says, 'Well, you will walk down that track!' I says, 'But for these twenty-one men that are here in my hands I wouldn't walk a foot for you.' He says, 'You get out. I am going to shoot all these things to pieces.' I says, 'You will shoot nothing to pieces, I bought them with my hard-earned money.' He says, 'All right, take them with you.' Then he shot up the cans and things, and he says, 'That is the track to Seattle and you go up it, and if I ever catch you in this county again you will get what you are looking for.'

"So we walked up the hill toward Seattle and there is a town, I think they call it Maltby, and we got there between four and five o'clock in the evening. Fellow Worker Thornton, Adams and Love were the committee men and they asked me how I felt. I told them my feet were pretty sore.

"I went over to the station agent and found out that there was a freight due at 9:30 but that sometimes it didn't get in until three in the morning. I then asked permission to light a fire and cook some coffee, and after we were thru eating we lay down.

"About 9:30 the train came along and I called the men. As the train was backing up I saw some light come, and one auto throwing her searchlight, and I counted four automobiles. That is all I could count but there were a whole lot of them coming. I says, 'Men, we have run up against a stone wall.'

"Fellow Worker Love and I—he came off the machine with me in Great Falls—we were first in line and Sheriff McRae and two other men with white handkerchiefs around their necks came forward first and he says, 'You son-of-a-b——, I thought you were going to Seattle?' I says, 'Ain't I going to Seattle? I can't go till the train goes,' I says, 'you've had me walking now till I have no foot under me. What do you mean by this outrage? My father fought for this country and I have a right here. I am on railroad property and have done nothing to anybody.' McRae then hit Fellow Worker Love on the head and I yelled 'Break and run, men, or they will kill you!' He turned around then and he said to me, 'You dirty old Irish bastard, now I will make you so you can't run. I'll show you!' With that he let drive and hit me, leaving this three cornered mark here (indicating place on head).

And when the others went up the track he says, 'Get now, God damn your old soul, or I will kill you!' I says, 'Sheriff, look here, you are a perfect gentleman, you are, to hit a fellow old enough to be your father.' He made as if to hit me again and then Fellow Worker Love came back and says, 'Have a heart!' I says 'You run,' and he says 'No, they are not going to kill you while I am here.' And Fellow Worker Paterson came back down the track and I says, 'What is the matter, Paterson, are you crazy? Get the men and tell them to go over the line. Don't stay in this county or they are liable to murder you!' Then Love and I went off the track into the thick bushes and lay down till next morning.

"At daylight we got up, went down to the junction and gathered up fifteen of the men. When the train pulled in the trainman asked me where I was going and I said I was going to Seattle. He says, 'Do you carry a card?' "Yes,' says I. 'Produce!' says he. That is the word the trainmen use. So I put my hand in my pocket and pulled it out. "You better get back in the caboose, you are hurt,' he said. He saw the blood where Fellow Worker Love had bandaged my head with his handkerchief. 'No,' says I, 'Where the men are riding is good enough for me.' So we went to where the interurban comes in and I was seven men short. I paid two-fifty into Seattle, and we came in, and I made a report to the Seattle locals."

Incidents similar to this were of almost daily occurrence, scores of deportations taking place during the month of September. Then on the 26th, despite his promises to refrain from molesting the hall, McRae entered the premises, forcibly seized Earl Osborne, the secretary, took him a long distance out in the country, and at the point of a gun made him start the thirty-mile trip on foot to Seattle. On the 29th of September the Everett authorities arrested J. Johnson and George Bradley in Seattle. Johnson was held on an arson charge but no legal warrant for his arrest was issued until October 17th, or until he had been in jail for nineteen days. Then the charge against him was that he had set fire to a box factory—but this was soon changed when it was learned by the authorities that the box factory had not caught fire until after Johnson was in jail, and for the first charge they substituted the claim that Johnson had burned the garage of one Walter Smith, a scab shingle weaver deputy. George Bradley, who had been deported from Everett after having served one day as secretary, was accused of second degree arson as an alleged accomplice. Each man was told that the other had confessed and the best thing to do was to make a clean breast of matters, but this scheme of McRae's fell thru for two reasons: the men were not guilty, and they had never seen or heard of each other before. Johnson was in jail fifty-eight days without a preliminary hearing. Both men were released on property bonds, and the trials were "indefinitely postponed," that still being their status at this writing.

No further attempts were made to open the hall after Osborne's deportation until October 16th when the organization in Seattle again selected a man to act as secretary in Everett. Thomas H. Tracy took charge on that date, remaining in Everett until a few days prior to November 5th, at which time he resigned, his place being taken by Chester Micklin.

During the month of October there were between three and four hundred deportations, the vigilantes operating mainly from the Commercial Club. Many of these "slugging parties" were attended by Mayor D. D. Merrill, Governor Clough, Captain Harry Ramwell, T. W. Anguish, W. R. Booth, Edward Hawse, and other "pillars of society" in Everett. Most of the men were deported without any formalities whatever, and the methods used in handling the others may well be judged by frequent entries on the police blotter to the effect that men arrested by Great Northern detective Fox were ordered turned over to Sheriff McRae by Mayor Merrill. The railroad company, acting in conjunction with the lumber trust, put on a private army, and had its men roughly dressed to resemble honest workingmen. Cases of "hi-jacking" became quite numerous about this time, but no redress from this highway robbery could be had.

On the question of the hiring of armed forces by the railroads the Industrial Relations Commission Report has this to say:

"Under the authority granted by the several states the railroads maintain a force of police, and some, at least, have established large arsenals of arms and ammunition. This armed force, when augmented by recruits from detective agencies and employment agencies, as seems to be the general practice during industrial disputes, constitutes a private army clothed with a degree of authority which should be exercised only by public officials; these armed bodies, usurping the supreme functions of the state and oftentimes encroaching on the rights of citizens, are a distinct menace to public welfare."

A number of the men deported during September and October were not members of the I. W. W., some even being opposed at the time to the tenet of the organization, "The working class and the employing class have nothing in common," but almost without exception the non-members who suffered deportation made it a point to join the union when the nearest branch or field delegate was reached. In Everett, delegates working quietly among the millmen, longshoremen, and other workers, were also getting numerous recruits as the class struggle stood forth in its naked form. All the efforts of the lumber trust to suppress the I. W. W. were as tho they had tried to quench a forest fire with gasoline.

It was on October 30th that forty-one men left Seattle by boat in a determined effort to reach the corner of Hewitt and Wetmore Avenues in order to test the validity of the alleged ordinance prohibiting free speech at that point. They were the first contingent of an army of harvesters who were just returning from a hard season's labor in the fields

Beverly Park

A close up view of Beverly Park showing cattle guards.

and orchards. The party was double the size of any free speech group that had tried to enter Everett at any previous time.

They were met at the dock by a drunken band of deputies, most of whom wore white handkerchiefs around their necks as a means of identification. The deputies were armed with guns and clubs, and they outnumbered the I. W. W. body five to one. Several of the lawless crew were so intoxicated they could scarcely stand, and one in particular had to be forcibly restrained by his less drunken associates from attempts to commit murder in the open. The I. W. W. men were clubbed with gun butts and loaded clubs whenever their movements were not swift enough to suit the fancies of the drunken mob. John Downs' face was an indistinguishable mass of blood where Sheriff McRae had "sapped up" on him and split open his upper lip. Boat passengers who remonstrated were promised the same treatment unless they kept still. In its mad frenzy the posse struck in all directions. So blindly drunk and hysterical was deputy Joseph Irving that he swung his heavy revolver handle with full force onto the head of deputy Joe Schofield. He continued the insane attack, while McRae, awry-eyed and lusting for blood, assisted in the brutal task until warning cried from the other vigilantes showed them their mistake. Schofield was carried to an automobile and hastened to the nearest drug store, where it was found necessary to call a physician to take three stitches to bind together the edges of the most severe wound.

The prisoners were loaded into large auto trucks and passenger cars, more than twenty of which were lined up in waiting, and were taken out to a lonely wooded spot near Beverly Park on the road to Seattle. McRae, with deputies Fred Luke, William Pabst and Fred Plymale, took one I. W. W. out in their five-passenger Reo, McRae afterward endeavored unsuccessfully to prove an alibi because his own car was in a garage. Deputy Sheriff Jefferson Beard also took out a prisoner.

Upon their arrival at Beverly the prisoners were made to dismount at the point of guns and stand in the cold drizzling rain until their captors had formed two lines reaching from the roadway to the interurban tracks. There in the darkness the men were forced to run stumbling over the uneven ground down a gauntlet that ended only with the cruel sharp blades of a cattle guard, while on their unprotected heads and shoulders the drunken outlaws rained blow after blow with gun-butts, black-jacks, loaded saps and pick-handles. In the confusion one boy escaped from Ed Hawse, but before he could get away into the brush this bully, weighing about 260 pounds, bore down upon him, and with a couple of other deputies proceeded to beat him well-nigh into insensibility. Deputies who lost their clubs in the scramble aimed kicks at the privates of the men as they passed down the line. Deputy Fred Luke swung at one man with such force that the leather wrist thong parted and the club disappeared into the woods. With drunken deliberation Joseph Irving cracked the head of man after man, informing each one that they were getting an extra dose because of his mistake in beating up a brother deputy. In the thick of it all, smashing, kicking, and screaming obscene curses at the helpless men and boys who dared demand free speech within the territory sacred to the lumber trust, was the deputy-sheriff of Snohomish County, Jefferson E. Beard!

A few of the men broke the lines and ran into the woods, a bullet past their heads warning others from a like attempt. Across the cattle guard, often sprawling on hands and knees from the force of the last blows received, went the men who had cleared the gauntlet. Legs sank between the blades of the guard and strained ligaments and sprained ankles were the result. One man suffered a dislocated shoulder at the hands of a Doctor Allison, another had the bridge of his nose broken by a blow from McRae, and dangerously severe wounds and bruises were sustained by nearly all of the forty-one.

So horrible were the moans and outcries of the

stricken men, so bestial were the actions of the infuriated deputies, that one of their own number, W. R. Booth, sickened at the sight and sound, went reeling up the roadway retching as he left the brutal scene.

Attracted by the curses of the deputies, the sound of the blows, and the moans and cries of the wounded men, Mrs. Ruby Ketchum came to the door of her house nearly a quarter of a mile away, and remained there listening to the hideous din, while her husband, Roy Ketchum, and his brother, Lew, went down to the scene of the outrage to investigate. The Ketchum brothers reported that the deputies were formed in two lines ending in six men, three on each side of the cattle guard. A man would be taken out of the car and two deputies would join his arms up behind him meanwhile hammering his unprotected face from both sides as hard as they could strike with their fists. Then the man was started down the line, one deputy following to club him on the back to make him hurry, and the other deputies striking with clubs and other weapons and kicking the prisoner as he progressed. Just before reaching the cattle guard he was made to run, and, in crossing the blades, the three men on the east side of the track would swing their clubs upon his back while the men on the west clubbed him across the face and stomach. This was repeated with the men as fast as they were dragged from the autos. They also heard the sound of blows and then cries of "Oh my God! Doc, don't hit me again, doc, you're killing me!" Lew Ketchum took deputy Fred Luke by the coat tails and pulled him back from the cattle guard, asking, "What are you doing, what is going on here?" and Luke replied, "We are beating up forty-one I. W. W.'s"

Harry Hubbard tells the story in these words from the time the autos arrived at Beverly:

"I got out of the car with another fellow, Rice, and I says, 'We had better stay together, it looks to me like we were going to get tamped up,' and somebody grabbed hold of him, and I stood a minute, and then I ran by one fellow up into the woods. Just as I got out of the radius of the automobile lights I fell over a stump on the edge of the embankment. I was in kind of a peculiar predicament and I had to get hold of the stump to pull myself up, and just as I did that some fellow behind me swung with a blackjack and grazed my temple, knocking me to my knees. I got up and he grabbed hold of me and we both fell down the bank together. Then two or three others grabbed me, and this Hawse had me by the collar, and Sheriff McRae walked up and said 'You are the son-of-a—— that was over here last week,' and I answered, 'I was working here last week.' Then he said, 'Are you an I. W. W.?' I said, 'Yes,' and he hit me an upward swing on the nose. He repeated, 'You are an I. W. W., are you?' and again I said, 'Yes.' He then swore at me and said, 'Say that you ain't!' and I replied, 'No, I won't say that I ain't,' and he hit me three more times on the nose.

"Then the man who was holding my left wrist with one hand and my shoulder with the other, said, 'Wait a minute until I get a poke at him,' and McRae said, 'All right, doc,' and then someone else said "All right Allison, hit him for me!' This fellow they called Doc Allison hit me and blackened my eye. McRae swore at me, he seemed to be intoxicater and he looked and acted like a maniac, he said 'If you fellows ever come back some of you will die, that's all there is to it.' I said, 'I don't think there is any necessity for killing anybody,' and he answered 'I will kill you if you come back,' and he raised his blackjack and said 'Run!' I said 'I wont run,' and he hit me again and I dropped to the ground. He raised his foot over my face, and used some pretty raw language, and as he stood there with his heel over my face I grabbed hold of a fellow's leg and pulled myself along so instead of hitting my face his heel scraped my side. Then I got some kicks, three of them in the small of the back around my kidneys.

"When I got up I walked thru the line, there

were twenty or thirty different ones hollered for me to run, but I was stubborn and wouldn't do it. And when I got to the cattle guard and stood at the other side kind of wiping the blood off my face I heard some one coming and I said, 'Four Hundred," and he said 'Yes,' and he was crying. It was a young boy and I walked down the track with him afterward.

"At the City Hospital in Seattle next day the doctor told me my nose was badly fractured and that I had internal injuries. A few days later my back pained me severely and I passed blood for a time after that."

C. H. Rice, whose shoulder was dislocated, gives about the same version.

"Two big fellows would hold a man until they were thru beating him and then turn him loose. I was turned loose and ran probably six or eight feet, something like that, and I was hit and knocked down. As I scrambled to my feet and ran a few feet again I was hit on the shoulder with a slingshot. This time I went down and I was dazed, I think I must have been unconscious for a moment because when I came to they were kicking me, and some of them said, 'He is faking,' and others said, 'No, he is knocked out.' I remember seeing some of the boys during that time running by me, and when they got me up I started to run a bit farther and was knocked down again.

"Then they called for somebody there, addressing him as Dr. Allison, and he grabbed my arm and pulled me up, and he raised my arm up and said, 'Aw, there is nothing the matter with you,' and jerked it down again. My arm was out of place, it seemed way over to one side, and I couldn't straighten it up.

"As I was going over the cattle guard several of them hit me and some one hollered 'Bring him back here, don't let him go over there.' They brought me back and this doctor said 'You touch your shoulder with your hand,' and I couldn't. He says 'There is nothing the matter with you.'

"Then the fellow who was on the dock, and who had been drinking pretty heavily, because they would have to shove him back every once in a while, he shouted out 'Let's burn him!' About that time Sheriff McRae came over and got hold of my throat and said, 'Now, damn you, I will tell you I can kill you right here and there never would be nothing known about it, and you know it.' And some one said, 'Let's hang him!' and this other fellow kept hollering 'Burn him! Burn him!' McRae kept hitting me, first on one side and then the other, smacking me that way, and then he turned me loose again and hit me with one of those slingshots, and finally he said 'Oh, let him go,' and he started me along, following behind and hitting me until I got over the cattleguard.

"I went down to the interurban track until I caught up with some of the boys. They tried to pull my shoulder back into place and then they took handkerchiefs and neckties, and one thing and another, and made a kind of a sling to hold it up. We then went down to the first station and the boys took up a collection and the eight of us who were hurt the worst got on the train and went to Seattle. The others had to walk the twenty-five miles into Seattle. Most of us had to go to the hospital next day."

Sam Rovinson was beaten with a piece of gaspipe, but taking advantage of the fact that the shooting when Archie Collins made his escape had attracted the attention of the deputies he got thru the gauntlet with only minor injuries. Rovinson testifies that McRae said to him:

"This time we will let you off with this, but next time you come up here we will pop you full of holes."

"I just came up here to exercise my constitutional right of free speech," expostulated Rovinson.

"To hell with free speech and the Constitution!" shouted McRae, "You are now in Snohomish county, and we are running the county!"

After the deputies had returned to town the two Ketchum brothers took their lanterns and went out to the scene thinking they might find some of the men out there hurt, with a broken leg, or arm or something, and that they could be taken to their house to be cared for. No men were seen, but three covered with blood were found and after examination were returned to where they had been picked up.

Early next morning some of the deputies, frightened at their cowardly actions of the previous night, were seen at Beverly Park making an examination of the ground. Two of them approached the Ketchum residence and asked if any I. W. W.'s had been found lying around there. After being assured that they had stopped short of murder, the deputies departed.

A little later an investigation committee composed of Rev. Oscar McGill of Seattle, and Rev. Elbert E. Flint, Rev. Jos. P. Marlatt, Jake Michel, Robert Mills, Ernest Marsh, E. C. Dailey, Commissioner W. H. Clay, Messrs. Fawcett, Hedge, Ballou, Houghton and others from Everett, made a close examination of the grounds. In spite of the heavy rain and notwithstanding the fact that deputies had preceded them, the committee found blood-soaked hats and hat bands and big brown spots of blood soaked into the cement roadway. In the cattle guard was the sole of a shoe, evidently torn off as one of the fleeing men escaped his assailants.

"Hearing of the occurrence I accompanied several gentlemen, including a prominent minister of the gospel of Everett, next morning to the scene. The tale of that struggle was plainly written. The roadway was stained with blood. The blades of the cattle guard were so stained, and between the blades was a fresh imprint of a shoe where plainly one man in his hurry to escape the shower of blows, missed his footing in the dark and went down between the blades. Early that morning workmen going into the city to work, picked up three hats from the ground, still damp with blood. There can be no excuse for nor extenuation of such an inhuman method of punishment," reported President E. P. Marsh to the State Federation of Labor.

J. M. Norland stated that "there were big brown blotches on the pavement which we took to be blood. They were perhaps two feet in diameter, and there were a number of smaller blotches for a distance of twenty-five feet. In the vicinity of the cattle guard the soil was disarranged and there were shoe marks near the cattle guard. You could also notice where, in their hurry to get across, they would go in between, and there would be little parts or shreds of clothing there, and on one there was a little hair."

All that day the talk in Everett centered around the crime of the preceding night. Little groups of citizens gathered here and there to discuss the matter. The deputies went about strenuously denying that they had a hand in the infamous affair, and friends of long standing refused to speak to those who were known positively to have been concerned in the outrage. A number of the ministers of the city conferred regarding a course of action, but finding the problem too deep for them to solve they left it to up to the individual. Various Everett citizens, representing a large degree of public sentiment, felt that the thing to do was to hold an immense mass meeting in order to present the facts of the hideous crime to the whole public. This plan met with immediate approval from many quarters, and the I. W. W. in Seattle was notified of this desire by mail, by telephone, and by means of citizens' delegations. Rev. Oscar McGill conferred with secretary Herbert Mahler and was quite insistent upon the necessity for such a meeting, as the Everett papers had carried no real information about the affair in Beverly. He brought out the fact that there had been thousands in attendance at the mass meeting in the Everett city park a month or so previous to this occurrence, and the speakers were then escorted by a large body of citizens from the interurban depot to the meeting place, and the feelings of the people were such that similar or even more adequate protection would be given were another meeting held. He suggested that the meeting he held in broad daylight and on a Sunday. That the plan met with the approval of the I. W. W. membership was shown by its adoption at a meeting the night following the trouble at Beverly Park. And the date selected was Sunday, November 5th.

Immdiately steps were taken to inform the various I. W. W. branches in the Northwest of the proposed action. Telegrams were sent to Solidarity, and a ringing call for two thousand men to help in the fight for free speech was published in the Industrial Worker. In addition to telegraphing the story and its attendant call for action to the unions of the Pacific Coast there were various members selected from among the forty-one who had been beaten, and these were dispatched to different points to spread the tale of Everett's atrocities, and to gain new recruits for the "invading army" of free speech fighters.

Seeking the widest possible publicity the free speech committee had printed and circulated thousands of handbills in Everett to call attention to the proposed meeting.

CITIZENS OF EVERETT

ATTENTION!

A meeting will be held at the corner of Hewitt and Wetmore Aves., on Sunday, Nov. 5th, 2 p. m. Come and help maintain your and our constitutional right. **Committee.**

The authorities in Everett were notified, the editors of all the Seattle daily papers were requested to have representatives present at the meeting, and reporters were called in and told of the intentions of the organization. During the week frequent meetings were held in the hall in Seattle to arrange for the incoming free speech fighters, and without an exception all these meetings were held with no examination of membership books and were open to the public. With their cards laid upon the table the members of the Industrial Workers of the World were preparing to call the hand of the semi-legalized outlaws of Snohomish county who had cast aside the law, abrogated the Constitution of the United States, and denied the right of free speech and free assembly.

Following the Beverly affair the Commercial Club redoubled its activities. Blackjacks and "Robinson clubs," so called because they were manufactured especially for the deputies by the Robinson Mill, were set aside for revolvers and high power rifles, and the ranks of the deputies were enlarged by the off-scouring and scum of the open shop persuasion.

McRae entered the I. W. W. hall on Friday, Nov. 3rd, the day Thomas H. Tracy turned the office over to Chester Micklin, and abruptly said "By God, I will introduce myself. I am Sheriff McRae! I won't have a lot of sons-of-bitches hanging around this place like in Seattle."

Micklin looked at the drunken sheriff a moment and replied, "The constitution guarantees us free speech, free assembly, and free——"

"To hell with the Constitution," broke in McRae. "We have a constitution here that we will enforce."

"You believe in unions, you believe in organized labor, don't you?" asked Micklin.

"Yes, I belonged to the shingle weavers at one time," returned McRae, "but when the shingle weavers went out on strike I donated $25.00 to their strike fund and they gave me a rotten deal and sent the check back to me, and to hell with the shingle weavers and the rest of the unions!"

Then, as he was leaving the hall, McRae pulled from his pocket a letter; took from it a black cat cut from pasteboard and stuck it in the secretary's face, saying "That's the kind of———s that is in your organization!"

Next morning the sheriff raided the hall and seized the men who were found there, with the exception of the secretary. Turning to Micklin he said boastfully "I'll bet you a hundred dollars you——s won't hold that meeting tomorrow!" McRae was drunk.

The arrested men were searched and deported and, as was the case in every previous arrest and deportation, there was no resistance offered, no physical violence threatened, and no weapons of any character found upon any of the I. W. W. men.

That night the deputies were secretly assembled at the Commercial Club where they were given their final instructions by the lumber trust and ordered to report fully armed and ready for action at the blowing of the mill whistles. With these preparations the open shop forces were ready to go to still greater lengths to uphold "law and order!"

The answer of the I. W. W. to this damnable act of violence at Beverly Park and to the four months of terrorism that had preceded it was a call for two thousand men to enter Everett, there to gain by sheer force of numbers that right of free speech and peaceable assembly supposed to have been guaranteed them by the Constitution of the United States.

---

* (The incidents in the foregoing chapter are corroborated by the sworn testimony of I. W. W. men who were shot at, beaten, robbed, and abused; by citizens of Everett and Seattle who were also beaten and mistreated or who witnessed the scenes; by physicians, attorneys, public officials, members of craft unions, and by deputies who hoped to make amends by testifying to the truth for the defense.)

The Ketchum Home near Beverly Park

CHAPTER IV.

BLOODY SUNDAY

How shall we enter the kingdom of Everett? was the question that confronted the committee in charge of affairs in Seattle on the morning of November 5th. Inquiries at the Interurban office developed the fact that sufficient cars could not be had to accommodate the crowd. The cost of making the trip by auto truck was found to be prohibitive. At the eleventh hour the committee, taking the money pooled by the members, secured the regular passenger steamship Verona, and an orderly and determined body of men filed down the steps leading from the I. W .W. headquarters and marched by fours to the Colman Dock.

Their mission was an open and peaceable one. Cheerful, optimistic, enthusiastic, the band of social crusaders felt that the conquest of free speech was assured. Not for a moment did they think that the Everett Klu-Klux-Klan would dare resort to violent and criminal tactics in the broad daylight of that beautiful sunny day and in plain view of a host of conscientious Everett citizens.

Assisted by Harry Feinberg and John T. (Red) Doran, Captain Chauncey Wiman checked the number of men who went on board, stopping further entry when the legal limit of two hundred and fifty persons was reached, Feinberg joining the men on board in order to serve as the main speaker at the proposed meeting. Among those who secured passage were several who were not members of the free speech party, but in the work of checking, the tickets of these persons were not collected, their fares being paid in the lump sum that was handed to the captain. Regular passengers of the Verona were informed that their tickets would be good for the steamer Calista, lying at Pier 3. Thirty-eight additional members of the free speech band joined the regular patrons who took passage on the Calista.

Laughter and jest were on the lips of the men who crowded the Verona, and songs of the One Big Union rang out over the sparkling waters of Puget Sound. Loyal soldiers were these in the great class war, enlightened workers who were willing to give their all in the battle for bread, happiness and liberty. Men of all callings these—logger, carpenter, laborer, railroad clerk, painter, miner, printer, seaman and farmhand, all united with one common aim—the desire to gain for Labor the right of free expression.

Among their number, however, were two individuals of a breed reckoned among the lowest order of the human species; two "stool pigeons," low informers upon whom even a regular detective looks down with contempt. One of these, carrying an I. W. W. card and in the employ of Snohomish county and the Everett Commercial Club under the direction of the Pinkerton Detective Agency, had sneaked out of the I. W. W. headquarters long enough to telephone Lieutenant Hedges of the Seattle Police force that there was a boatload of I. W. W. men leaving for Everett. There was no secret in connection with the trip, but that there exist such class traitors, relatively few as they are, to whom the enemies of the workers can look for information is one of the sad features of the class struggle. The "stool's" message was relayed to the Everett authorities and, after being revised by the advocates of the open shop, it finally reached the deputies in the form of a report that a boatload of I. W. W.'s, armed to the teeth, were about to invade, pillage, and burn the city.

At one o'clock the mill whistles blew, the mill deputies armed with their mill clubs, mill revolvers, rifles and shotguns, assembled at the mill headquarters—the Commercial Club—and from there were transported in mill automobiles down the alleys and back streets to the City Dock.

Citizens were driven from the dock and a rope, guarded by armed deputies, was stretched across the land end to prevent access by any save men with guns. Part of the equipment of the Naval Militia was stored in readiness at the Commercial Club—a stubborn fact for those who deny that government is a class institution. At the Pacific Hardware Company, deputy Dave Oswald had an auto load of rifles and ammunition prepared for immediate transportation and use. In Captain Ramwell's office, at the point where the rope was stretched, there were stacked a number of high-power rifles, brought there from the same source. It is even rumored that there was a machine gun on the dock. On the scab tugboat Edison, moored at the north side of the dock, men armed with rifles lay in waiting. The Everett Improvement Dock to the south was also prepared for action. Hundreds of deputies were admitted to the City Dock and were lined up under the direction of Sheriff McRae, Deputy-Sheriff Jefferson Beard, and Lieutenant Charles O. Curtis, of the Officers' Reserve Corps of the National Guard of Washington. Boards were removed from the sides of the warehouses so as to command a view of the landing place, and sacks of potatoes and lumber were used as partial barricades. A few of the deputies were in the west warehouse at the extreme end of the dock, but the majority of them were in the larger warehouse to the east of the open docking space. Plentifully supplied with ammunition and "booze," the cowardly deputies lay hidden in this ambush. The scene was set and the tragedy of November Fifth about to be staged.

As the Verona cleaved the placid, sunlit waters of the Bay and swung up to the City Dock at Everett, shortly before two o'clock, the men were merrily singing the English Transport Workers' strike song,

"HOLD THE FORT!"

We meet today in Freedom's cause,
  And raise our voices high;
We'll join our hands in union strong,
  To battle or to die.

CHORUS

Hold the fort for we are coming,
Union men be strong.
Side by side we battle onward,
Victory will come!

Look, my comrades, see the union,
  Banners waving high.
Reinforcements now appearing,
  Victory is nigh.

See our numbers still increasing;
  Hear the bugle blow:
By our union we shall triumph
  Over every foe.

Fierce and long the battle rages,
  But we will not fear.
Help will come whene'er it's needed,
  Cheer, my comrades, cheer!

From a hillside overlooking the scene thousands upon thousands of Everett citizens sent forth cheer after cheer as a hearty welcome to the "invading army." High up on the flag-pole of the Verona clambered Hugo Gerlot, a youthful free speech enthusiast, to wave a greeting to the throng that lined the shore. Passenger Oscar Carlson and his friend Ernest Nordstrom, from their position on the very bow of the boat, caught the spirit of the party and endeavored to join in the song that resounded louder and clearer as many of the men left the cabins to go out upon the deck.

Completely filling the bow of the boat and blocking the passageway on either side, the singers crowded to the rail in the usual joyously impatient manner of holiday excursionists, and then for the first time observed a body of deputies march from the large warehouse and settle into lines across the back and sides of the open landing space on the dock, where Curtis, McRae, and Beard were stationed.

Waiting until Captain Ramwell's wharfinger, William Kenneth, had made fast the bowline to prevent the boat from backing out, Sheriff Donald McRae gave his belt holster a hitch to bring his gun directly across his middle and then lurched forward to the face of the dock. Holding up his left hand to check the singing, he yelled to the men on board:

"Who is your leader?"

Immediate and unmistakable was the answer from practically every member of the Industrial Workers of the World:

"We are all leaders!"

Angrily jerking his gun from its holster and flourishing it in a threatening manner, McRae cried:

"You can't land here!"

"The hell we can't!" came the reply as the men stepped toward the partly thrown-off gang plank.

A shot rang out from the immediate vicinity of deputy W. A. Bridges, then another, closely followed by a volley that sent them staggering backward. Many fell to the deck. Evidently the waving of McRae's revolver was the prearranged signal for the carnage to commence. The long months of lumber trust lawlessness had culminated in cowardly, deliberate, premeditated and foul murder!

Young Gerlot crumpled up and slid part way down the flag pole, then suddenly threw out both arms and crashed lifeless to the deck, his bullet-torn and bleeding body acting as a shield for several who had thrown themselves prostrate. Passenger Oscar Carlson threw himself flat upon the forward deck and while in that position seven bullets found their way into his quivering flesh, life clinging to the shattered form by a strange vagary of fate. With a severe bullet wound in his abdomen, Ed Roth swayed back and forth for a moment and then toppled forward on his face.

When a bullet whistled past the head of Captain Chauncey Wiman, and another tore a spoke as thick as a man's wrist from the pilot wheel beneath his hand, he deserted his post to barricade himself behind the safe with a mattress, remaining in that position until the close of the hostilities.

At the first shot and during the first volley the unarmed men wildly sought cover from the deadly leaden hail. Those who had not dropped to the deck, wounded or seeking shelter, surged to the starboard side of the boat, causing it to list to an alarming degree, the fastened bowline alone preventing it from capsizing. Several men lost their footing on the blood-slimed decks and were pitched headlong overboard. There, struggling frantically in the water,—by no possible chance combatants—a storm of rifle bullets churning little whirlpools around their heads, one by one they were made the victims of lumber trust greed by the Hessianized deputies stationed at the shore end of the City Dock and upon the dock to the south. The bay was reddened with their blood. Of all who went overboard, James Hadley alone regained the deck, the rest disappearing beneath the silent waters to be dragged by the undertow out to an unknown and nameless ocean grave.

Young Joe Ghilezano seized the rail preparatory to jumping overboard, but seeing two men shot dead while they were in the water he lay down on the deck instead. While there a bullet pierced his hip, another went thru his back close to the spine, and a third completely tore off his left knee cap. Harry Parker slipped over the starboard side in order to gain the lower deck, and a rifle bullet from the vicinity of the tug Goldfinch, along the Everett Improvement Company Dock, ranged thru his back from left to right, just as his friend, Walter Mulholland, also wounded, pulled him in thru a hole torn in the canvas wind shield. An abdominal wound laid Felix Baran low. The thud of bullets as they struck the prostrate men added to the ghastly sound caused by the firing of rifles and revolvers, the curses of the deputies and the moans of the wounded men.

Following the first volley the deputies who had been out in the open scuttled into the warehouses on either side. Thru their scattering ranks the scabs on the tug Edison poured their rifle fire toward the men on the Verona. Lieutenant C. O. Curtis pitched forward and fell dead upon the dock—the victim of a rifle bullet. One of the fleeing deputies paused behind the corner of the waiting room just long enough to flinchingly reach out his hand and, keeping his head under cover, emptied his revolver without taking aim. Deputy Sheriff Jefferson Beard fell mortally wounded as he turned to run, and was dragged into the warehouse by some of the less panic stricken murderers. Sheriff McRae, with a couple of slight wounds in his left leg and heel, was forced to his knees by the impact of bullets against the steel jacket which he wore, remaining in a supplicating attitude for a few seconds while he sobbed out in a quavering tone, "O-o-oh! I'm hit! I-I'm hit!! I-I-I'm hit!!!"

Placed on board the Verona to serve the interests of the lumber trust, what were the two Pinkerton operatives doing while the boat was landing and just before the first heavy firing commenced? Their actions were shrouded in mystery. But, as if anticipating something, one was seen directly after the first shot scurrying into hiding where he lay shivering until long after the firing had ceased. The other, while under cover, was struck on the head by a glancing bullet. He became so enraged at this lack of thoughtfulness on the part of his degenerate brothers that he emptied his revolver at their backs as they broke for cover. From a safe position on the dock, deputy H. D. Cooley, with a pair of field glasses, was tremblingly trying to spy for the approach of the Calista.

Inside the waiting room and the warehouses the drink-crazed deputies ran amuck, shooting wildly in all directions, often with some of their own number directly in the line of fire—bullet holes in the floor and a pierced clock case high up on the waiting room wall giving mute evidence of their insane recklessness. One deputy fled from the dock in terror, explaining to all who would listen that a bullet hole in his ear was from the shot of one of his associates on the dock.

"They've gone crazy in there!" he cried excitedly. "They're shootin' every which way! They shot me in the ear!"

Thru the loopholes already provided, and even thru the sides of the warehouses they blazed away in the general direction of the boat, using revolvers and high powered rifles with steel and copper-jacketed missles. Dum-dums sang their deadly way to the Verona and tore gaping wounds in the breasts of mere boys—an added reward by the industrial lords for their first season of hard labor in the scorching harvest fields. John Looney was felled by a rifle bullet and even as he fell shuddering to the deck another leaden missile shattered the woodwork and impaled one of his eyeballs upon a spear of wood, gouging it from the socket.

At the foot of the dock, protected by the Klatawa slip, (Indian name for runaway) C. R. Schweitzer, owner of a scab plumbing establishment, fired time after time with a magazine shotgun, the buckshot scattering at the long range and raking the forward deck with deadly effect. The pilot house was riddled and the woodwork filled with hundreds of the little leaden messengers that carried a story of "mutual interests of Capital and Labor." Deputy Russell and about ten others assisted in the dastardly work at that point, pouring shot after shot into the convulsive struggling heaps of wounded men piled four and five deep on the deck. One boy in a brown mackinaw suddenly rose upright from a tangled mass of humanity, the blood gushing from his wounds, and with an agonized cry of "My God! I can't stand this any longer!" leaped high in the air over the side of the boat, sinking from sight forever, his watery resting place marked only by a few scarlet ripples.

Two bodies, one with the entire throat shot away, were found next morning washed up on the beach, and that fact was reported to the Everett police by Ed. and Rob. Thompson. That night some men fishing in a little sailboat far out in the bay saw five weighted objects about six feet long, and apparently wrapped in canvas, thrown overboard from a launch, but in none of the daily papers was there any mention of bodies having been found. Six uncalled-for membership cards, deposited by men who took passage on the Verona, may represent as many murders by the cowards on the dock. Those cards are made out to Fred Berger, William Colman, Tom Ellis, Edward Raymond, Peter Viberts, and Chas. E. Taylor. Some of the deputies gloatingly declared that the death toll of the workers was twelve men at the lowest count.

So wanton was the slaughter of the helpless men and boys that strong men who witnessed the scene turned away vomiting. From the hillside the women —those whom the deputies were pretending to protect from the "incoming horde,"—casting aside all womanly fears, raced to the dock in a vain endeavor to stop the commission of further crime, crying out in their frenzy, "The curs! The curs! The dirty curs! They're nothing but murderers!" They, as well as the men who tried to launch boats to rescue the men in the water, were halted by the same citizen deputies whose names head the list of Red Cross donors.

For a short period of time, seemingly endless hours to the unarmed and helpless men on the boat, the rain of lead continued. Tho the boat had righted itself, the men were still unable to extricate themselves from the positions into which they had been thrown. Near the top of one heap lay Abraham Rabinowitz, a young Jewish college graduate, and as he struggled to regain his footing a bullet tore off the whole back part of his head, his blood and brains splashing down over Raymond Lee and Michael Reilly who lay just beneath Rabinowitz died in the arms of Leonard Broman, his "pal" in the harvest fields, without ever having regained consciousness.

"Hold me up, fellow workers!" suddenly called out Gus Johnson as he was fatally stricken by a bullet. "I want to finish the song." Then, above the din of the gunfire and curses of the deputies, the final verse of "Hold the Fort" rang out in defiance of industrial tyranny, and with the termination of the words "Cheer, my comrades, cheer!" the bright red death-foam flecked the ever-to-be silent lips of the brave Swedish revolutionist.

Splintering the stairways, seats and woodwork, and wounding many of the men crouched in hiding, thousands of rounds of ammunition found their way into the boat during the ten long minutes of the onslaught. Finally, with a 41 Colts revolver to enforce his demand, J. F. Billings ordered engineer Ernest Shellgren to back the boat away from the dock. With no pilot at the wheel the propeller churned madly backward for a moment, the bowline drew taut and snapped, and the Verona pulled away from the murderous crew of vigilantes. Not content with the havoc they had wrought at close quarters some of the deputies continued to fire as long as the boat was within range, a bullet from a high powered rifle shattering the left leg of Harry Golden, a youth of twenty-two years, when the boat was far out in the bay. Amputation of the limb was necessary, a cork leg daily reminding young Golden of the majesty of the law.

The Verona with its grim cargo of dead and wounded steamed toward Seattle, meeting the steamer Calista about four miles out, stopping just long enough for Captain Wiman to shout thru his megaphone, "For God's sake don't land! They'll kill you! We have dead and wounded on board now."

With unaccustomed fingers the uninjured men bathed the wounded, tearing up shirts and underclothing in order to bind up their injuries, and making the men as comfortable as possible during the two and one half hour return trip.

A few of the men on board had been armed. These voluntarily threw overboard their revolvers, together with the few empty shells that lay scattered upon the deck, George Reese alone having to be forced to discard the "souvenirs" he had picked up.

It was a quiet crowd that pulled into Seattle, not only because they realized that the class struggle is not all jokes and songs, but also in deference to the sufferings of their wounded comrades. This same spirit animated the men when they were met by drawn cordons of police at the Seattle dock, their first thought and first words being, "Get the wounded fellows out and we will be all right." In the city jail, located on the floor above the hospital, the same generous consideration of their wounded fellow workers' condition led them to forego the demonstration usually attending the arrest and jailing of any body of I. W. W. members.

The four dead members, their still forms covered with blankets, were first removed from the boat and taken to the morgue. Police and hospital ambulances were soon filled with the thirty-one wounded men, who were taken to the city hospital. The uninjured men were then lined up and slowly marched to the city jail. From the Calista the thirty-eight I. W. W. members were taken and placed in the county jail.

At the hospital, Felix Baran, shot in the abdomen, slowly and painfully passed away from internal hemorrhage. Dr. Mary Equi, of Portland, Ore., who examined the body, stated that with surgical attention there would have been more than an even chance of recovery.

No one will ever know how many brave workers were swept out to sea and lost, but Sunday, November Fifth, of the year Nineteen-sixteen, wrote in imperishable letters of red on the list of Labor's martyrs who gave up their lives in Freedom's Cause the names of

FELIX BARAN;
HUGO GERLOT;
GUSTAV JOHNSON;
JOHN LOONEY;
ABRAHAM RABINOWITZ.

French, German, Swedish, Irish, and Russian Jew,—these are the true internationalists of the world-wide brotherhood of toil who died for free speech and the right to organize in this "land of liberty." To them Courtenay Lemon's tribute to the I. W. W. applies with full force.

"Again and again its foot-free members, burning with an indignation and a militant social idealism which is ever an inscrutable puzzle to local authorities, have hastened to towns where free speech fights were on, defied the police, braved clubbings, and voluntarily filled the jails to overflowing, to the rage and consternation of the police and taxpayers. It has acted as the flying squadron of liberty, the unconquered knight-errantry of all captive freedoms; and the migratory workers who constitute a large part of its membership, ever on the march and pitching their camp wherever the industrial battle is thickest, form a guerilla army which is always eager for a fight with the powers of tyranny. Whether they disagree with its methods and aims, all lovers of liberty everywhere owe a debt to this organization for its defense of free speech. Absolutely irreconcilable, absolutely fearless, and unsuppressibly persistent, it has kept alight the fires of freedom, like some outcast vestal of human liberty. That the defense of traditional rights to which this government is supposed to be dedicated should devolve upon an organization so often denounced as 'unpatriotic' and 'un-American,' is but the usual, the unfailing irony of history."(*)

Baran, Gerlot, Johnson, Looney, Rabinowitz,—these names will be a source of inspiration to the workers when their cowardly murderers have long been forgotten.

Those who survived their wounds, saving as pocket pieces the buckshot, copper and steel jacketed and dum-dum bullets extracted from their persons, were; mentioning their more serious wounds:

Harry Golden, age 22, shot in left leg, making amputation necessary.

Joseph Ghilazano, age 20, shot in shoulder and both legs, entire knee-cap shot off and replaced with a silver substitute.

Albert Scribner, age 32, severely wounded in hip, probably lamed for life.

Mario Marino, age 18, shot thru the lungs.

Edward Roth, age 30, severely wounded in abdomen.

Walter Mulholland, age 18, shot in buttock.

Carl Bjork, age 25, wounded in back.

Harry Parker, age 22, shot above abdomen, in back, and in legs.

John Ryan, age 21, wounded in right shoulder and left leg.

Leland E. Butcher, age 28, shot in the left leg.

J. A. Kelly, age 31, shot in right leg.

Hans Peterson, age 32, wounded in head.

Fred Savery, age 25, wounded in hip.

Steve Sabo, age 21, shot in left shoulder.

Robert Adams, age 32, shot in left arm.

Owen Genty, age 26, wounded in right kidney.

C. C. England, age 27, shot in left knee.

Nick Canaeff, age 35, shot in left arm.

Albert Doninger, age 20, wounded in left arm.

Brockman B. Armstrong, age 35, wounds on head.

E. J. Shapeero, age 24, wounded in right leg.

Carl Burke, age 25, shot in back and shoulder.

(*) Courtenay Lemon, "Free Speech in the United States." Pearson's Magazine, December 1916.

Ira Luft, age 27, shot in right side of back.

George Turnquist, age 26, wounded in left leg.

George Brown, age 21, shot in back.

D. J. McCarthy, age 37, shot in side of head and in right leg.

John Adams, age 28, wounded in right elbow.

Edward Truitt, age 28, shot in right elbow.

Others on the boat who were wounded were Oscar Carlson, passenger, nine severe bullet wounds in all parts of his body; L. S. Davis, ship steward, wounded in the arm, and Charles Smith, Pinkerton "stool pigeon" with a slight scalp injury.

The wounded men were none too well treated at the city hospital, only a part of the neglect being due to the overcrowded condition of the wards. Wounds were hastily dressed and in some cases the injured men were placed in jail at once where they had to care for themselves as best they might.

In Everett the deputies left the dock when the Verona had steamed out of the range of their rifle fire, taking with them the corpse of gunman C. O. Curtis, office manager of the Canyon Lumber Company, and deputy-sheriff Jefferson Beard, whose wounds caused his death the following morning. The injured deputies were H. B. Blackburn, James A. Broadbent, R. E. Brown, E. P. Buehrer, Owen Clay, Louis Connor, Jr., Fred Durr, A. J. Ettenborough, Athol Gorrell, Thomas Hedley, Joe Irving, James Meagher; Donald McRae, J. C. Rymer, Edwin Stuchell, and Charles Tucker. Hooted, hissed, and jeered at by the thousands of citizens on the viaduct and hill above the dock, these self-immolated prostitutes to the god of greater profits were taken to the hospitals for treatment.

Among the crowd of citizens was Mrs. Edith Frennette, who had been in Everett a couple of days in connection with a lumber trust charge against her, and with her were Mrs. Lorna Mahler and Mrs. Joyce Peters, who had come from Seattle to attend the proposed street meeting. Making the claim that Mrs. Frenette had threatened the life of Sheriff McRae with a gun and had tried to throw red pepper into his eyes as he was being transported from the dock, the Everett authorities caused the arrest of the three women in Seattle as they were returning in an auto to meet the Verona at the Seattle dock. They were held several days before being released, no charges having been placed against Mrs. Mahler or Mrs. Peters, and the case against Mrs. Frenette was eventually dismissed, just as had been all previous charges made by McRae. These three arrests brought the total number of free speech prisoners up to two hundred and ninety-four.

What were the feelings of the Everett public directly following the massacre can best be judged from the report of an Everett correspondent to the Seattle Union Record, the official A. F. of L. organ.

"Your correspondent was on the street at the time of the battle and at the dock ten minutes afterward. He mingled with the street crowds for hours afterwards. The temper of the people is dangerous. Nothing but curses and execrations for the Commercial Club was heard. Men and women who are ordinarily law abiding, who in normal times mind their own business pretty well, pay their taxes, send their children to church and school, pay their bills, in every way comport themselves as normal citizens, were heard using the most vitriolic language concerning the Commercial Club, loudly sympathizing with the I. W. W.'s. And therein lies the great harm that was done, more menacing to the city than the presence of any number of I. W. W.'s, viz., the transformation of decent, honest citizens into beings mad for vengeance and praying for something dire to happen. I heard gray-haired women, mothers and wives, gentle, kindly, I know, in their home circles, openly hoping that the I. W. W.'s would come back and 'clean up.'"

Corroborating this is the report of President E. P. Marsh to the State Federation of Labor.

"A dangerous situation existed in Everett after the battle of November 5. Public feeling ran high and anything might have happened. Half a thousand citizens were under arms enraged at the Industrial

Workers of the World and deadly determined to stamp out their organization in Everett. It is no exaggeration to say that literally thousands of the working people of Everett were just as enraged toward the members of the Commercial Club who participated in the gun battle. * * * As an instance of how high the feeling ran let me tell you that on the following morning the mayor of the city appeared on the (shingle weavers') picket line with a high power rifle and told the union pickets that he had every reason to believe that an attempt might be made by snipers to pick them off. He asked them to scatter as much as possible, make no demonstration whatever, and declared he would defend them with his life if necessary."

Mayor Merrill, equally guilty with the deputies who were on the dock, taking advantage of a means of spreading information that was denied to the workers, directly after the massacre spoke from a soap box on the corner of Wetmore and California Avenues, telling all who would listen that he was not responsible for the trouble as the Commercial Club had taken the power away from him and put it in the hands of McRae. The insincerity of this vacillating lackey of the lumber trust was demonstrated by his brutal treatment of young Louis Skaroff, who with Chester Micklin and Osmond Jacobs, had been arrested and thrown into jail when the three, bravely taking their lives in their hands, attempted to speak on the corner of Hewitt and Wetmore two hours after the tragedy. It was on Monday night about ten o'clock that the night jailer took Skaroff into a room where Mayor Merrill and a man posing as an immigration officer were seated. The fake immigration officer tried to frighten the prisoner with threats of deportation, after which the jailer beat Skaroff across the head. Merrill arose and took a hand in the proceedings, buffeting the boy back and forth until he fell to the floor. Then, with the aid of the jailer, Skaroff's fingers were placed, one by one, beneath the legs of an iron bed in the room while the ponderous mayor jumped up and down on the bed, mashing and tearing flesh and knuckles. Upon regaining consciousness the mutilated boy found himself in the jail corridor, crushed beneath Merrill's massive form, the mayor having grasped Skaroff by the hair in order to repeatedly hammer the lad's head against the hard cement floor. Finding that Skaroff's spirit could not be broken the cowards finally desisted. Skaroff was released at the end of eleven days.

Chaos reigned in Everett following the tragedy. That night over five hundred deputies patrolled the streets, fearing just retribution for their criminal misdeeds. Those who had been on the dock as parties to the massacre were overheard saying to each other, "We must stick together on this story about the first shot coming from the boat." Certain officials called for the state militia which was mobilized in Seattle but not used. One militiaman, a young lad named Ted Kennedy, refused to serve, claiming that it was the same as strike duty. The fact that the militia was mobilized at once, and that Governor Ernest Lister went to Everett to confer with officials and mill owners there, when he had refused to furnish protection or even to make an investigation at the request of the I. W. W. a short time before showed the governor's bias in favor of the employers. In this lumber district the militia was apparently the property of the mill owners.

A hastily gathered coroner's jury in Everett on November 6th brought in a verdict that C. O. Curtis and Jefferson F. Beard met death from "gunshot wounds inflicted by a riotous mob on the Steamer Verona at the city dock." If any of the jury dissented from its false statement they were too spineless to express their opinion. The deliberations were under the direction of Coroner A. R. Maulsby and the members of the jury were Adam Hill, C. E. Anthony, O. H. King, Chris Culmback, C. Sandstein, and Charles F. Manning.

The inquest was a farce. Those who were outside the "deadline" and who were willing to swear that the first shots came from the dock were not permitted to testify, only sympathizers with the Commercial Club being called as witnesses. No real attempt to take testimony was made. The Seattle Central Labor Council on November 8th appropriated $100 for a more complete investigation after branding the Everett inquest as fraudulent in the following resolution:

"Whereas, It appears to this council that, following a lockout and open-shop campaign by Roland H. Hartley and others of Everett, Wash., the police and business men of that city have attempted to ruthlessly and lawlessly suppress all street speaking and demonstrations by labor organizations, and that unarmed men have been brutally beaten and terrorized, and

Whereas, This policy culminated in a bloody battle on Sunday, November 5, resulting in the death of seven or more men and the wounding of many more, and

Whereas, A fair inquest should be held to fix responsibility for this crime, and it appears that this has not been done, but that only witnesses favorable to the bosses have been heard;

Therefore, we demand another inquest, free from control by the forces opposed to labor, and a change of venue, if that be necessary."

Capitalism stood forth in all its hideous nakedness on that day of red madness, and public opinion was such that the striking shingle weavers had but to persistently press their point in order to win. A conference of prominent men, held in Everett on Monday, decided that the situation could be relieved only by a settlement of the strike. The mill men, when called in, abruptly refused to grant a single demand so long as the men were still out, an attitude they could not have maintained for long. Listening to the false advice of "friends of labor" and "labor leaders" the shingle weavers, albeit grudgingly, returned to their slavery, unconditional surrender being the price they were forced to pay for the doubtful privilege of "relieving the social tension." But with the pay envelopes that could not be stretched to cover the increased cost of living, the weavers, discouraged to an extent and lacking their former solidarity, were forced to down tools again within a few weeks by the greatest of all strike agitators —Hunger.

The prisoners in Seattle were held incommunicado for several days. They were fed upon the poorest grade of prison fare, and were made to sleep on the winter-chilled cement floors without blankets. But Mayor Hiram Gill, realizing that public sentiment was with the imprisoned men, ordered that they be placed upon a proper

MAYOR GILL SAYS I. W. W. DID NOT START RIOT

Seattle Executive Places Blame for Sunday Tragedy on Citizens of Everett—Gives Prisoners Tobacco.

Providing the I. W. W.'s, whose attempted armed invasion of Everett last Sunday resulted in seven deaths and injuries to forty-nine persons, with every comfort possible, Mayor H. C. Gill yesterday afternoon personally directed the carrying of 300 warm blankets and an assortment of tobacco to the 250 prisoners now held in the city jail.

In this manner Gill replied to criticism in Seattle and Everett for not having stopped the I. W. W's from going to the Snohomish County city. He supplemented this today by assailing Sheriff Donald McRae, of Snohomish County, and the posse of special deputies who met the invading I. W. W.'s at the boat.

"In the final analysis," the mayor declared, "it will be found these cowards in Everett who, without right or justification, shot into the crowd on the boat were the murderers and not the I. W. W.'s.

Calls Them Cowards.

"The men who met the I. W. W.'s at the boat were a bunch of cowards. They outnumbered the I. W. W.'s five to one, and in spite of this they stood there on the dock and fired into the boat, I. W. W.'s, innocent passengers and all.

"McRae and his deputies had no legal right to tell the I. W. W.'s or anyone else that they could not land there. When the sheriff put his hand on the butt of his gun and told them they could not land, he fired the first shot, in the eyes of the law, and the I. W. W.'s can claim that they shot in self-defense."

Mayor Gill asserted the Everett authorities have no intention of removing the I. W. W.'s now in jail here to Snohomish County.

"They are afraid to come down here and get them," he declared, "because Everett is in a state of anarchy and the authorities don't know where they're at."

Asked what he would have done at Everett Sunday when the I. W. W.'s appeared at that city, the mayor said he would have permitted them to land.

"After they had been allowed to come ashore," he said, "I would have had them watched. Then if they violated the law I would have had them thrown in jail. There would have been no trouble that way."

No Fight in Seattle.

"Because Everett has been reduced to a state of anarchy by their high-handed methods of dealing with this situation it is no reason they are going to attempt to bring their fight down in Seattle, at least while I am mayor.

"If I were one of the party of forty I. W. W.'s who was almost beaten to death by 300 citizens of Everett without being able to defend myself, I probably would have armed myself if I intended to visit Everett again.

"If the Everett authorities had an ounce of sense, this tragedy would have never happened. They have handled the situation like a bunch of imbeciles, and they have been trying to unload these men onto Seattle. You don't see any disturbances here, because we don't use nickel methods."

The mayor charged that Everett officials were inconsistent in their handling of this situation. He said that they permit candidates for office to violate the city ordinances by speaking on the streets and yet run the I. W. W.'s out of town if they endeavor to mount a soap box.

violen
preach
structi
they m
city th
pal an
larg
corne
nance,
anarch
"Pre
dertoo
ous n
minat
Seat
armed
the p
the le

we
who,
infor
ceed
repli
ing s
ing o
"Ir
these
ere

diet, be given blankets and be allowed to see relatives and friends. On November 8th in the Seattle Times there appeared a statement by Gill that played a very important part in riveting the attention of the people upon the real criminals in the case. As the Times is a notoriously conservative and labor-hating sheet, being largely responsible for the raid on the I. W. W. and Socialist Halls on July 19, 1913, and for the attack by drunken sailors and soldiers on the I. W. W. hall on June 16, 1917, it can hardly be accused of exaggeration in favor of the workers in this interview.

Following the publication of this interview the Seattle Chamber of Commerce, Seattle's "Commercial Club," endeavored to father a movement looking to the recall of Gill from office. Back of this attempt were Judge Thomas Burke, Louis Lang, Jay Thomas, and four stall-fed ministers, the Reverends W. A. Major, E. V. Shailer, Wood Stewart and

Carter Helm Jones. Of these, Thomas represented the liquor interests, Lang was the former police chief who had been discharged in disgrace and was herding scabs on the waterfront, Burke was chief spokesman for the low-wage open-shop interests, and as to the preachers—the less said the better. The lumber and shipping trusts had adequate representation at the "Law and Order" meeting as the attempted recall gathering was styled. But the whole thing fell flat when Gill himself offered to sign the recall for the opportunity it would give him to tell the real facts about the Everett case and the interests lined up behind the prosecution and the recall.

On the night of the tragedy a report was circulated in Seattle to the effect that every known I. W. W. would be arrested on sight. The answer to this was a street meeting at which nearly ninety dollars were collected as the first money toward the Everett Prisoners' Defense, and the packing of the hall for weeks thereafter by members and sympathizers who had not attended meetings for a long time. A temporary committee was chosen to handle the work of the defense of the imprisoned men, and this committee acted until November 16th, at which time at a mass meeting of I. W. W. members Herbert Mahler was elected secretary of the Everett Prisoners' Defense Committee, Charles Ashleigh, publicity agent, and W. J. Houser, Morris Levine and Thomas Murphy as the committee. Richard Smith was afterward chosen to take the place vacated by Levine. This committee functioned thruout the case and up until the final audit of their account on June 12, 1917.

Within the jail a process of selection had gone on. One by one the free speech prisoners were taken from their cells and slowly led past a silent and darkened cell into whose gloomy depths the keenest eye was unable to penetrate. Again and again they were marched past the peephole, first with hats on and then with them off, while two sinister looking fingers were slid out of a narrow opening from time to time to indicate those who should be held.

"I'd give two of my fingers," muttered one of the prisoners bitterly, "to know the skunk that belongs to those two fingers."

Little did he and his fellow workers realize that they were to learn later, thru the development of the trial, that the principal person engaged in the despicable work was George Reese, a member of the I. W. W. and of the I. L. A. It was on learning this that many of the actions of Reese were made clear; his connection with dock riots during the longshoremen's strike, his establishment of a "flying squadron" to beat up scabs on the waterfront, his open boast on the floor of I. L. A. meetings that his pockets were lined with money gained by robbing the strike-breakers after they had been beaten up and his advice to other strikers to do likewise, his activities just prior to the various dock fires, his seemingly miraculous escape in every instance when strikers were arrested, his election as delegate from the longshoremen to the Seattle Central Labor Council, his requests of prominent I. W. W. members that they purchase various chemicals for him, his giving of phosphorus to members of the I. L. A. and the I. W .W. with instructions as to how and where to use it, his attempts to advocate violence at an Everett street meeting, his gathering of "souvenirs" on the Verona—all actions designed either to aid the employers in their fights against the workers or to furnish an excuse for his further employment as an "informer."

Well may the question be asked—What was Reese doing just as the Verona docked in Everett on November 5th? Was Reese merely a "stool pigeon" or was he an "agent provocateur?"

Aiding Reese in the selective process was Charles Smith, the other Pinkerton operative who had been on the boat. One of the men first picked out was I. P. McDowell, alias Charles Adams, and this individual was weak enough to fall for the promise of immunity offered by agents of the lumber trust if he would point out the "leaders" and then take the stand to swear that the men on the boat were armed and the first shot came from one of them. McDowell pointed out some of the men, but lacking the nerve to carry out the last part of the program he was held with the rest for trial. The seventy-four men thus picked were formally charged with murder in the first degree. The first charge carried the names of C. O. Curtis as well as that of Jefferson Beard, but later the name of Curtis was dropped from the information. The men so charged were:

Charles Auspos, alias Austin, age 38, teamster, born in Wisconsin.

James D. Bates, age 29, steam fitter, born in Illinois.

E. M. Beck, age 45, laborer, born in New York.

Charles Berg, age 22, laborer, born in Germany.

J. H. Beyer, age 56, painter, born in Michigan.

J. F. Billings, age 35, cook, born in Nebraska.

Charles Black, age 23, laborer, born in Pennsylvania.

J. J. Black, age 27, longshoreman, born in Massachusetts.

John W. Bowdoin, age 35, laborer, born in Sweden.

Frank Boyd, age 43, laborer, born in Illinois.

Pete Breed, age 26, laborer, born in Holland.

W. H. Brown, age 40, laborer, born in Maryland.

H. T. Cheetman, age 25, carpenter, born in Florida.

Fred Crysler, age 26, laborer, born in Canada.

Charles H. Cody, age 46, painter, born in Montana.

William Coffin, age 34, motorman, born in California.

Clarence Cyphert, age 35, logger, born in Washington.

Roy Davis, age 47, laborer, born in California.

William Davis, age 35, cook, born in Maryland.

Axel Downey, age 17, laborer, born in Iowa.

John Downs, age 28, sailor, born in Colorado.

Adolph Ersson, age 26, laborer and sailor, born in Sweden.

Harry Feinberg, age 25, cleaner and dyer, born in Illinois.

Charles Hawkins, age 28, laborer, born in Indiana.

Charles Haywood, age 46, miner, born in Minnesota.

E. F. Hollingsworth, age 29, fireman, born in North Carolina.

J. E. Houlihan, age 36, miner, born in Ireland.

Alfred Howard, age 28, coal packer, born in New York.

Harvey Hubler, age 21, teamster, born in Illinois.

Oscar Johnson, age 24, laborer, born in Sweden.

Victor Johnson, age 37, laborer, born in Finland.

J. A. Kelly, age 31, logger, born in Ohio.

Theodore Lauer, age 29, laborer, born in New York.

William Lawson, age 32, laborer, born in Washington.

Jack Leonard, age 27, laborer, born in Kentucky.

Pat Lyons, age 48, laborer, born in England.

Jim Mack, age 31, laborer, born in Ireland.

Joseph Manning, age 28, automobile repairer, born in Pennsylvania.

Laurence Manning, age 26, laborer, born in New York.

Ed Miller, age 48, painter, born in New York.

Harold Miller, age 21, gas fitter, born in Kansas.

John Mitchell, age 38, miner, born in Illinois.

George Murphy, age 28, laborer, born in Kentucky.

Louis McCall, age 24, laborer, born in Texas.

I. P. McDowell, alias Charles Adams, age 28, printer, born in Illinois.

C. D. McLennan, age 48, longshoreman, born in Georgia.

Carl Newman, age 30, laborer, born in Sweden.

John Nugent, age 38, laborer, born in New York,

Malachi O'Neill, age 34, blacksmith, born in Ireland.

Earl Osborne, age 33, logger, born in North Carolina.

Jack Paterson, age 24, laborer, born in Illinois.

Harston Peters, age 32, laborer, born in Virginia.

James Powers, age 47, sheet metal worker, born in Massachusetts.

John Rawlings, age 26, laborer, born in Wisconsin.

Michael J. Reilly, age 23, laborer, born in New York.

John Ross, age 36, laborer, born in Massachusetts.

Ed. Roth, age 31, longshoreman, born in New York.

Thomas Savage, age 50, machinist, born in New York.

E. J. Shapeero, age 23, timekeeper, born in Pennsylvania.

William Shay, age 28, laborer, born in Massachusetts.

H. Shebeck, age 24, laborer, born in Wisconsin.

Albert Shreve, age 40, laborer, born in Iillinois.

H. Sokol, age 26, laborer, born in Russia.

D. Stevens, age 21, longshoreman, born in Canada

Robert Struick, age 24, farmer, born in Michigan.

Frank Stewart, age 35, logger, born in Canada.

Tom Tracy, age 30, crane driver, born in Pennsylvania.

Thomas H. Tracy, age 36, teamster, born in Nebraska.

Edwart Truitt, age 28, longshoreman, born in Pennsylvania.

F. O. Watson, age 35, blacksmith, born in Louisiana.

James Whiteford (Kelly), age 36, cook, born in New York.

Abraham B. Wimborne, age 22, buss-boy, born in England.

William Winn, age 44, miner, born in Maryland.

All of these men, with the exception of J. H. Beyer, were heavily handcuffed and secretly transferred to Everett, forty-one being taken in the first contingent and the balance later.

Meanwhile the I. W. W. branches in Seattle had communicated with the General Headquarters of the organization and steps had been taken to secure legal aid. Attempts to enlist the services of Frank P. Walsh, former chairman of the Industrial Relations Commission, were unsuccessful. For various reasons other well known attorneys refused to ally themselves with the defense.

Attorney Fred H. Moore of Los Angeles, responding to the call from Seattle, reached Seattle just one week after the tragedy, on Sunday, November, 12th. Moore acted as chief counsel for the defense. He had first come into prominence thru his connection with the great free speech fight waged in Spokane, Wash., during the fall of 1909 and the spring of 1910. During that fight he handled the legal end of the cases of many hundreds of free speech fighters whose arrests ran into the thousands. He was also connected with various other cases in connection with the Industrial Workers of the World, notably that of Jack Whyte and others arrested in the contest for free speech in San Diego, Cal., and the famous Ettor-Giovannitti case that developed from the great strike of textile workers in Lawrence, Mass., in 1912. His sympathy with the workers and his understanding of the class struggle made him invaluable to the defense.

Of equal importance was attorney George F. Vanderveer, who was called into the case a little later than Moore. Vanderveer was formerly the prosecuting attorney for King county, in which position he won a reputation for clever and merciless cross-examination. One of Seattle's most prominent and brilliant lawyers, his wide acquaintance with all classes of people and his comprehensive knowledge of conditions in King and Snohomish counties, coupled with his keen satire and compelling logic, gave a force to the case that cannot be underestimated.

Attorney E. C. Dailey of Everett, Caroline A. Lowe of Kansas City, Mo., and Harry Sigmond and J. L. Finch, both of Seattle, completed the list of counsel for the defense.

After being held in the Seattle city jail for nine days without any charge having been placed against them, one hundred twenty-eight men who were on the Verona were released, small bodies of them being sent out at different periods in order to avoid demonstrations from the public. Those who were released were:

James Agen, Frank Andrews, Brockman Armstrong, W. D. Beachy, J. H. Beyer, John Bolan, J. Bonfield, Elmer Brisbon, Leonard Broman, George Brown, James Burns, Martin Cable, Val Calze, A. L. Cameron, James Carlough, J. H. Carr, Ray Clark, Joseph Cline, Archie Collins, Robert Conning, Nick Conaieff, Joseph Costello, R. F. Dalton, Frank Dante, C. W. Davis, Lawrence Davis, Albert Doninger, John Donohue, William Dott, Joseph Dougherty, Ned Dustard, J. H. Elliott, C. C. England, John Fitzpatrick, A. Fletcher, Russell Free, Alfred Freeman, Ben Freeman, James Freeman, John Gibson, Frank Gillarkey, P. A. Gragler, Charles Gray, James Gray, Paul Grossman, Ed Gruberg, Raymond Gurber, Robert Hansen, Joe Harris, L. W. Harris, Arnold Hensel, Roy Howell, G. H. Isenberg, Carl Jacobson, George Johnson, Ray Johnson, John Karne, Henry Krieg, Fred Laveny, Henry Lea, Raymond Lee, William Ledingham, Charles Leider, Ira Luft, Ed Lynn, George Maguire, William Micklenburg, August Miller, Dennis Miller, Frank C. Miller, John Miller, Frank Millet, Roy Mitchell, William Montgomery, William Moore, James Murray, Leo McCabe, J. McCoy, Bernard Narvis, Al. Nickerson, Ben Noll, Tom Norton, Tom O'Connor, Jack Osborne, E. Peckman, Hans Peterson, A. Pilon, Ira Porter, Max Ramsey, Edward Rays, Herman Rechlenberg, Frank Reiner, Ernest Rich, John J. Riley, C. H. Ross, M.

Rountell, Steve Sabo, J. L. Samuel, Joe Sarracco, Ed Schwartz, Carl Schultz, H. Stredwick, Arthur Shumek, Charles Smith, Harry Smith, E. J. Smith, Cecil Snedegar, Frank Sofer, Stanley Stafl, Raymond St. Clair, John Stroka, Mike Stysco, C. Thomas, Richard Tibbs, John Utne, Joseph Vito, John Walker, Benny Warshawsky, F. Westwood, Ben Whitehead, Arley Whiteside, William Wilke, H. Wilson, Frank Wise, and Charles Wolskie.

Most of these were mere boys. Mere boys—but undaunted by their recent terrible experience on the Verona where the open shop fiends had fired upon them without warning. Mere boys—and yet they loyally marched straight to the I. W. W. hall as soon as they were released, there to inquire about the condition of their wounded fellow workers and to gain news of those who had been taken to Everett to answer charges of first degree murder. Mere boys—youthful enthusiasm shining on their beardless faces. Scattered among them were a few men of middle years, and here and there a grey head stood out in bold relief—but the majority of them were mere boys, youthful soldiers in the Social Revolution, fine and clean and loyal material called together by the compelling ideal of a New Society.

The predominance of young blood in the organization was noted in the report of the 1912 convention, where it was shown that ninety per cent of the membership were under thirty years of age, due of course to the fact that the modern tendency is to displace the older men in industry. As one wit has put it "If a man works as hard as the employers want him to he is worn out at forty-five; if he isn't worn out at forty-five he is not the kind of worker the employers want." Others have noted the percentage of the very young. John Graham Brooks, for instance, in "American Syndicalism—The I. W. W." has this to say:

"Of the same nature as a characteristic is the **youth** of the membership. The groups I saw in the West bore this stamp so unmistakably as to suggest bodies of students at the end of a rather jolly picnic. The word 'bum' usually applied to them in that region does not fit them. There are plenty of older men, as there are men with every appearance of being 'down and out'—with trousers chewed off at the heels, after the manner of tramps, but in face and bearing they are far from 'bums.' In one of the speeches the young were addressed as 'best material;' because they could stand the wear and tear of racking journeys. They were free from family responsibilities, and could at any moment respond to the call of duty."

Bearing out this idea, tho along a somewhat different line, is an excerpt from an article by Anna Louise Strong which appeared in the Survey magazine just prior to the trial. This and other articles, together with the personal efforts of Miss Strong, whose official standing as a member of the Seattle School Board and as Executive Secretary of the Seattle Council of Social Agencies gave weight to her opinion, did much toward creating a favorable public sentiment during the trial. Says Miss Strong:

"The boys in jail are a cheerful lot. The 'tanks' which contain them are the tanks of the usual county jail, much overcrowded now by the unusual number. Bunks crowded above each other, in full sight thru the bars; a few feet away, all the processes of life open to the casual beholder. But they sit in groups playing cards or dominoes; they listen to tunes played on the mouth-organ; most of all they sing. They sing whenever visitors come, and smile thru the bars in cheerful welcome. Theirs is the spirit of the crusader of all ages, and all causes, won or lost, sane or insane. Theirs is the irresponsibility and audacious valor of youth. When they disliked their food, says a conservative newspaper, they went on strike and 'sang all night.' Sang all night! What sane adults in our drab, business-as-usual world would think of doing that? Who, in fact, could think of doing it but college boys or Industrial Workers of the World, cheerfully defying authority?"

Thru an absurd and laughable error J. H. Beyer, one of the seventy-four men charged with first degree murder, was among those who were released. Beyer immediately sought out and told attorney Moore his story. Then this "hardened criminal" walked the street of Seattle after public announcement had been made that he was willing to be taken to Everett to be incarcerated with the rest of his fellow workers, and that he awaited rearrest. The prosecution made no move to apprehend him, so on December 14th Beyer went to Everett and asked the authorities to lock him up. The Snohomish officials shamefacedly granted this unique request but they absolutely refused to refund the money Beyer had paid to deliver himself up to "Justice."

Before leaving Seattle Beyer made this statement: "I have waited here nearly a month since my release from the Seattle jail, yet no officer from Everett has come for me. In justice to the other boys accused I feel that I should share their lot as well as the accusation. I do not fear returning to Everett and giving myself up for I am confident that we shall be all exculpated. I am fifty-three years of age and have had many and varied experiences in my career, but I never expected to be accused of crime because I endeavored to assert my constitutional right of Free Speech."

The same day that Beyer surrendered himself, bonds of $50 each were secured for thirty-eight men who had been selected from the Verona and Calista and held on charges of unlawful assembly. Bail was given by James Duncan, Secretary of the Central Labor Council, and E. B. Ault, editor of the Union Record, both of Seattle. The released men were Dewey Ashmore, E. Belmat, C. Burke, L. E. Butcher, James Callahan, Harry Chase, Charles Day, A. J. Deach, Charles Ellis, J. Ford, Owen Genty, Hy Gluckstad, Frank Goff, James C. Hadley, Steve Heletour, A. O. Hooper, C. C. Hulbert, H. P. Hunsberger, C. L. Johnson, R. W. Jones, Joe Kelley, F. Lansing, W. O. Lily, E. McBride, William Mc-

Gregor, R. Nicholson, David O'Hern, Harry Parker, J. Ryan, Sam Scott, Mark Skomo, Thomas Smye, and F. Thorpe.

Altho an inquest had been held over the dead gunmen at such an early date after the tragedy and with such haste as to seem suspicious, repeated demands for an inquest over Labor's dead were of no avail. No such inquest was ever held. Only by strong protest were the bodies kept from the potter's field.

Thirty-eight charged with unlawful assembly, seventy-four in jail accused of first degree murder, thirty-two severely wounded and at least two of these crippled for life, six unaccounted for and probably shot and drowned, and five known dead in the city morgue,—this was the answer of the tyrannical timber barons to Labor's demand for free speech and the right to organize within the confines of the Lumber Kingdom.

CHAPTER V.

BEHIND PRISON BARS

"One of the greatest sources of social unrest and bitterness has been the attitude of the police toward public speaking. On numerous occasions in every part of the country the police of cities and towns have, either arbitrarily, or under the cloak of a traffic ordinance, interfered with or prohibited public speaking, both in the open and in halls, by persons connected with organizations of which the police or those from whom they receive their orders did not approve. In many instances such interference has been carried out with a degree of brutality which would be incredible if it were not vouched for by reliable witnesses. Bloody riots frequently have accompanied such interference, and large numbers of persons have been arrested for acts of which they were innocent or which were committed under the extreme provocation of brutal treatment by police or private citizens.

"In some cases this suppression of free speech seems to have been the result of sheer brutality and wanton mischief, but in the majority of cases it undoubtedly is the result of a belief by the police or their superiors that they were 'supporting and defending the Government' by such invasion of personal rights. There could be no greater error. Such action strikes at the very foundation of government. It is axiomatic that a government which can be maintained only by the suppression of criticism should not be maintained. Furthermore, it is the lesson of history that attempts to suppress ideas result only in their more rapid propagation."

The foregoing is the view of the Industrial Relations Commission as it appears on page 98 and 99 of Volume One of their official report to the United States Government.

Jail at EVERETT

The growth of a public sentiment favorable to the Industrial Workers of the World was clearly shown on November 18th, at which time the bodies of Felix Baran, Hugo Gerlot and John Looney were turned over to the organization for burial. Gustav Johnson had already been claimed by relatives and a private funeral held, and the body of Abraham Rabinowitz sent to New York at the request of his sister.

Thousands of workers, each wearing a red rose or carnation, formed in line at the undertaking parlors and then silently marched four abreast behind the three hearses and the automobiles containing the eighteen women pall bearers and the floral tributes to the martyred dead.

To the strains of the "Red Flag" and the "Marseillaise" the grim and imposing cortege wended its way thru the crowded city streets, meeting with expressions of sorrow and sympathy from those who lined the sidewalk. Delegations of workers from Everett, Tacoma, and other Washington cities and towns were in line, and a committee from Portland, Ore., brought appropriate floral offerings. The solidarity of labor was shown in this great funeral procession, by all odds the largest ever held in the Northwest.

Arriving at the graveside in Mount Pleasant cemetery the rebel women reverently bore the coffins from the hearses to the supporting frame, surrounded by boughs of fragrant pine, above the yawning pit. A special chorus of one hundred voices led the singing of "Workers of the World, Awaken," and as the song died away Charles Ashleigh began the funeral oration.

Standing on the great hill that overlooks the whole city of Seattle, the speaker pointed out the various industries with their toiling thousands and referred to the smoke that shadowed large portions of the view as the black fog of oppression and ignorance which it was the duty of the workers to dispel in order to create the Workers' Commonwealth. The entire address was marked by a simple note of resolution to continue the work of education until the workers have come into their own, not a trace of bitterness evincing itself in the remarks. Ashleigh called upon those present never to falter until the enemy had been vanquished. "Today," he said, "we pay tribute to the dead. Tomorrow we turn, with spirit unquellable, to give battle to the foe!"

As the notes of "Hold the Fort!" broke a moment of dead silence, a shower of crimson flowers, torn from the coats of the assembled mourners, covered the coffins and there was a tear in every eye as the bodies slowly descended into their final resting place. As tho loath to leave, the crowd lingered to sing the "Red Flag" and "Solidarity Forever." Those present during the simple but stirring service were struck with the thought that the class struggle could never again be looked upon as a mere bookish theory, the example of those who gave their lives in the cause of freedom was too compelling a call to action.

But the imperious exactions of the class war left no time for mourning, and ere the last man had left the graveside the first to go was busily spreading the news of an immense mass meeting to be held in Dreamland Rink on the next afternoon. At this meeting five thousand persons from all walks of life gathered to voice their protest against the Everett outrage and to demand a federal investigation. The labor unions, the clergy, public officials and the general citizenry, were represented by the speakers. This was the first of many mass meetings held by the aroused and indignant people of Seattle until the termination of the case.

The "kept" press carried on a very bitter campaign against the I. W. W. for some few days after the dock tragedy, but dropped that line of action when the public let them understand that they were striking a wrong note. Thereafter their policy was to ignore, as far as possible, the entire affair. Practically the only time this rule was broken was in the printing of the song "Christians At War" by John F. Kendrick, taken from the I. W. W. song book.

Funeral of GERLOT,
LOONEY and BARAN

The Seattle Post-Intelligencer gave a photographic reproduction of the cover page of the book and of the page containing the song. The obvious intent was to have people think that this cutting satire was an urge for the members of the I. W. W. to do in times of peace those inglorious things that are eminently respectable in times of war. Later the Times, and several other papers, reproduced the same cover and song, the only change being that certain words were inked out to make it appear that the song was obscene. And tho the P.—I. had published the song in full the Times placed beneath their garbled version these words, "The portions blotted out are words and phrases such as never appear in The Times or in any other decent newspaper." The simultaneous appearance of this song in a number of papers was merely a coincidence, no doubt; there is no reason to believe that the lumber trust inspired the attack!

Allied as usual with the capitalist press and "stool pigeons" and employers' associations in a campaign to discredit the workers involved in the case, was the moribund Socialist Labor Party thru its organ, the Weekly People.

The entire I. W. W. press came to the support of the imprisoned men as a matter of course. The Seattle Union Record and many other craft union papers, realizing that an open shop fight lay back of the suppression of free speech, also did great publicity work. But no particular credit is due to those "labor leaders" who, like J. G. Brown, president of the Shingle Weavers' Union, grudgingly gave a modicum of assistance under pressure from radicals in their respective organizations.

The Northwest Worker of Everett deserves especial praise for its fearless and uncompromising stand in the face of the bitterest of opposition. This paper had practically to suspend publication because of pressure the lumber trust brought to bear on the firm doing their printing. This, with the action recorded in the minutes of the Commercial Club, "decided to go after advertisements in labor journals and the Northwest Worker," shows that a free press is as obnoxious to the lumber lords as are free speech and free assembly.

It scarcely needs noting that the International Socialist Review rendered yeoman service, as that has been its record in all labor cases since the inception of the magazine. Several other Socialist publications, to whom the class struggle does not appear merely as a momentary quadrennial event, also did their bit. Diverse foreign language publications, representing varying shades of radical thought, gave to the trial all the publicity their columns could carry.

Just why seventy-four men were picked as prisoners is a matter of conjecture. Probably it was because the stuffy little Snohomish county jail could conveniently, to the authorities, hold just about that number. The men were placed four in a cell with ten cells to each tank, there being two tanks of steel resting one above the other. Even with all the windows thrown open the ventilation was so poor that the men were made ill by the foul air.

For almost two full months after being transported to Everett the men were held incommunicado; were not allowed to see papers or magazines or to have reading matter of any description; were subjected to the brutalities of Sheriff McRae and other jail officials who had been prominent in previous outrage and participants in the massacre at the dock; and were fed on the vilest prison fare. Mush was the principal article of diet; mush semi-cooked and cold; mush full of mold and maggots; mush that was mainly husks and lumps that could not be washed down with the pale blue prison milk; mush—until the prisoners fitfully dreamed of mush and gagged at the mere mention of the word. Finding themselves slowly starving the men decided that it were better to complete the job at once rather than to linger in misery. A hunger strike was declared! Meal after meal—or mush after mush—passed and the men refused to eat. Those who were thought to be leaders in the miniature revolt were thrown in the blackhole where there was neither light nor fresh air. Still the men refused to eat, so the authorities were forced to surrender and the men had something to eat besides mush.

Great discomfort was experienced by the prisoners from having to sleep on the cold steel floors of the unheated cells during the chill November nights. Deciding to remedy the condition they made a demand for mattresses and blankets from the authorities, not a man of them being willing to have the Defense Committee purchase such supplies. The needed articles were refused and the men resorted to a means of enforcing their demands known as "building a battleship."

With buckets and tins, and such strips of metal as could be wrenched loose, the men beat upon the walls, ceilings, and floors of the steel tanks. Those who found no other method either stamped on the steel floors in unison with their fellows, or else removed their shoes to use the heels to beat out a tattoo. To add to the unearthly noise they yelled concertedly with the full power of their lungs. Three score and ten men have a noise-making power that words cannot describe. The townspeople turned out in numbers, thinking that the deputies were murdering the men within the jail. The battleship construction workers redoubled their efforts. Acknowledging defeat, the jail officials furnished the blankets and mattresses that had been demanded.

A few days later the men started their morning meal only to find that the mush was strongly "doped" with saltpeter and contained bits of human manure and other refuse—the spite work, no doubt, of the enraged deputies. Another battleship was started. This time the jailers closed all the windows in an effort to suffocate the men, but they broke the glass with mop-handles and continued the din. As before, the deputies were defeated and the men received better food for a time.

On November 24th an official of the State Board of Prisoners took the finger prints and photographs of the seventy-four men who were innocent until proven guilty under the "theory" of law in this country, and, marking these Bertillion records with prison serial numbers, sent copies to every prison in the United States. In taking the prints of the first few men brute force was used. Lured from their cells the men were seized, their hands screwed in a vise, and an imprint taken by forcibly covering their hands with lampblack and holding them down on the paper. When the others learned that some had thus been selected they voted that all should submit to having their prints taken so the whole body of prisoners would stand on the same footing. Attorney Moore was denied all access to the prisoners during the consummation of this outrage.

After obtaining permission of the jail officials a committee of Everett citizens, with the voluntary assistance of the Cooks' and Waiters' Union, prepared a feast for the free speech prisoners on Thanksgiving Day. When the women arrived at the jail they were met by Sheriff McRae who refused to allow the dinner to be served to the men. McRae was drunk. In place of this dinner the sheriff set forth a meal of moldy mush so strongly doped with chemicals as to be unfit for human consumption. This petty spite work by the moon-struck tool of the lumber trust was in thoro keeping with the cowardly characteristics he displayed on the dock on November 5th. And the extent to which the daily press in Everett was also under the control of the lumber interests was shown by the publication of a faked interview with attorney Fred Moore published in the Everett Herald under date of November 29th, Moore having been credited with the statement that the prison food deserved praise and the prisoners were "given as good food and as much of it as they could wish."

During the whole of McRae's term as sheriff

there was no time that decent food was given voluntarily to the prisoners as a whole. At times, with low cunning, McRae gave the men in the upper tank better food than those confined below, and also tried to show favoritism to certain prisoners, in order to create distrust and suspicion among the men. All these attempts to break the solidarity of the prisoners failed of their purpose.

On one occasion McRae called "Paddy" Cyphert, one of the prisoners whom he had known as a boy, from his cell and offered to place him in another part of the jail in order that he might escape injury in a "clubbing party" the deputies had planned. Cyphert told McRae to put him back with the rest for he wanted the same treatment as the others and would like to be with them in order to resist the assault. In the face of this determination, which was typical of all the prisoners, the contemplated beating was never administered.

McRae would oftentimes stand outside the tanks at a safe distance and drunkenly curse the prisoners and refer to them as cowards, to which the men would reply by repeating the words of the sheriff on the dock, "O-oh, I'm hit! I-I'm h-hit!! I-I-I'm h-h-hit!!!" Then they would burst forth with a song written by William Whalen in commemoration of the exploits of the doughty sheriff, a song which since has become a favorite of the migratory workers as they travel from job to job, and which will serve to keep the deeds of McRae fresh in the minds of the workers for many years to come.

TO SHERIFF McRAE

Call out your Fire Department, go deputize your bums;
Gather in your gunmen and stool pigeons from the slums;
You may resolute till doomsday, you ill-begotten knave;
We'll still be winning Free Speech Fights when you are in your grave!

You reprobate, you imp of hate, you're a traitor to the mind
That brought you forth in human shape tó prey upon mankind.
You are lower than the snakes that cawl or the scavengers that fly;
You're the living, walking image of a damn black-hearted lie!

We'll still be here in Everett when your career is ended,
And back among the dregs of life your dirty hide has blended;
When you shun the path of honest wrath and fear the days to come,
And bow your head to the flag of red, you poor white-livered bum!

For the part you played in Everett's raid that fateful Sunday morn,
May your kith and kindred live to curse the day that you were born;
May the memory of your victims haunt your conscience night and day,
Until your feeble, insect mind beneath the strain gives way!

Oh, Don McRae, you've had your day; make way for Freedom's host:
For Labor's sun is rising, soon 'twill shine from coast to coast!
The shot you fired at Everett re-echoes thru the night
As a message to the working class to organize and fight!

Those graves upon the hillside as monuments will stand
To point the way to Freedom's goal to slaves thruout the land;
And when at last the working class have made the masters yield,
May your portion of the victory be a grave in the Potter's Field!

The end of the first week in January brought about the change in the administrative force of Snohomish county that had been voted at the November election. A new set of lumber trust lackeys were placed in office. James McCullogh succeeded Donald McRae as sheriff, and Lloyd Black occupied the office vacated by Prosecuting Attorney O. T. Webb.

The advent of a new sheriff made some slight difference in the jail conditions, but this was more than offset by the underhanded methods used from that time on with the idea of breaking the solidarity of the free speech fighters. Liquor was placed in the bathrooms where the men could easily get hold of it, but even among those who had been hard drinkers on the outside there were none who would touch it. Firearms were cunningly left exposed in hopes that the men might take them and attempt a jail break, thus giving the jailers a chance to shoot them down or else causing the whole case to be discredited. The men saw thru the ruse and passed by the firearms without touching them.

Working in conjunction with the prosecuting attorney was H. D. Cooley. This gentleman was one of the deputies on the dock, having displayed there his manly qualities by hiding behind a pile of wood at first, and later by telling others to go with rifles to head off the Calista which he had spied approaching from the direction of Mukilteo. Cooley had a practice among the big lumbermen, and in the case against the I. W. W. he was hired by the state with no stipulation as to pay. The general excuse given for his activities in the case, which dated from November 6th, was that he was retained by "friends of Jefferson Beard" and other "interested parties."

Attorney A. L. Veitch was also lined up with the prosecution. He was the same gentleman who had lectured to the deputies during the preceding fall as a representative of the Merchants' and Manufacturers' Association, and had told the deputies how to handle "outside agitators." Veitch was also employed by the state as a matter of record, but there was a direct stipulation that he receive no pay from state funds. He also was employed by "friends of Jefferson Beard" and other "interested parties."

With Veitch there was imported from Los Angeles one Malcolm McLaren, an M. and M. detective and office partner with Veitch, to act as "fix-it" man for the lumber trust. McLaren was at one time an operative for the infamous Wm. J. Burns, and Burns has well said "Private detectives, ninety per cent of them, as a class, are the worst of crooks, blackmailers and scoundrels." Under McCullogh's regime this open-shop gumshoe artist had free access to the jail with instructions to go as far as he liked.

Just what the prisoners thought about jail conditions during the time they were incarcerated is given in the following report which was smuggled out to the Industrial Worker and published on March 3rd:

" 'Everything is fine and dandy on the outside, don't worry, boys.' "

"This is the first thing we heard from visitors ever since we seventy-four have been incarcerated in the Snohomish County Jail at Everett.

"While 'everything is fine and dandy on the outside' there are, no doubt, hundreds who would like to hear how things are on the inside. Let us assure everyone on the outside that 'everything is fine and dandy' on the inside. We are not worrying as it is but a short time till the beginning of the trials, the outcome of which we are certain will be one of the greatest victories Labor has ever known, if there exists a shadow of justice in the courts of America.

"One hundred days in jail so far—and for nothing! Stop and think what one hundred days in jail means to seventy-four men! It means that in the aggregate the Master Class have deprived us of more than twenty years of liberty. Twenty years! Think of it, and a prospect of twenty more before all are at liberty.

"And why?

"There can be but one reason, one answer: We are spending this time in jail and will go thru the mockery of a trial because the masters of Everett are trying to shield themselves from the atrocious murders of Bloody November Fifth.

"After being held in Seattle, convicted without a trial, except such as was given us by the press carrying the advertising of the boss and dependent on him for support, on November 10th forty-one of us were brought to Everett. A few days later thirty more were brought here.

"We found the jail conditions barbarous. There were no matresses and only one blanket to keep off the chill of a Puget Sound night in the cold, unheated steel cells. There were no towels. We were supplied with laundry soap for toilet purposes, when we could get even that. Workers confined in lower cells were forced to sleep on the floors. There were five of them in each cell and in order to keep any semblance of heat in their bodies they had to sleep all huddled together in all their clothing.

"The first few days we were in the jail we spent in cleaning it, as it was reeking with filth and probably had never been cleaned out since it was built. It was alive with vermin. There were armies of bedbugs and body lice. We boiled up everything in the jail and it is safe to say that it is now cleaner than it had ever been before, or ever will be after the Wobblies are gone.

"When we first came here the lower floor was covered with barrels, boxes and cases of whiskey and beer. This was moved in a few days, but evidently not so far but McRae and his deputies had access to it, as their breath was always charged with the odor of whiskey. It was an everyday occurrence to have several of the deputies, emboldened by liquid courage and our defenseless condition—walk around the cell blocks and indulge in the pastime of calling us vulgar and profane names. Threats were also very common, but we held our peace and were content with the thought that 'a barking dog seldom bites.'

"The worst of these deputies are gone since the advent of sheriff McCullogh, but there are some on the job yet who like their 'tea.' About two weeks ago every deputy that came into the jail was drunk; some of them to the extent of staggering.

"When we first entered the jail, true to the principles of the I. W. W., we proceeded to organize ourselves for the betterment of our condition. A 'grub' committee, a sanitary committee and a floor committee were appointed. Certain rules and regulations were adopted. By the end of the week, instead of a growling, fighting crowd of men, such as one would expect to find where seventy-four men were thrown together, there was an orderly bunch of real I. W. W.'s, who got up at a certain hour every morning, and all of whose actions were part of a prearranged routine. Even tho every man of the seventy-four was talking as loudly as he could a few seconds before ten p. m., the instant the town clock struck ten all was hushed. If a sentence was unfinished, it remained unfinished until the following day.

"When the jailer came to the door, instead of seventy-four men crowding up and all trying to talk at once, three men stepped forward and conversed with him. Our conduct was astonishing to the jail officials. One of the jailers remarked that he had certainly been given a wrong impression of the I. W. W. by McRae. He said, 'this bunch is sure different from what I heard they were. You fellows are all right.' The answer was simply: 'Organization.' Instead of a cursing, swearing, fighting mob of seventy-four men, such as sheriff McRae would like to have had us, we were entirely the opposite.

"Time has not hung heavy on our hands. One scarcely notices the length of the days. Educational meetings are frequent and discussions are constantly in order. Our imprisonment has been a matter of experience. We will all be better able to talk Industrial Unionism than when we entered the jail.

"The meals! Did we say 'meals?' A thousand

pardons! Next time we meet a meal we will apologize to it. Up to the time we asserted our displeasure at the stinking, indigestible messes thrown up to us by a drunken brute who could not qualify as head waiter in a 'nickel plate' restaurant, we had garbage, pure and simple. Think of it! Mush, bread and coffee at 7:30 a. m., and not another bite until 4 p. m. Then they handed us a mess which some of us called 'slumgullion,' composed of diseased beef. Is it any wonder that four of the boys were taken to the hospital? But we will not dwell on the grub. Suffice it to say we were all more or less sick from the junk dished out to us. We were all hungry from November 10th until January 22nd. One day in November we had beans. Little did we surmise the pains, the agony contained in that dish of innocent looking nutriment, beans. At two in the morning every man in the jail was taken violently ill. We aroused the guards and they sent for a doctor. He came about eight hours later and looked disappointed upon learning that we were not dead. This doctor always had the same remedy in all cases. His prescription was, 'Stop smoking and you will be all right.' This is the same quack who helped beat up the forty-one members of the I. W. W. at Beverly Park on October 30th, 1916. His nerve must have failed him or his pills would have finished what his pickhandle had started.

"During the entire time of our confinement under McRae, drunken deputies came into the jail and did everything in their power to make conditions as miserable as possible for us. McRae was usually the leader in villification of the I. W. W.

"When on January 8th a change of administration took place, we called a meeting which resulted in an interview with Sheriff McCullogh. Among other things we demanded a cook. For days the sheriff stalled us off. He professed that he wanted to do things for our comfort. We gave him ample time —but there was no change in the conditions. On January 15th the matter came to a climax. For five days prior to this we had been served with what some called 'mulligan.' In reality it was nothing more or less than water slightly colored with the juice of carrots. If there had ever been any meat in it that meat was taken out before the mulligan was served. We called for the sheriff and were informed that he had gone away. We called for one of our attorneys who was in one of the outer offices at the time, but Jailer Bridges refused to let us see him. Having tried peaceful methods without success, we decided to forcibly bring the matter to the attention of the authorities. We poured the contents of the container out thru the bars and onto the floor. The boys in the upper tank did the same thing. For doing this we were given a terrible cursing by Jailer Bridges and the drunken cook, the latter throwing a piece of iron thru the bars, striking one of the boys on the head, and inflicting a long, ugly wound. The cook also threatened to poison us.

"That night when we were to be locked in, one of our jailers, decidedly under the influence of liquor, was in such a condition that he was unable to handle the levers properly and in some manner put the locking system out of commission. After probably three quarters of an hour, during which all of us and every I. W. W. in the world were consigned to hell many times, the doors were finally locked.

" 'By God, you s—s-of-b——s will wish you ate that stew,' was the way in which the jailer said 'good night' to us. The significance of his words was brought back to us next morning when the time came for us to be unlocked. We were left in our cells without food and with the water turned off so we could not even have a drink. We might have remained there for hours without toilet facilities had we not taken matters into our hands. With one accord we decided to get out of the cells. There was only one way to do this—'battleship!'

"Battleship we did! Such a din had never before been heard in Everett. Strong hands and shoulders were placed to the doors which gave up

An all-I. W. W. crew raising a spar tree 160 ft. long, 22½ inches at top and 54½ inches at butt, at Index, Wash.

Another view of the same operation.

their hold on the locks as if they had been made of pasteboard, and we emerged into the recreation corridors. The lumber trust papers of Everett, which thought the events of November 5th and the murder of five workers but a picnic, next day reported that we had wrecked the jail and attempted to escape. We did do a little wrecking, but as far as trying to escape is concerned that is a huge joke. The jail has not been built that can hold seventy-four I. W. W. members if they want to escape. We had but decided to forcibly bring the jail conditions to the attention of the authorities and the citizens. We were not willing to die of hunger and thirst. We told Sheriff McCullogh we were not attempting to escape; he knew we were not. Yet the papers came out with an alleged interview in which the sheriff was made to say that we were. It was also said that tomato skins had been thrown against the walls of the jail. There were none to throw!

Summing up this matter: we are here, and here we are determined to remain until we are freed. Not a man in this jail would accept his liberty if the doors were opened. This is proven by the fact that one man voluntarily came to the jail here and gave himself up, while still another was allowed his liberty but sent for the Everett authorities to come and get him while he was in Seattle. This last man was taken out of jail illegally while still under the charge of first degree murder, but he preferred to stand trial rather than to be made a party to schemes of framing up to perjure away the liberties of his fellow workers.

"Signed by the workers in the Snohomish County Jail."

If the authorities hoped to save money by their niggardly feeding policy the battleship of January 19th, mentioned in the foregoing account, convinced them of their error. With blankets tied to the cell doors they first tore them open and then twisted them out of shape. Taking a small piece of gaspipe they disarranged the little doors that controlled the locking system above each cell, and then demolished the entire system of locks. Every bolt, screw and split pin was taken out and made useless. While some were thus engaged others were busy getting the food supplies which were stacked up in a corner just outside the tanks. When Sheriff McCullogh finally arrived at the jail, some three hours later, he found the prisoners calmly seated amid the wreckage eating some three hundred pounds of corned beef they had obtained and cooked with live steam in one of the bath tubs. Shaking his head sadly the sheriff remarked, "You fellows don't go to the same church that I do." The deputy force worked for hours in cleaning up the jail, and it took a gang of ironworkers nine working days, at a cost of over $800.00, to repair the damage done in twenty minutes. Twenty of the "hard-boiled Wobblies" were removed to Seattle shortly after this, but it was no trouble for the men to gain their demands from that time on. They had but to whisper the magic word "battleship" to remind the jailers that the I. W. W. policy, as expressed in a line in Virgil, was about to be invoked:

"If I cannot bend the powers above,
I will rouse Hell."

Lloyd Black, prosecuting attorney only by a political accident, soon dropped his ideals and filled the position of prosecutor as well as his limited abilities allowed, and it was apparent that he felt the hands of the lumber trust tugging on the strings attached to his job and that he had succumbed to the insidious influence of his associates. He called various prisoners from their cells and by pleading, cajoling and threatening in turn, tried to induce them to make statements injurious to their case.

Fraudulently using the name of John M. Foss, a former member of the General Executive Board of the I. W. W. and then actively engaged in working for the defense, Black called out Axel Downey, a boy of seventeen and the youngest of the free speech prisoners, and used all the resources of his department to get the lad to make a statement. Downey refused to talk to any of the prosecution lawyers or detectives and demanded that he be returned to his cell. From that time on he refused to answer any calls from the office unless the jail committee was present. Nevertheless the name of Axel Downey was endorsed, with several others, as a witness for the prosecution in order to create distrust and suspicion among the prisoners.

About this time the efforts of Detective McLaren and his associates were successful in "influencing" one of the prisoners, and Charles Auspos, alias Charles Austin, agreed to become a state's witness. Contrary to the expectation of the prosecution, the announcement of this "confession" created no sensation and was not taken seriously on the outside, while the prisoners, knowing there was nothing to confess, were concerned only in the fact that there had been a break in their solidarity. "We wanted to come out of this case one hundred per cent clean," was the sorrowful way in which they took the news.

Auspos had joined the I. W. W. in Rugby, North Dakota, on August 10th, 1916, and whether he was at that time an agent for the employers is not known, but it is evident that he was not sufficiently interested in industrial unionism to study its rudimentary principles. It may be that the previous record of Auspos had given an opportunity for McLaren to work upon that weak character, for Auspos started his boyhood life in Hudson, Wisconsin, with a term in the reformatory, and his checkered career included two years in a military guard house for carrying side-arms and fighting in a gambling den, a dishonorable discharge from the United States Army, under the assumed name of Ed. Gibson, and various arrests up until he joined the I. W. W.

This Auspos was about 33 years of age, five foot eleven inches tall, weight about 175 pounds, brown hair, brown eyes, medium complexion but face inclined to be reddish, slight scar on side of face, and was a teamster and general laborer by occupation, his parents living in Elk River, Minn.

And while Auspos had by his actions descended to the lowest depths of shame, there were those among the prisoners who had scaled the heights of self-sacrifice. There were some few among them whose record would look none too well in the light of day, but the spirit of class solidarity within them led them to say, "Do with me as you will, I shall never betray the working class." James Whiteford, arrested under the name of James Kelly, deserves the highest praise that can be given for he was taken back to Pennsylvania, which state he had left in violation of a parole, to serve out a long penitentiary sentence which he could have avoided by a few easily told lies implicating his fellow workers in a conspiracy to do murder on November 5th.

Shortly after the attempted "frame-up" with Axel Downey there was a strong effort made to bring pressure upon Harvey Hubler. A "lawyer" who called himself Minor Blythe, bearing letters obtained by misrepresentation from Hubler's father and sister, attempted to get Hubler from his cell on an order signed by Malcolm McLaren, the detective. With the experience of Downey fresh in mind, Hubler refused to go out of the tank, even tho the "lawyer" stated that he had been sent by Hubler's father and could surely get him out of jail.

The next day twelve armed deputies came into the jail to force Hubler to accompany them to the office. The prisoners as a whole refused to enter their cells, and armed themselves with such rude weapons as they could find in order to repulse the deputies. The concerted resistance had its effect and a committee of three, Feinberg, Peters and Watson, acompanied Hubler to the office. Hubler there refused to read the letter, asking that it be read aloud in the presence of the other men. The detectives refused to do this and the men were put back in the tank.

That afternoon, with two other prisoners, Hubler went out of the tank to wash his clothes. The jailers had been awaiting this opportunity and immediately locked the men out. The gunmen then overpowered Hubler and dragged him struggling to the office. The letter was then read to Hubler, who made no comment further than to say that the I. W. W. had engaged attorneys to defend him and he wished to be taken back where the rest of the men were.

Meanwhile the men in the tanks had started another battleship. A hose had been installed in the jail since the previous battleship and the deputies turned this upon the men as soon as the protest started. The prisoners retaliated by taking all mattresses, blankets, clothing and supplies belonging to the county and throwing them where they would be ruined by the water, and not knowing what was happening to Hubler they shouted "Murder" at the top of their voices. While the trouble was going on several members of the I. W. W., many Everett citizens, and one attorney tried to gain admittance to the jail office to learn the cause of the disturbance, but this was denied for more than an hour. Hubler was finally brought back and the battleship ceased. The county had to furnish new bedding and clothing for the prisoners.

After this occurence the prisoners were allowed the run of the corridors and were often let out to play ball upon the jail lawn, with only two guards to watch them. There were no disorders in the jail from that time on.

A committee of Everett women asked permission to serve a dinner to the imprisoned men and when this was granted they fairly outdid themselves in fixing up what the boys termed a "swell feed." This was served to the men thru the bars but tasted none the less good on that account.

The Seattle women, not to be outdone, gave a banquet to the prisoners who had been transported to the Seattle county jail. The banquet was spread on tables set the full length of the jail corridor, and

Judge J. T. Ronald

the menu ran from soup to nuts. An after dinner cigar, and a little boutonniere of fragrant flowers furnished by a gray-haired old lady, completed the program.

These banquets and the jail visitors, together with numerous books, magazines and papers—and a phonograph that was in almost constant operation—made the latter part of the long jail days endurable.

The defense was making strong efforts, during this time, to secure some judge other than Bell or Alston, the two superior court judges of Snohomish County, finally winning a victory in forcing the appointment of an outside judge by the governor of the state.

Judge J. T. Ronald, of King County, was selected by Governor Lister, and after the men had pleaded "Not Guilty" on January 26th, a change of venue on account of the prejudice existing in Everett's official circles was asked and granted, Seattle being selected as the place where the trial would take place.

Eleven of the prisoners were named on the first information, the men thus arraigned being F. O. Watson, John Black, Frank Stuart, Charles Adams, Harston Peters, Thomas H. Tracy, Harry Feinberg, John Downs, Harold Miller, Ed Roth and Thomas Tracy. The title of the case was "State vs. F. O. Watson et, al.," but the first man to come to trial was Thomas H. Tracy. The date of the trial was set for March 5th.

On November 5th, when he was taken from the Verona to jail, Thomas H. Tracy gave his name at the booking window as George Martin, in order to spare the feelings of relatives to whom the news of his arrest would have proven a severe shock. When the officers were checking the names later he was surprised to hear them call out "Tracy, Thomas Tracy." Thinking that his identity was known because of his having been secretary in Everett for a time, he stepped forward. An instant later a little fellow half his size also marched to the front. There were two Tom Tracys among the arrested men! Neither of them knew the other! Tracy then gave his correct name and both he and "Little Tom Tracy" were later held among the seventy-four charged with murder in the first degree.

During all the time the free speech fighters were awaiting trial the lumber trust exerted its potent influence at the national capital to the end of preventing any congressional investigation of the tragedy of November 5th and the circumstances surrounding it. The petitions of thousands of citizens of the state of Washington were ignored. All too well the employers knew what a putrid state of affairs would be uncovered were the lumber trust methods exposed to the pitiless light of publicity. That the trial itself would force them into the open evidently did not enter into their calculations.

In changing the information charging the murder of C. O. Curtis to the charge of murdering Jefferson Beard the prosecution thought to cover one point beyond the possibility of discovery, which change seems to have been made as a result of the exhuming of the body of C. O. Curtis in February. Curtis had been buried in a block of solid concrete and this had to be broken apart in order to remove the body. Just who performed the autopsy cannot be ascertained as the work was covered in the very comprehensive bill of $50.50 for "Exhuming the body of C. O. Curtis, and autopsy thereon," this bill being made out in the name of the superintendent of the graveyard and was allowed and paid by Snohomish County. This, together with the fact that at no time during the trial did the prosecution speak of C. O. Curtis as having met his death at the hands of the men on the Verona, seems to bear out the contention of the defense that Curtis was the victim of the rifle fire of one of his associates.

So on March 5th, after holding the free speech prisoners for four months to the day, the lumber trust, in the name of the State of Washington, brought the first of them, Thomas H. Tracy, to trial, on a charge of first degree murder, in the King County Court House at Seattle, Washington.

CHAPTER VI.

THE PROSECUTION

The King County Court House is an imposing, five story, white structure, covering an entire block in the business section of the city of Seattle. Its offices for the conduct of the county and city business are spacious and well appointed. Its corridors are ample, and marble. The elevator service is of the best. But the courtrooms are stuffy little dens, illy ventilated, awkwardly placed, and with the poorest of acoustics. They seem especially designed to add to the depressing effect that invariably attends the administration of "law and order." The court of Judge Ronald, like many other courts in the land, is admirably designed for the bungling inefficiencies of "justice." Yet it was in this theater, thru the medium of the Everett trial, that the class struggle was reproduced, sometimes in tragedy and sometimes in comedy.

To reach the greatest trial in the history of labor unionism, perhaps the greatest also in the number of defendants involved and the number of witnesses called, one had to ascend to the fourth floor of the court house and line up in the corridor under the watchful eyes of the I. W. W. "police," C. R. Griffin and J. J. Keenan, appointed by the organization at the request of the court. There, unless one were a lawyer or a newspaper representative, it was necessary to wait in line for hours until the tiny courtroom was opened and the lucky hundred odd persons were admitted to the church-like benches of J. T. Ronald's sanctum, where the case of State versus Tracy was on trial.

Directly in front of the benches, at the specially constructed press table, were seats provided for the representatives of daily, weekly and monthly publications whose policies ranged from the ultra conservative to the extreme radical. Here the various reporters were seen writing madly as some important point came up, then subsiding into temporary indifference, passing notes, joking in whispers, drawing personal cartoons of the judge, jury, counsel, court functionaries and out-of-the-ordinary spectators,—the only officially recognized persons in the courtroom showing no signs of reverence for the legal priesthood and their mystic sacerdotalism.

Just ahead of the press table were the attorneys for the prosecution: Lloyd Black, a commonplace, uninspired, beardless youth as chief prosecutor; H. D. Cooley, a sleek, pusillanimous recipient of favors from the lumber barons, a fixture at the Commercial Club, and an also-ran deputy at the dock on November 5th, as next counsel in line; and A. L. Veitch, handsome in a gross sort of a way, full faced, sensual lipped, with heavy pouches beneath the eyes, a self-satisfied favorite of the M. & M., and withal the most able of the three who by virtue of polite fiction represented the state of Washington. From time to time in whispered conference with these worthy gentlemen was a tall, lean, grey, furtive-eyed individual who was none other than the redoubtable Californian detective, Malcolm McLaren.

At right angles to this array of prosecutors the counsel for the defense were seated, where they remained until the positions were reversed at the close of the prosecution's case. Chief counsel Fred H. Moore, serious, yet with a winning smile occasionally chasing itself across his face and adding many humorous wrinkles to the tired-looking crow-feet at the corners of his eyes; next to him George F. Vanderveer, a strong personality whose lightning flashes of wit and sarcasm, marshalled to the aid of a merciless drive of questions, were augmented by a smile second only to Moore's in its captivating quality; then E. C. Dailey, invaluable because of his knowledge of local conditions in Everett and personages connected with the case; and by his side, at times during the trial, was H. Sigmund, special counsel for Harry Feinberg.

Seated a little back, but in the same group, was a man of medium height, stocky built, slightly ruddy complexion, black hair, and twinkling blue eyes. He was to all appearances the most composed man in the courtroom. A slight smile crept over his face, at times almost broadened into a laugh, and then died away. This was Thomas H. Tracy, on trial for murder in the first degree.

To the rear of the defendant and forming a deep contrast to the determined, square-jawed prisoner was the guard, a lean, hungry-looking deputy with high cheek bones, unusually sharp and long nose and a pair of moustachios that drooped down upon his chest, a wholly useless and most uncomfortable functionary who could scarce seat himself because of the heavy artillery scattered over his anatomy.

The court clerk, an absurdly dignified court bailiff, a special stenographer, and Sheriff McCullogh of Snohomish county, occupied the intervening space to the pulpit from which Judge J. T. Ronald delivered his legal invocations.

The judge, a striking figure, over six feet in height and well proportioned, of rather friendly countenance and bearing in street dress, resembled nothing so much as a huge black owl when arrayed in his sacred "Mother Hubbard" gown, with tortoise-shell rimmed smoked glasses resting on his slightly aquiline nose and surmounting the heavy, closely trimmed, dark Vandyke beard.

To the right of the judge as he faced the audience was the witness chair, and across the whole of the corner of the room was a plat of the Everett City Dock and the adjacent waterfront, together with a smaller map showing part of the streets of the city. The plat was state's exhibit "A." Below these maps on a tilted platform was a model of the same dock, with the two warehouses, waiting room, Klatawa Slip, and the steamer Verona, all built to scale. This was defendant's exhibit "1."

Extending from these exhibits down the side of

the railed enclosure, were seats for two extra jurors. The filling of this jury box from a long list of talesmen was the preliminary move to a trial in which the defendant was barely mentioned, and which involved the question of Labor's right to organize, to assemble peaceably, to speak freely, and to advocate a change in existing social arrangements. Capital was lined up in a fight against Labor. There was a direct reflection in the courts of the masters of the age-long, world-wide class struggle.

The examination of talesmen occupied considerable time. Each individual was asked whether he had read any of the following papers: The Industrial Worker, The Socialist World, or the Pacific Coast Longshoreman. The prosecution also inquired as to the prospective juror's familiarity with the I. W. W. Song Book and the various works on Sabotage. Union affiliations were closely inquired into, and favorable mention of the right to organize brought a challenge from the state. The testing of the talesmen was no less severe on the part of the defense.

Fifty-one talesmen were disqualified, after long and severe legal battles, before a jury was finally secured from among the voters and property owners who alone were qualified to serve. The jury, as selected, was rather more intelligent than was to be expected when consideration is taken of the fact that any person who acknowledged having an impression, an opinion, or a conclusion regarding the merits of the case was automatically excused from service. Those who were chosen to sit on the case were:

Mrs. Mattie Fordran, wife of a steamfitter; Robert Harris, a rancher; Fred Corbs, bricklayer, once a member of the union, then working for himself; Mrs. Louise Raynor, wife of a master mariner; A. Peplan, farmer; Mrs. Clara Uhlman, wife of a harnessmaker in business for himself; Mrs. Alice Freeborn, widow of a druggist; F. M. Christian, tent and awning maker; Mrs. Sarah F. Brown, widow, working class family; James R. Williams, machinist's helper, member of union; Mrs. Sarah J. Timmer, wife of a union lineman, and T. J. Byrne, contractor. The two alternate jurors, provided for under the "Extra Juror" law of Washington, passed just prior to this trial, were: J. W. Efaw, furniture manufacturer, president of Seattle Library Board and Henry B. Williams, carpenter and member of a union.

Judge Ronald realized the importance of the case as was shown in his admonition to the jury, a portion of which follows:

"It is plain, from both sides here, that we are making history. Let us see that the record that we make in this case,—you and I, as a court,—be a landmark based upon nothing in the world but the truth. We may deceive some people and we may, a little, deceive ourselves; but we cannot deceive eternal truth."

On the morning of March 9th Judge Ronald, the tail of his black gown firmly in hand, swept into the courtroom from his private chambers, the assembled congregation arose and stood in deep obeisance before His Majesty The Law, the pompous bailiff rapped for order and delivered an incantation, the Judge seated himself on the throne of "Justice," the assemblage subsided into their seats —and the trial was opened in earnest. Prosecuting Attorney Lloyd Black then gave his opening statement, the gist of which is contained in the following quotations:

"You are at the outset of a murder trial, murder in the first degree. The defendant, Thomas H. Tracy, alias George Martin, is charged with murder in the first degree, in having assisted, counselled, aided, abetted and encouraged some unknown person to kill Jefferson Beard on the 5th of November, 1916.

"* * * As far as the state is concerned, no one knows or can know or could follow the course of the particular bullet that struck and mortally wounded and killed Jefferson Beard.

"* * * The evidence further will show that the first, or one of the first, shots fired was from the steamer Verona and was from a revolver held in the hand of Thomas H. Tracy.

"* * * As to the killing of Jefferson Beard itself the probabilities are, as the evidence of the state will indicate, that he was killed by someone on the hurricane deck of the Verona because the evidence will show that the revolver shots went thru his overcoat, missing his coat, and thru his vest, and had a downward course, so that it must have come from the upper deck. The evidence will show that Thomas H. Tracy was on the main deck firing thru an open cabin window.

"* * * Of the approximately 140 special and regular deputies of Snohomish County about one-half were armed, some with revolvers, some with rifles and some with clubs.

"* * * When the fusilade had come from the I. W. W.'s on the Verona, a portion of the deputies ran thru a door into this warehouse, (indicating): a portion of them went into that warehouse, and used some of the knotholes there, and some shot holes thru which they could see, * * *"

Black then gave a recital of the lumber trust version of the events leading up to November 5th, bringing in the threats of an alleged committee who were said to have declared "that they would call thousands of their members to the city of Everett, flood the jails, demand separate trials, and tie up and overwhelm the court machinery, and that the mayor should consider that they had beaten Spokane and killed its chief, killed Chief Sullivan of that city, that they had defeated Wenatchee and North Yakima, and now it was Everett's turn."

"* * * That in furtherance of their threats that they would burn the city of Everett, that a number of mysterious fires took place, fires connected with some person who was opposed to the I. W. W. * * * And in addition, the I. W. W. members were arrested at different times preceding this trouble on the 5th of November and phosphorus was found upon their person either in cans or wrapped up.

"* * * At different times, the evidence will show, Sheriff Donald McRae and other peace officers of the city of Everett, including Mayor Merrill, received anonymous letters, and also received direct statements from the I. W. W. that they would get them; and, as one speaker put it, he says 'Sheriff McRae will wake up some day and say '"Good morning, Jesus!"'

Black continued his recital of events, admitting the "Wanderer" incident, but he tried to sidestep the criminal actions at Beverly Park.

"Now, there happened at Beverly Park an incident that the State in this action doesn't feel that it has anything to do with this particular cause."

Ironical laughter at this juncture caused the removal of several spectators from the courtroom. So disconcerted was Black that he proceeded to give away the real cause of action against the I. W. W.

"The I. W. W. organization itself is an unlawful conspiracy, an unlawful conspiracy in that it was designed for the purpose of effecting an absolute revolution in society and in government, effecting it not by the procedure of law thru the ballot, but for effecting it by direct action. The I. W. W. meant to accomplish the change in society, not by organization as the labor unions hope to get higher wages, not to get into effect their theory of society by the ballot, as the Socialists hope, but that they expressly state that the election of a Socialist president will accomplish no good, and that sabotage should be employed against government ownership as well as against private production, so that directly they might put into effect their theories of government and society."

The defense reserved the right to make their opening statement at the close of the prosecution's case, thus leaving the state in the dark as to the line of defense, and forcing them to open their case at once.

Lester L. Beard and Chester L. Beard, twin sons of the deceased deputy sheriff, testified as to the condition of their father's clothing, Attorney Vanderveer drawing from Lester Beard the admission that his father was an employment agent in Seattle in 1914.

Following them, Drs. William O'Keef Cox, H. P. Howard, and William P. West testified to having performed an autopsy on Beard and described the course of the bullet upon entering the body. Dr. West was an armed guard at the land end of the City Dock on November 5th, Dr. Cox was also on the dock as a deputy, and Dr. Howard carried a membership in the Commercial Club. They were the physicians present when the autopsy was performed.

The next witness, Harry W. Shaw, a wood and coal dealer of Everett, admitted having joined the citizen deputies because of a call issued by the sheriff thru the Commercial Club. Shaw went to the dock on November 5th, carrying, as he claimed, a revolver with a broken firing pin which he had hoped to have repaired on that Sunday on the way to the dock. He was close to Beard when the latter fell and helped to carry him from the open space on the dock into the warehouse. He afterward accompanied Beard to the hospital in an automobile and returned to the dock with Beard's unfired revolver in his possession. He swore that he had seen McRae sober three times in succession! When asked by Attorney Moore he gave an affirmative answer to this pertinent question:

"You knew that the matter of the enforcement of the city ordinances of Everett was peculiarly within the powers of the police department of the city, didn't you?"

Owen Clay was then called to the stand. Clay had been made bookkeeper of the Weyerhouser Mill about a year and a half before this, and had been given a membership in the Commercial Club at the time. He was injured in the right arm in the trouble at the dock and then ran around the corner of the ticket office, after which he emptied his revolver with his left hand. Attorney Vanderveer questioned this witness as follows:

"Who shot Jeff Beard in the right breast?"

"I don't know."

"Did you do it?"

"I don't know."

"Thank you! That's all," said Vanderveer with a smile.

The next witness was C. A. Mitchell, employee of the Clark-Nickerson Mill. He testified that he belonged to Company "B" under the command of Carl Clapp. His testimony placed Sheriff McRae in the same position as that given by the preceding witness, about eight to ten feet from the face of the dock in the center of the open space between the two warehouses, but unlike Clay, who testified that McRae had his left hand in the air, he was positive that the sheriff had his right hand in the air at the time the shooting started.

W. R. Booth, engaged in real estate and insurance business, a member of the Commercial Club, and a deputy at the dock, was next called. Attorney Cooley asked this witness about the speech made at an unspecified street meeting. Vanderveer immediately objected as follows:

"We object to that as immaterial and calling for a conclusion of the witness. He does not know who was speaking, nor whether he was authorized to do it, or brought there by the Industrial Workers of the World, or a hireling of the Merchants' and Manufacturers' society. It has happened time and time again that people are employed by these capitalists themselves to go out and make incendiary speeches and cause trouble, and employed to go out and fire buildings and do anything to put the opposition in wrong."

When questioned about McRae's position on the dock, Booth stated that the sheriff had both hands in the air. This witness admitted having been a member of the "Flying Squadron" and being a participant in the outrage at Beverly Park. He named others who went out with him in the same automobile, Will Seivers and Harry Ramwell, and stated that A. P. Bardson, clerk of the Commercial Club, was probably there as he had been out on all the other occasions. He said that he would not participate in the beating up of anyone, and that when the affair started he went up the road for purposes of his own. He was asked by Vanderveer as to the reason for continuing to associate with people who had abused the men at Beverly Park, to which he replied:

"Because I believe in at least trying to maintain law and order in our city."

During the examination of this witness, and at various times thruout the long case, it was only with evident effort that Attorney Vanderveer kept on the unfamiliar ground of the class struggle, his natural tendencies being to try the case as a defense of a pure and simple murder charge.

W. P. Bell, an Everett attorney representing a number of scab mills, a member of the Commercial Club and a deputy on the dock, testified next, contradicting the previous witnesses but throwing no additional light upon the case. He was followed by Charles Tucker, a scab and gunman employed by the Hartley Shingle Company and a deputy on the dock. Tucker lied so outrageously that even the prosecution counsel felt ashamed of him. He was impeached by his own testimony.

Editor J. A. MacDonald of the Industrial Worker was called to the stand to show the official relation of the paper to the I. W. W. and to lay a foundation for the introduction of a file of the issues prior to November 5th. A portion of the file was introduced as evidence and at the same time the state put in as exhibits a copy of the I. W. W. Constitution and By-Laws, Sabotage by Elizabeth Gurley Flynn, Sabotage by Walker C. Smith, The Revolutionary I. W. W. by Grover H. Perry, The I. W. W., Its History, Structure and Methods by Vincent St. John, and the Joe Hill Memorial Edition of the Song Book.

Herbert Mahler, former secretary of the Seattle I. W. W. and at the time Secretary-Treasurer of the Everett Prisoners' Defense Committee, was next upon the stand. He was asked to name various committees and to identify certain telegrams. The unhesitatingly clear answers of both MacDonald and Mahler were in vivid contrast to the mumbled and contradictory responses of the deputies.

William J. Smith, manager of the Western Union Telegraph Company was then called to further corroborate certain telegrams sent and received by the I. W. W.

As the next step in the case prosecutor Black read portions of the pamphlet "Sabotage" by Smith, sometimes using half a paragraph and skipping half, sometimes using one paragraph and omitting the next, provoking a remonstrance from Attorney Vanderveer which was upheld by the Court in these words:

"You have a right to do what you are doing, Mr. Black, but it don't appeal to my sense of fairness if other omissions are as bad as the one you left out. You are following the practice, but I don't know of an instance where there has been such an awful juggling about, and it is discretionary with the Court, and I want to be fair in this case. I want to let them have a chance to take the sting out of it so as to let the jury have both sides, because it is there. Now, Mr. Vanderveer, I am going to leave it to you not to impose upon the Court's discretion. Any new phases I don't think you have the right to raise, but anything that will modify what he has read I think you have the right to."

Thereupon Vanderveer read all the omitted portions bearing upon the case, bringing special emphasis on these two parts:

"Note this important point, however. Sabotage does not seek nor desire to take human life."

"Sabotage places human life—and especially the life of the only useful class—higher than all else in the universe."

With evidences of amusement, if not always approval, the jury then listened to the reading of numerous I. W. W. songs by Attorney Cooley for the prosecution, tho some of the jurymen shared in the bewilderment of the audience as to the connection between the song "Overalls and Snuff" and defendant Tracy charged with a conspiracy to commit murder in the first degree.

D. D. Merrill, Mayor of Everett, next took the stand. He endeavored to give the impression that the I. W. W. was responsible for a fire loss in Everett of $100,000.00 during the latter part of the year 1916. Vanderveer shot the question:

"From whom would you naturally look for information on the subject of fires?"

"From the Fire Chief, W. C. Carroll," replied the mayor.

"We offer this report in evidence," said Vanderveer crisply.

The report of the Fire Chief was admitted and read. It showed that there were less fires in 1916 that in any previous year in the history of Everett, and only four of incendiary origin in the entire list!

The prosecution tried to squirm out of this ticklish position by stating that they meant also the fires in the vicinity of Everett, but here also they met with failure for the principal fire in the surrounding district was in the co-operative mill, owned by a number of semi-radical workingmen at Mukilteo.

The mayor told of having been present at the arrest of several men taken from a freight train at Lowell, just at the Everett city limits. Some of these men were I. W. W.s, and on the ground afterward there was said to have been found some broken glass about which there was a smell of phosphorus. The judge ruled out this evidence because there were other than I. W. W. men present, no phosphorus was found on the men, and if only one package were found it would not indicate a conspiracy but might have been brought by an agent of the employers. This was the nearest the prosecution came at any time in the trial in their attempt to connect the I. W. W. with incendiary fires.

A tense moment in this sensational trial came during the testimony of Mayor Merrill, when young Louis Skaroff was suddenly produced in court and the question flashed at the cringing witness:

"Do you recognize this boy standing here? Do you recognize him, Louis Skaroff?"

"I think I have seen him," mumbled the mayor.

"Let me ask you if on the 6th day of November at about ten o'clock at night in a room in the City Hall at Everett where there was a bed room having an iron bedstead in it, in the presence of the jailer, didn't you have an interview with this man?"

Merrill denied having mutilated Skaroff's fingers beneath the casters of the bed, but even the capitalist press reported that his livid face and thick voice belied his words of denial.

And Prosecutor Lloyd Black remarked heatedly, "I don't see the materiality of all this."

Merrill left the stand, having presented the sorriest figure among the number of poor witnesses produced by the prosecution.

Carl Clapp, superintendent of the Municipal Waterworks at Everett, and commander of one of the squads of deputies, followed with testimony to the effect that sixty rifles from the Naval Militia were stored in the Commercial Club on November 5th. At this juncture the hearing of further evidence was postponed for a half day to allow Attorney Vanderveer to testify on behalf of Mayor H. C. Gill in a case then pending in the Federal Court.

On several other occasions Vanderveer was called to testify in this case and there were times when it was thought that he also would be indicted and brought to trial, yet with this extra work and the threat of imprisonment hanging over him, Vanderveer never flagged in his keen attention to the work of the defense. It was commonly thought that the case against Gill and the attempt to involve

Vanderveer were moves of the lumber trust and Chamber of Commerce directed toward the I. W. W., for in the background were the same interested parties who had been forced to abandon the recall against Seattle's mayor. Gill's final acquittal in this case was hailed as an I. W. W. victory.

Upon the resumption of the trial the prosecution temporarily withdrew Clapp and placed Clyde Gibbons on the stand. This witness was the son of James Gibbons, a deceased member of the I. W. W., well and favorable known in the Northwest. James Gibbons was killed by a speeding automobile about a year prior to the trial, and his widow and son, Clyde, were supprted by the I. W. W. and the Boiler Makers' Union for several months thereafter.

Clyde Gibbons, altho but seventeen years old, joined the Navy by falsifying his age. Charity demands that the veil be drawn over the early days of Clyde's training, yet his strong imagination and general untruthfulness are matters of record. He was shown in court to have stolen funds left in trust with him by Mrs. Peters, one of the persons against whom his testimony was directed. It is quite probable that the deceit about his age, or some other of his queer actions, were discovered and used to force him to testify as the prosecution desired. The following testimony bears out this idea:

"Who was it that you met at the Naval Recruiting Station and took you to McLaren?"

"I don't know his name."

"Well, how did you get to talking to this total stranger about the Everett matter?"

"He told me he wanted to see me in the judge's office."

"And they took you down to the judge's office, did they?"

"Yes, sir."

"And when you got to the judge's office you found you were in Mr. McLaren's and Mr. Veitch's and Mr. Black's office in the Smith Building?"

"Yes, sir."

Gibbons testified as to certain alleged conversations in an apartment house frequented by members of the I. W. W., stating that a party of members laid plans to go to Everett and to take with them red pepper, olive oil and bandages. Harston Peters, one of the defendants, had a gun that wouldn't shoot and so went unarmed, according to this witness. Gibbons also stated that Mrs. Frenette took part in the conversation in this apartment house on the morning of the tragedy, whereupon Attorney Moore asked him:

"On directing your attention to it, don't you remember that you didn't see Mrs. Frenette at all in Seattle, anywhere, at any time subsequent to Saturday night; that she went to Everett on Saturday night?"

"Well, I am quite sure I saw her Sunday, but maybe I am mistaken."

The judge upheld the defense attorneys in their numerous objections to the leading questions propounded by prosecutor Black during the examination of this witness.

Clapp was recalled to the stand and testified further that Scott Rainey, head of the U. S. Naval Militia at Everett, had ordered Ensign McLean to take rifles to the dock, and that the witness and McLean had loaded the guns, placed them in an auto and taken them to the dock, where they were distributed to the deputies just as the Verona started to steam away.

Ignorance as to the meaning of simple labor terms that are in the every-day vocabulary of the "blanketstiff" was shown by Clapp in his answers to these queries:

"What is direct action?"

"Using force instead of lawful means."

"What do you mean?"

"Well, either physical force, or conspiracy."

"You understand conspiracy to be some kind of force, do you?"

"It may be force."

When asked where he had obtained information about sabotage, this witness said that he had looked up the word in Webster's Unabridged Dictionary, a work in which the term is strangely absent.

Clapp was the first witness to admit the armed character of the deputy body and also to state that deputies with guns were stationed on all of Everett's docks.

After excusing this witness, Cooley brought in copies of two city ordinances covering street speaking in Everett. One of them which allowed the holding of meetings at the corner of Hewitt and Wetmore Avenues was admitted without question, but the other which purported to have been passed on September 19, 1916, was objected to on the ground that it had not been passed, was never put upon passage and never moved for passage in the Everett City Council.

Richard Brennan, chauffeur of the patrol wagon, A. H. Briggs, city dog catcher, and Floyd Wildey, police officer, all of Everett, then testified regarding the arrest of I. W. W. members during August and September. Wildey stated that on the night of August 30 four or five members of the I. W. W. came away from their street meeting carrying sections of gaspipe in their hands. This was thought to be quite a blow against the peaceful character of the meeting until it was discovered on cross-examination that the weapons were the removable legs of the street speaking platform.

David Daniels, Arthur S. Johnson, Garland Queen, J. R. Steik. M. J. Fox and, later on, Earl Shaver, all of whom were police officers in Everett, gave testimony along somewhat the same lines as the other witnesses from Everett who owed their jobs to the lumber trust. They stated that the I. W. W. men deported on August 23rd, had made threats against McRae and several police officers.

Ed. M. Hawes, proprietor of a scab printing and stationery company, member of the Commercial Club and citizen deputy, gave testimony similar to that of other vigilantes as to the trouble on November 5th. When asked if he had ever known any I. W. W. men offering resistance, Hawes replied that one had tried to start a fight with him at Beverly Park. Having thus established his connection with this infamous outrage, further questioning of this witness developed much of the story of the brutal gauntlet and deportation. Hawes told of one of his prisoners making an endeavor to escape, and when asked whether he blamed the man for trying to get away, answered that he thought the prisoner was a pretty big baby.

"You thought he was a pretty big baby?" queried Vanderveer.

"Yes, sir."

"Or do you think the men were pretty big babies and cowards who were doing the beating?"

The witness had no answer to this question.

"How much do you weigh?" demanded Vanderveer sharply.

"I weigh 260 pounds," replied Hawes.

Frank Goff and Henry Krieg, two young lads who were severely beaten at Beverly Park, were suddenly produced in court and the big bully was made to stand alongside of them. He outweighed the two of them. It was plainly evident who the pretty big baby was!

Howard Hathaway, law student and assistant to the state secretary of the Democratic Central Committee, was forced to admit his connection with the raid upon the launch "Wanderer" and also upon the men peacefully camping at Maltby. His testimony was mainly for the purpose of making it appear that James P. Thompson had advocated that the shingle weavers set fire to the mills and win their strikes by methods of terrorism.

Two newspaper reporters, William E. Jones of the Seattle Post-Intelligencer, and J. J. Underwood of the Seattle Times, were placed upon the stand in order to lay the foundation for an introduction of an article appearing in the P-I on Sunday morning,

November 5th. Jones testified that he was present at the Seattle police station when Philip K. Ahern, manager of the Pinkerton Detective Agency, requested the release of Smith and Reese, two of his operatives who had been on the Verona. Underwood stated that upon hearing of the treatment given the I. W. W. men at Beverly Park he had exclaimed, "I would like to see anybody do that to me and get away with it."

"You meant that, did you?" asked Vanderveer.

"You bet I meant it!" asserted the witness positively.

The two reporters proved to be better witnesses for the defense than for the prosecution.

Sanford Asbury, T. N. Henry, Ronald Johnson, John S. Donlan, and J. E. Gleason, then testified regarding the movements of the men who left Seattle on the Verona and Calista on the morning of November 5th. They uniformly agreed that the crowd was in no way disorderly, nor were their actions at all suspicious. The defense admitted that the Verona had been chartered but stated that there were passengers other than I. W. W. members on board.

The first witness from the Verona was Ernest Shellgren, the boat's engineer, who testified that he was in the engine pit when the boat landed and heard crackling sounds telegraphed down the smoke stack that he knew an instant later were bullets. He was struck by a spent bullet and ran to various places on the boat seeking shelter from the hail of lead that appeared to come from all directions, finally returning to the boiler as the safest place on the boat. He stated that he saw one man firing a blue steel revolver from the boat, only the hand and revolver being in his line of vision. The only other gun he saw was one in the hands of the man who asked him to back the boat away from the dock during the firing. He also stated that the I. W. W. men on the way over to Everett comported themselves as was usual with any body of passengers.

Shellgren was asked if he could identify John

Downs or Thomas H. Tracy as being connected with the firing in any way and he stated that he could not do so. The defense objected to the use of Down's picture, as it did on every occasion where a picture of one of the prisoners was used, on the grounds that the photographs were obtained by force and in defiance of the constitutional rights of the imprisoned free speech fighters.

Seattle police detectives, Theodore Montgomery and James O'Brien, who made a search of the Verona upon its return to Seattle, testified to having found a little loose red pepper, two stones the size of a goose egg tied up in a cloth, and a few empty cartridges. These two witnesses also developed the fact that in no case were regular bandages used on the wounded men, thus establishing the fact that no serious trouble was anticipated.

James Meagher, occupation "home owner," member of the Commercial Club and citizen deputy, testified that a hundred shots were fired from the Verona before a gun was pulled on the dock, one of the first shots striking him in the leg. This witness was asked:

"Did you see a single gun on the boat?"

"No sir," was his mumbled response.

The prosecution witnesses disagreed as to the number of lines of deputies stretched across the back and sides of the open space on the dock, the statements varying from one to four files.

Chad Ballard, Harry Gray, and J. D. Landis, of the Seattle police detective bureau, and J. G. McConnell, Everett Interurban conductor, testified to the return and arrest of Mrs. Frenette, Mrs. Mahler and Mrs. Peters, after the trouble on November 5th. The police officers also told of a further searching of the Verona on its return. The defense admitted that some of the members had red pepper in their possession and stated that they would ask the judge to instruct the jury that red pepper is a weapon of defense and not of offense and that murder cannot be committed with red pepper.

Elmer Buehrer, engineer at the Everett High School, and citizen deputy, gave testimony that was halting, confused and relatively unimportant. He was prompted by the prosecution to such an extent that Attorney Vanderveer at the close of one question said, "Look at me and not at counsel."

"Look where you please," cried Cooley angrily.

"Well, look where you please," rejoined Vanderveer. "He can't help you."

It was apparent that the only reason for putting on this witness and former witness Meagher was because of a desire to create sympathy thru the fact that they had been wounded on the dock.

Edward Armstrong, master mariner on the Verona, testified that he had thrown out the spring line and lifted out the gate when the firing started. He fell to the deck behind a little jog, against the bulkhead, and while in that position two bullets went thru his cap. Altho this witness stated that he judged from the sound that the first shot came from some place to the rear of him, his testimony as to the attitude of McRae was as follows:

"I seen him with his right hand hanging on the butt of the gun."

"And that was before there was any shooting?"

"Yes sir."

As to the condition of the boat after the trouble he gave an affirmative answer to the question:

"You know that the whole front of the pilot house and the whole front of this bulkhead front of the forward deck leading to the hurricane deck is full of B. B. shot, don't you?"

James Broadbent, manager of the Clark-Nickerson Mill, and a citizen deputy, followed Armstrong with some unimportant testimony.

L. S. Davis, steward on the Verona, also stated that McRae committed the first overt act in taking hold of his gun. He was asked:

"He had his hand on his gun while he was still facing you?"

"Yes sir. I could see it plainly," answered Davis.

Pilot house of the "Verona"
riddled with rifle bullets
at EVERETT

"That was before he started to turn, before he was hit?"

"Yes sir."

Davis was wounded in the arm as he was on the pilot house steps.

He was asked about the general disposition, manner and appearance of the men on the Verona on the way over to Everett, and answered:

"I thought they were pretty nicely behaved for men—for such a crowd as that."

"Any rough talk; any rough, ugly looks?"

"No sir."

"Any guns?"

"No."

"Any threats?"

"I didn't hear any threats."

"Jolly, good-natured bunch of boys?"

"Yes."

"Lots of young boys among them, weren't there?"

"Yes, quite a few."

Davis stated that three passengers got off at Edmunds on the way up to Everett, thus establishing the fact that there were other than I. W. W. men on board.

R. S. "Scott" Rainey, commercial manager of the Puget Sound Telephone Company and a citizen deputy, was called and examined at some length before it was discovered that he was not an endorsed witness. This was the second time that the prosecution had turned this trick. Vanderveer objected, stating that there would be two hundred endorsed witnesses who would not be used.

"Oh no!" returned Mr. Veitch.

"Well," said Vanderveer, "a hundred then. A hundred we dare you to produce!"

"We will take that dare," responded Veitch. But the prosecution failed to keep their word, and deputy Dave Oswald of the Pacific Hardware Company, who during the various deportations tried to have the I. W. W. men stripped, covered with hot tar, rolled in feathers and ridden out of town on a rail, and a number of his equally degenerate brother outlaws were never produced in court.

Rainey testified that he had seen a quantity of murderous looking black-jacks in the Commercial Club for distribution to the deputies. He also saw men fall overboard from the Verona and saw none of them rescued. He thought there were twenty-five men with guns on the boat, and he did his firing at the main deck.

"And you didn't care whether you hit one of the twenty-five or one of the other two hundred and twenty-five?" scornfully inquired Vanderveer.

"No sir," said the miserable witness.

The next witness called was William Kenneth, city dock wharfinger in the employ of Captain Ramwell. This witness testified that there were numerous holes in the warehouses that were smooth on the inside and splintered on the outside, thus indicating that they were from shots blindly fired thru the walls from within. On being recalled on the Monday morning session of March 26th the witness said he wished to state that he was unable to testify from which direction the holes in the warehouses had been made. It appeared that he had discovered the bullet marks to have been whittled with a penknife since he had last viewed them.

Arthur Blair Gorrell, of Spokane, student at the State University, was on the dock during the trouble and was wounded in the left shoulder blade. He stated that he knew that McRae had his gun drawn before he was shot.

Captain K. L. Forbes, of the scab tugboat Edison, next took the witness chair. He didn't like the idea of calling his crew scabs for the engineer carried a union card. When questioned about the actions of the scab cook on the Edison, this witness would not state positively that the man was not firing directly across the open space on the dock at the Verona and in line with Curtis and other deputies.

Thomas E. Headlee, ex-mayor of Everett, bookkeeper at the Clark-Nickerson mill, and a citizen deputy, said he went whenever and wherever he was called to go by the sheriff.

"Then it's just like this," said Vanderveer, "when you pull the string, up jumps Headlee?"

This witness tried to blame all the fires in Everett onto the I. W. W. and the absurdity of his testimony brought this question from the defense:

"Just on general principles you blame it on the I. W. W.?"

"Sure!" replied the witness, "I got their reputation over in Wenatchee from my brother-in-law who runs a big orchard there."

Lewis Connor, member of the Commercial Club, and his friend, Edwin Stuchell, university student, both of whom were deputies on the dock on November 5th, then testified, but developed nothing of importance. Stuchell's father was part owner of the Eclipse mill and was said to have been on the board of directors of the Commercial Club. These witnesses were followed by Raymond E. Brown, owner of an Everett shoe store, a weak-kneed witness who had been sworn in as a deputy by W. W. Blain, secretary of the Commercial Club.

One of the greatest sensations in this sensational trial was when former sheriff Donald McRae took the stand on Tuesday, March 27th.

McRae was sober!

The sheriff was fifty years of age, of medium height, inclined to stoutness, smooth-shaven, with swinish eyes set closely on either side of a pink-tinted, hawk-like nose that curved just above a hard, cruel and excessively large mouth. The sneering speech and contemptible manner of this witness lent weight to the admissions of his brutality that had been dragged from reluctant state's witnesses thru the clever and cutting cross-examination conducted by Moore and Vanderveer.

McRae told of his former union affiliations, having once been International Secretary of the Shingle

Weavers' Union, and on another occasion the editor of their paper—but he admitted that he had never in his life read a book on political economy.

He detailed the story of the arrests, deportations and other similar actions against the striking shingle weavers and the I. W. W. members, the recital including an account of the "riot" at the jail, the deportation of Feinberg and Roberts, the shooting at the launch "Wanderer" and the jailing of its passengers, and the seizing of forty-one men and their deportation at Beverly Park. McRae's callous admissions of brutality discounted any favorable impression his testimony might otherwise have conveyed to the jury.

He admitted having ordered the taking of the funds of James Orr to pay the fares of workers deported on August 23rd, but denied the truth of an account in the Everett Herald of that date in which it was said that I. W. W. men had made some remarks to him "whereupon Sheriff McRae and police officer * * promptly retaliated by cracking the I. W. W.'s on the jaw with husky fists."

Regarding the launch "Wanderer" the sheriff was asked:

"Did you strike Captain Mitten over the head with the butt of your gun?"

"Certainly did!" replied McRae with brutal conciseness.

"Did any blood flow?"

"A little, not much."

"Not enough to arouse any sympathy in you?"

"No," said the sheriff unfeelingly.

"Did you strike a little Finnish fellow over the head with a gun?"

"I certainly did!"

"And split his head open and the blood ran out, but not enought to move you to any sympathy?"

"No, not a bit!" viciously answered McRae.

"Did you hit any others?" inquired Vanderveer.

"No, not then."

"Why not?"

"They probably seen what happened to the captain and the other fellow for getting gay."

As to the holding of Mitten in jail for a number of days on a charge of resisting an officer, and his final release, McRae was asked:

"Why didn't you try him on that charge?"

"Because when we let the I. W. W.'s go they insisted on him going, too, and I said, 'all right, take him along.'"

"You did whatever the I. W. W.'s wanted in that?"

"Well, I was glad to get rid of them," remarked the sheriff.

McRae said that none of the men taken to Beverly Park were beaten on the dock before being placed in automobiles for deportation, but on cross-examination he admitted that one of the deputies got in a mix-up and was beaten by a brother deputy. The sheriff stated that he took one man out to Beverly Park in a roadster, and had then returned to Everett to attend a dance given by the Elks' lodge.

In relating the events on November 5th, McRae's story did not differ materially from that of the witnesses who had already testified. He stated that a bullet passed thru his foot, striking the heel of his shoe, and coming out of the side. The shoe was then offered in evidence. He testified that another shot struck the calf of his leg and passed completely thru the limb. Both these wounds were from the rear. His entire suit was offered in evidence. The coat had nine bullet holes in it, yet McRae was not injured at all in the upper portion of his body! The sheriff stated that he fired twenty shots in all, and was then removed to the Sister's Hospital while the shooting was still in progress.

McRae then identified Ed Roth, James Kelly and Thomas H. Tracy as three of the I. W. W. men who were most active in firing from the Verona. In his identification of Tracy, McRae stated that the defendant was in the second or third cabin window aft the door, and was hanging out of the window with his breast against the sill and his elbow on the ledge. Vanderveer then placed himself in the position described by the sheriff and requested McRae to assume the same attitude he was in at the time he saw Tracy. Upon doing this it was apparent that the edge of the window sill would have cut off all view of Tracy's face from the sheriff, so McRae endeavored to alter his testimony to make it appear that Tracy's face was a foot or more inside the cabin window. This was the first identification of Tracy or other men on the boat that was attempted by the prosecution.

The sheriff stated that there were only twenty or twenty-five armed men on the Verona, and he admitted, before he left the stand, that he had told Attorney Vanderveer it was a pity that the spring line on the Verona did not break when the boat tilted so as to drown all the I. W. W.'s in the Bay.

Charles Auspos, alias Charles Austin, followed McRae as the state's witness second in importance only to the ex-sheriff. The testimony of these two was relied upon for a conviction.

Just why Auspos joined the I. W. W. will never be known, but his claim was that he could not work in the Dakota harvest fields or ride on the freight trains without an I. W. W. card. He was asked:

"When you did line up, you were then willingly a member, were you?"

"Yes sir."

"And you did not go to Yakima and come back to Seattle to fight for free speech because you were compelled to do so?" asked Moore.

"No," replied Auspos, "there was no compulsion."

Auspos stated that he was willing to take a chance in the fight for free speech and that the worst he expected was something similar to the happenings at Beverly Park. That he was not so willing in his testimony was shown by the uneasy actions of the prosecution lawyers, who moved from place to place around the court room during the examination

Arrival of the
"VERONA" at SEATTLE
1008

of this witness, with the view of having him look one of them in the eyes at all times during his recital. At one time Black nearly climbed into the jury box, while Cooley fidgeted in his chair placed directly in the middle of the aisle, and Veitch stood back of the court clerk on the opposite side of the court room, trying to engage the attention of the hesitating witness.

The testimony was to the effect that Auspos had reached Seattle on Saturday, November 4th, and had slept in the I. W. W. hall that night. Next morning at about eleven o'clock he returned from breakfast and was again admitted with examination for a membership card. A meeting was in progress in the gymnasium but was too crowded for him to be able to get in. There was no secrecy, however, just as there was no oath of fealty demanded of a worker upon joining the organization. The witness claimed that he and one of the defendants, J. E. Houlihan, were standing together in the hall when "Red" Doran called Houlihan aside into the gymnasium. Two minutes later Houlihan returned and said, "I made it." "What did you get?" Auspos declared he then asked his partner, receiving the reply, "A thirty-eight." Auspos claimed he saw Earl Osborne cleaning a gun in the gymnasium that same morning, and there was a rifle or shotgun in a canvas case in one corner. He said that men were breaking up chairs to obtain legs as clubs and that he, with others, was furnished with a little package of red pepper.

Regarding his actions upon the Verona the witness stated that he and James Hadley came up the steps from the freight deck to the passenger deck just as the boat was nosing against the dock and that he walked across the deck to a point within three feet of the rail. His description of the motion of McRae's hands differed from that given by the deputy witnesses and was such as would indicate the drawing of a gun from a belt holster. He testified that McRae swung around to the right just before being shot, thus contradicting McRae, who had declared that the turn he had made was to the left. The witness in a rather indefinite manner stated that the first shot came from the boat. All the damaging claims in the testimony of Auspos were severely shaken by the cross-examination conducted by Moore, and Auspos finally admitted that the only point on which he wished to have his evidence differ from the statement he had made to Vanderveer prior to the trial was in the matter of the firing of the first shot. Auspos made no attempt to identify anyone on the boat as having a firearm.

During the examination some reference was made to "Red" Downs, at which Judge Ronald remarked:

"I am a little confused. Did he say 'Red' Downs or 'Red' Doran?"

"There are two of them," responded Moore.

"Lots of red in this organization," cut in prosecutor Cooley, amid laughter from the spectators.

Attorney Moore brought from Auspos the admission that the plea of "Not Guilty" was a true one and he still believed that he and the other prisoners were not guilty of any crime. Yet such are the peculiarities of the legal game that an innocent man can turn state's evidence upon his innocent associates.

After uncovering the previous record of Auspos, he was asked about his "confession" as follows:

"Mr. McLaren and you had reached an understanding in your talk before Mr. Cooley came?"

"Yes sir."

"The question of what you are to get in connection with your testimony here has not as yet been definitely decided?"

"I am going to get out of the country."

"You are not going to get a trip to Honolulu?" asked Moore with a smile as he concluded the cross-examination of Auspos.

"No sir," stammered the tool of the prosecution unconvincingly.

It was at this point that the prosecution introduced several additional leaflets and pamphlets issued by the I. W. W. Publishing Bureau, the principal reason being to allow them to appeal to the patriotism of the jury by referring to Herve's pamphlet, "Patriotism and the Worker," and Smith's leaflet, "War and the Workers."

The next witness after Auspos was Leo Wagner, another poor purchase on the part of the prosecution. He merely testified that a man on the Calista had said that the men were armed and were not going to stand for being beaten up. Objection was made to the manner in which Cooley led the witness with his questions, and when Cooley stated that it was necessary to refresh the memory of the witness, Vanderveer replied that the witness had been endorsed but a few days before and his recollection should not be so very stale.

When this witness was asked what he was paid for his testimony he squirmed and hesitated until the court demanded an answer, whereupon he said:

"I got enough to live on for a while."

William H. Bridge, deputy sheriff and Snohomish county jailer, was the next witness. He stated on his direct examination that the first shot came from the second or third window back from the door on the upper cabin. Black asked Bridge:

"How do you know there was a shot from that place?"

"Because I saw a man reach out thru the window and shoot with a revolver."

"In what position was he when shooting?"

"Well, I could see his hand and a part of his arm and a part of his body and face."

"Who was the man, if you know?"

"Well, to the best of my judgement, it was the defendant, Thomas H. Tracy."

Under Vanderveer's cross-examination this witness was made to place the model of the Verona with its stern at the same angle as it had been at the time of the shooting. The witness was then asked to assume the same position he had been in at the time he said he had seen Tracy. The impossibility of having seen the face of a man firing from any of the cabin windows was thus demonstrated to the jury.

Then to clinch the idea that the identification was simply so much perjury, Vanderveer introduced into evidence the stenographic report of the coroner's inquest held over Jefferson Beard in which the witness, Bridge, had sworn that the first shot came from an open space just beneath the pilot house and had further testified that he could not recognize the person who was doing the firing.

Walter H. Smith, a scab shingle weaver, and deputy on the dock, followed with a claim to have recognized Tracy as one of the men who was shooting from the Verona. He also stated that he could identify another man who was shooting from the forward deck. He was handed a number of photographs and failed to find the man he was looking for. Instead he indicated one of the photographs and said that it was Tracy. Vanderveer immediately seized the picture and offered it in evidence.

"I made a mistake there," remarked Smith.

"I know you did," responded Vanderveer, "and I want the jury to know it."

The witness had picked out a photograph of John Downs and identified it as the defendant.

The prosecution then called S. A. Mann, who had been police judge in Spokane, Wash., from 1908 into 1911, and questioned him in regard to the Spokane Free Speech fight and the death of Chief of Police John Sullivan. Here attorney Fred Moore was on familiar ground, having acted for the I. W. W. during the time of that trouble. Moore developed the fact that there had been several thousand arrests with not a single instance of resistance or violence on the part of the I. W. W., not a weapon found on any of their persons, and no incendiary fires during the entire fight. He further confounded the prosecution by having Judge Mann admit that in the Spokane fight a prisoner arrested on a city charge was always lodged in the city jail and one arrested on a county charge was always placed in the county jail—a condition not at all observed in Everett.

Moore also brought out the facts of the death of Chief Sullivan so far as they are known. The witness admitted that Sullivan was charged with abuse of an adopted daughter of Mr. Elliott, a G. A. R. veteran; that desk officer N. V. Pitts charged Sullivan with having forced him to turn over certain Chinese bond money and the Chief resigned his position while under these charges; that the Spokane Press bitterly attacked Sullivan and was sued as a consequence, the Scripps-McRae paper being represented by the law firm of Robertson, Miller and Rosenhaupt, of which Judge Frank C. Robertson was the head; that the Chronicle and Spokesman-Review joined in the attack upon the Chief; and that when Sullivan was dying from a shot in the back the following conversation occurred between himself and the dying man: "I said to him 'John, who do you suppose did this?' He says, 'Judge F. C. Robertson and the Press are responsible for this.' I said, 'John, you don't mean that, you can't mean it?' He says, 'That is the way I feel.' "

Judge Ronald prevented the attorneys from going very deeply into the Spokane affair, saying:

"I am not going to wash Spokane linen here; we have some of our own to wash!"

C. R. Schweitzer, owner of a scab plumbing shop, aged 47, yet grey-haired, brazenly admitted having emptied a shotgun into the unarmed boys on the Verona. It was the missiles from the brand-new shotgun—probably furnished by Dave Oswald—that riddled the pilot house and wounded many of the men who fell to the deck when the Verona tilted. Schweitzer fired from a safe position behind the Klatawa slip. Why the prosecution used him as a witness is a mystery.

W. A. Taro, Everett Fire Chief, testified regarding the few incendiary fires that had occurred in Everett during the year 1916, but failed to connect them with the I. W. W. in any way. D. Daniels, Everett police officer, testified to a phosphorous fire which did no damage and was in no way connected with the I. W. W.

Mrs. Jennie B. Ames, the only woman witness called by the prosecution, testified that Mrs. Frennette was on the inclined walk at the Great Northern Depot, at a point overlooking the dock, and was armed with a revolver at the time the Verona trouble was on. Police officer J. E. Moline also swore to the same thing, but was badly tangled when confronted with his own evidence given at the preliminary hearing of Mrs. Frennette on December 6th, 1916.

Never was there a cad but who wished himself proclaimed as a gentleman; never a bedraggled and maudlin harlot but who wanted the world to know that she was a perfect lady. The last witness to be called by the prosecution was John Hogan—"Honest" John Hogan if prosecutor Lloyd Black was to be credited.

"Honest" John Hogan was a young red-headed regular deputy sheriff, who was a participant in the outrage on the City Dock on November 5th. "Honest" John Hogan claimed to have seen the defendant, Thomas Tracy, firing a revolver from one of the forward cabin windows. "Honest" John Hogan had the same difficulty as the other "identifying" witnesses when he also was asked to state whether it was possible to see a man firing from a cabin window when the stern of the boat was out and the witness in his specified position on the dock. "Honest"

John Hogan was sure it was Tracy that he saw because the man had a week's growth of whiskers on his face.

And this ended the case for the prosecution.

As had been predicted there were hundreds of witnesses who were endorsed and not called, and almost without an exception those who testified were parties who had a very direct interest in seeing that a conviction was secured. But thru the clever work of the lawyers for the defense what was meant to have been a prosecution of the I. W. W. was turned into an extremely poor defense of the deputies and their program of "law and order." From the state's witnesses the defense had developed nearly the whole outline and many of the details of its side of the case.

When the state rested its case, Tracy leaned over to the defense lawyers and, with a smile on his face, said:

"I'd be willing to let the case go to the jury right now."

CHAPTER VII.

THE DEFENSE

The case for the defense opened on Monday morning of April 2nd when Vanderveer, directly facing the judge and witness chair from the position vacated by the prosecution counsel, moved for a directed verdict of not guilty on the ground that there had been an absolute failure of evidence upon the question of conspiracy, any conspiracy of which murder was either directly or indirectly an incident, and there was no evidence whatever to charge the defendant directly as a principal in causing the death of Jefferson Beard. The motion was denied and an exception taken to the ruling of the court.

Fred Moore made the opening statement for the defense. In his speech he briefly outlined the situation that had existed in Everett up to and including November 5th and explained to the jury the forces lined up against each other in Everett's industrial warfare. Not for an instant did the attention of the jury flag during the recital.

Herbert Mahler, secretary of the I. W. W. in Seattle during the series of outrages in Everett, was the first witness placed upon the stand. Mahler told of the lumber workers' convention and the sending of organizer James Rowan to make a survey of the industrial situation in the lumber centers, Everett being the first point because of its proximity to Seattle and not by reason of any strikes that may have existed there. The methods of conducting the free speech fight, the avoidance of secrecy, the ardent desire for publicity of the methods of the lumber trust as well as the tactics of the I. W. W., were clearly explained.

Cooley cross-examined Mahler regarding the

song book with reference to the advocacy and use of sabotage, asking the witness:

"How about throwing a pitchfork into a threshing machine? Would that be all right?"

"There are circumstances when it would be, I suppose," replied Mahler. "If there was a farmer deputy who had been at Beverly Park, I think they certainly would have a right to destroy his threshing machine."

"You think that would justify it?" inquired Cooley.

"Yes," said the witness, "I think that if the man had abused his power as an officer and the person he abused had no other way of getting even with him and that justice was denied him in the courts, I fully believe that he would be. That would not hurt anybody; it would only hurt his pocketbook."

"Now what is this Joe Hill Memorial Edition?"

"Joe Hillstrom, known as Joe Hill, had written a number of songs in the I. W. W. Song Book and he was murdered in Utah and the song book was gotten out in memory of him," responded Mahler.

"He was executed after having been convicted of murder in the first degree, and sentenced to death. And you say he was murdered?" said Cooley.

"Yes," said Mahler with emphasis. "Our contention has been that Hillstrom did not have a fair trial and we are quite capable of proving it. I may say that President Wilson interceded in his behalf and was promptly turned down by Governor Spry of Utah. Hillstrom was offered a commutation of sentence and he refused to take it. He wanted a retrial or an acquittal. When the President of the United States had interceded with the Governor of Utah, when various labor organizations asked that he be given a retrial, and a man's life is to be taken from him, and people all over the country ask for a retrial, that certainly should be granted to him."

James P. Thompson was placed upon the stand to explain the principles of the I. W. W. The courtroom was turned into a propaganda meeting during the examination of the witness. One of the first features was the reading and explanation of state's exhibit "K," the famous I. W. W. preamble which has been referred to on various occasions as the most brutally scientific exposition of the class strug-gle ever penned:

I. W. W. PREAMBLE

The working class and the employing class have nothing in common. There can be no peace so long as hunger and want are found among millions of the working people and the few, who make up the employing class, have all the good things of life.

Between these two classes a struggle must go on until the workers of the world organize as a class, take possession of the earth and the machinery of production, and abolish the wage system.

We find that the centering of the management of industries into fewer and fewer hands makes the trade unions unable to cope with the ever growing power of the employing class. The trade unions foster a state of affairs which allow one set of workers to be pitted against another set of workers in the same industry, thereby helping defeat one another in wage wars. Moreover, the trade unions aid the employing class to mislead the workers into the belief that the working class have interests in common with their employers.

These conditions can be changed and the interests of the working class upheld only by an organization formed in such a way that all its members in any one industry, or in all industries, if necessary, cease work whenever a strike or lockout is on in any department thereof, thus making an injury to one an injury to all.

Instead of the conservative motto, "A fair day's wage for a fair day's work," we must inscribe on our banner the revolutionary watchword, "Abolition of the wage system."

It is the historic mission of the working class to do away with capitalism. The army of production must be organized, not only for the every day struggle with capitalists, but also to carry on production when capitalism shall have been overthrown. By organizing industrially we are forming the structure of the new society within the shell of the old.

"Men in society represent economic categories," said Thompson. "By that I mean that in the world of shoes there are shoemakers, and in the world of boats there are seamen, and in this society there are economic categories called the employing class and the working class. Now, between them as employing class and working class there is nothing in common. Their interests are diametrically opposed as such. It is not the same thing as saying that human beings have nothing in common. The working class and the employing class have antagonistic interests, and the more one gets the less remains for the other.

"Labor produces all wealth," continued Thompson, "and the more the workers have to give up to anyone else the less remains for themselves. The more they get in wages the less remains for the others in the form of profits. As long as labor produces for the other class all the good things of life there will be no peace; we want the products of labor ourselves and let the other class go to work also.

"The trades unions are unable to cope with the power of the employers because when one craft strikes the others remain at work and by so doing help the company to fill orders, and that is helping to break the strike. If a group of workers strike and win, other workers are encouraged to do likewise: if they strike and lose, other workers are discouraged and employers are encouraged to do some whipping on their own account.

"We believe in an industrial democracy; that the industry shall be owned by the people and operated on a co-operative plan instead of the wage plan; that there is no such thing as a fair day's pay; that we should have the full product of our labor in the co-operative system as distinguished from the wage system.

"Furthermore," went on the witness, as the jury leaned forward to catch his every word, "our ideas were suggested to us by conditions in modern industry, and it is the historical mission of the workers to organize, not only for the preliminary struggles, but to carry on production afterward."

"We object to this!" shouted Mr. Cooley, and the court sustained the objection.

Despite continual protests from the prosecution Thompson gave the ideas of the I. W. W. on many questions. Speaking of free speech the witness said:

"Free speech is vital. It is a point that has been threshed out and settled before we were born. If we do not have free speech, the children of the race will die in the dark."

The message of industrial unionism delivered thru the sworn testimony of a labor organizer was indeed an amazing spectacle. Judge Ronald never relaxed his attention during the entire examination, the jury was spell-bound, and it was only by an obvious effort that the spectators kept from applauding the various telling points.

"There is overwork on one hand," said Thompson, "and out-of-work on the other. The length of the working day should be determined by the amount of work and the number of workers. You have no more right to do eight or ten or twelve hours of labor when others are out of work, despondent, committing suicide, than you have to drink all the water, if that were possible, while others are dying of thirst.

"Solidarity is the I. W. W. way to get their demands. We do not advocate that the workers should organize in a military way and use guns and dynamite. The most effective weapon of labor is economic power: the modern wage workers are the living parts of industry and if they fold their arms, they immediately precipitate a crisis, they paralyze the world. No other class has that power. The other class can fold their arms, and they do most of the time, but our class has the economic power. The

I. W. W. preaches and teaches all the time that a far more effective weapon than brickbats or dynamite is solidarity.

"We have developed from individual production to social production, yet we still have private ownership of the means of production. One class owns the industries and doesn't operate them, another class operates the industries and does not own them. We are going to have a revolution. No one is more mistaken than those who believe that this system is the final state of society. As the industrial revolution takes place, as the labor process takes on the cooperative form, as the tool of production becomes social, the idea of social ownership is suggested, and so the idea that things that are used collectively should be owned collectively, presents itself with irresistible force to the people of the twentieth century. So there is a struggle for industrial democracy. We are the modern abolitionists fighting against wage slavery as the other abolitionists fought against chattel slavery. The solution for our modern problems is this, that the industries should be owned by the people, operated by the people for the people, and the little busy bees who make the honey of the world should eat that honey, and there should be no drones at all in the hives of industry.

"When we have industrial democracy you will know that the mills, the mines, the factories, the earth itself, will be the collective property of the people, and if a little baby should be born that baby would be as much an owner of the earth as any other of the children of men. Then the war, the commercial struggles, the clashes between groups of conflicting interests, will be a night-mare of the past. In the place of capitalism with its one class working and its other class enjoying, in the place of the wages system with its strife and strikes, lockouts and grinding poverty, we will have a co-operative system where the interests of one will be to promote the interests of all—that will be Industrial Democracy."

Thompson explained the meaning of the sarcastic song, "Christians at War," to the evident amusement of the jury and spectators. The witness was then asked about Herve's work on anti-patriotism in this question by attorney Moore:

"What is the attitude of your organization relative to internationalism and national patriotism?"

"We object to that as incompetent and immaterial," cried Veitch of the prosecution.

"What did you put this book in for then?" said Judge Ronald in a testy manner as he motioned the witness to proceed with his answer.

"In the broader sense," answered Thompson, "there is no such thing as a foreigner. We are all native born members of this planet, and for the members of it to be divided into groups or units and to be taught that each nation is better than the other leads to clashes and the world war. We ought to have in the place of national patriotism—the idea that one people is better than another,—a broader conception, that of international solidarity. The idea that we are better than others is contrary to the Declaration of Independence which declares that all men are born free and equal. The I. W. W. believes that in order to do away with wars we should remove the cause of wars; we should establish industrial democracy and the co-operative system instead of commercialism and capitalism and the struggles that come from them. We are trying to make America a better land, a land without child slaves, a land without poverty, and so also with the world, a world without a master and without a slave."

When the lengthy direct examination of Thompson had been finished, the prosecution questioned him but five minutes and united in a sigh of relief as he left the stand.

The next witness called was Ernest Nordstrom, companion of Oscar Carlson who was severely wounded on the Verona. Nordstrom testified rather out of his logical order in the trial by reason of the fact that he was about to leave on a lengthy fishing trip to Alaska. His testimony was that he purchased a regular ticket at the same time as his friend Carlson, but these tickets were not taken up by the purser. The original ticket of this passenger was then offered in evidence. The witness stated that the first shot came from almost the same place on the dock as did the words "You can't land here." He fell to the deck and saw Carlson fall also. Carlson tried to rise once, but a bullet hit him and he dropped; there were nine bullet holes in him. Nordstrom was asked:

"Did you have a gun?"

"No sir."

"Did Carlson have a gun?"

"No sir."

"Did you see anybody with a gun on the boat?"

"No. I didn't."

Organizer James Rowan then gave his experiences in Everett, ending with a vivid recital of the terrible beating he had received at the hands of deputies near Silver Lake. Upon telling of the photograph that was taken of his lacerated back he was asked by Veitch:

"What was the reason you had that picture taken?"

"Well," said Rowan, in his inimitable manner, "I thought it would be a good thing to get that taken to show up the kind of civilization that they had in Everett."

Dr. E. J. Brown, a Seattle dentist, and Thomas Horner, Seattle attorney, corroborated Rowan's testimony as to the condition of his back. They had seen the wounds and bruises shortly after the beating had been administered and were of the opinion that a false light was reflected on the photograph in such a way that the severest marks did not appear as bad as they really were.

Otto Nelson, Everett shingle weaver, gave testimony regarding the shingle weavers' strikes of 1915 and 1916 but was stopped from going into detail by the rulings of the court. He told also of the peaceful character of all the I. W. W. meetings in Everett, and stated that on one occasion police officer Daniels had fired two shots down one of the city streets at an I. W. W. man who had been made to run the gauntlet.

H. P. Whartenby, owner of a five-ten-fifteen cent store in Everett, said that the I. W. W. meetings were orderly, and further testified that he had been ordered out of the Commercial Club on the evening of November 5th but not until he had seen that the club was a regular arsenal, with guns stacked all over the place.

To establish the fact that the sidewalks were kept clear, that there was no advocacy of violence, that no resistance was offered to arrest, and that the I. W. W. meetings were well conducted in every particular, the defense put on in fairly rapid succession a number of Everett citizens: Mrs. Ina M. Salter, Mrs. Elizabeth Maloney, Mrs. Letelsia Fye, Bruce J. Hatch, Mrs. Dollie Gustaffson, Miss Avis Mathison, Mrs. Peter Aiken, Mrs. Annie Pomeroy, Mrs. Rebecca Wade, F. G. Crosby, and Mrs. Hannah Crosby. The fact that these citizens, and a number of other women who were mentioned in the testimony, attended the I. W. W. meetings quite regularly, impressed the jury favorably. Some of these women witnesses had been roughly handled by the deputies. Mrs. Pomeroy stated that the deputies, armed with clubs and distinguished by white handkerchiefs around their necks, invaded one meeting and struck right and left. "And they punched me at that!" said the indignant witness.

"Punched you where?" inquired Vanderveer in order to locate the injury.

"They punched me on the sidewalk!" answered the witness, and the solemn bailiff had to rap for order in the court room.

Cooley caught a Tartar in his cross-examination of Mrs. Crosby. He inquired:

"Did you hear the I. W. W.'s say that when they got a majority of the workers into this big union they would take possession of the industries and run them themselves?"

"Why certainly!"

"You did hear them say they would take possession?"

"Why certainly!" flashed back the witness. "That's the way the North did with the slaves, isn't it? They took possession without ever asking them. My people came from the South and they had slaves taken away from them and never got anything for it, and quite right, too!"

"Then you do believe it would be all right, yourself?" said Cooley.

"I believe that confiscation would be perfectly right in the case of taking things that are publicly used for the public good of the people——."

"That's all," hastily cut in Cooley.

"That they should be used then by the people and for the people!" finished the witness.

"That's all!" cried Cooley loudly and more anxiously.

Frank Henig, the next witness, told of having been blackjacked by Sheriff McRae and exhibited the large scar on his forehead that plainly showed where the brutal blow had landed. He stated that he had tried to secure the arrest of McRae for the entirely unwarranted attack but was denied a warrant.

Jake Michel, secretary of the Everett Building Trades Council, gave evidence regarding a number of the I. W. W. street meetings. He was questioned at length about what he had inferred from the speeches of Rowan, Thompson and others. Replying to one question he said:

"I think the American Federation of Labor uses the most direct action that any organization could use."

"In a strike?"

"Yes."

"And by that you mean a peaceful strike?" said Cooley suggestively.

"Well, I haven't seen them carry on very many peaceful ones yet," replied Michel.

Cooley asked Michel whether Rowan had said that "the workers should form one great industrial union and declare the final and universal strike; that is, that they should remain within the industrial institutions and lock the employers out for good as owners?"

"I never heard him mention anything about locking anyone out; I think he wanted to lock them in and make them do some of the work!" answered Michel.

"You haven't any particular interest in this case, have you?" asked Cooley with a sneer.

"Yes, I have!" replied Michel with emphasis.

When asked what this particular interest was, Michel caused consternation among the ranks of the prosecution by replying:

"The reason I have that interest is this; I have two sons and two daughters. I want to see the best form of organization so that the boys can go out and make a decent living; I don't want my girls to become prostitutes upon the streets and my boys vagabonds upon the highways!"

Harry Feinberg, one of the free speech prisoners named on the first information with Watson and Tracy, was then placed on the stand and questioned as to the beating he had received at the hands of deputies, as to the condition of Frank Henig after McRae's attack, and upon matters connected with various street meetings at which he had been the speaker. Mention of the name of George Reese brought forth an argument from the prosecution that it had not been shown that Reese was a detective. After an acrimonious discussion Vanderveer suddenly declared:

"Just to settle this thing and settle it for now and all the time, I will ask a subpoena forthwith for Philip K. Ahern and show who Reese is working for."

The subpoena was issued and a recess taken to

allow it to be served. As Vanderveer stepped into the hall, detective Malcolm McLaren said to him, "You can't subpoenae the head of the Pinkerton Detective Agency!"

"I have subpoenaed him," responded Vanderveer shortly as he hurried to the witness room.

While awaiting the arrival of this witness, Feinberg was questioned further, and was then taken from the stand to allow the examination of two Everett witnesses, Mrs. L. H. Johnson and P. S. Johnson, the latter witness being withdrawn when Ahern put in an appearance.

Vanderveer was very brief, but to the point, in the examination of the local head of the Pinkerton Agency.

"Mr. Ahern, on the fifth day of November you had in your employ a man named George Reese?"

"Yes sir."

"For whom was he working, thru you, at that time?"

"For Snohomish County."

"That's all!" said Vanderveer triumphantly.

Cooley did not seem inclined to cross-examine the witness at any length and Vanderveer in another straightforward question brought out the fact that Reese was a Pinkerton employe during the Longshoremen's strike—this being the time that Reese also was seated as a delegate to the Seattle Trades Council of the A. F. of L.

A portion of the testimony of Mrs. L. H. Johnson was nearly as important as that concerning Reese. She recited a conversation with Sheriff McRae as follows:

"McRae said he would stop the I. W. W. from coming to Everett if he had to call out the soldiers. And I told him the soldiers wouldn't come out on an occasion like this, they were nothing but Industrial Workers of the World and they had a right to speak and get people to join their union if they wanted to. And he said he had the backing of the millmen to keep them out of the city, and he was go-

Cutting off top of tree to fit block for flying machine.

ing to do it if he had to call the soldiers out and shoot them down when they landed there, when they came off the dock."

This clearly indicated the bloodthirsty designs of the millmen and the sheriff at a time long before November 5th.

G. W. Carr, Wilfred Des Pres, and J. M. Norland testified to the breaking up of peaceably conducted I. W. W. meetings, Des Pres also telling of rifles having been transported from the Pacific Hardware Company to the dock on November 5th. All three were Everett citizens. Black asked Norland if he knew what sabotage was, to which Norland replied:

"Everybody that follows the labor movement knows what sabotage is."

There was a sensation in court at this question for it was the first and only time that any of the prosecution counsel correctly pronounced the word sabotage!

W. W. Blain, secretary of the Commercial Club, altho an unwilling witness, gave much information of value to the defense. He was forced to produce the minutes of the "open shop committee" and give up the story of how control of the club was purchased by the big interests, how the boycott was invoked against certain publications, and finally to tell of the employment of Pinkerton detectives prior to November 5th, and to give a list of the deputies furnished by the Commercial Club.

During the examination of this witness some telegrams, in connection with the testimony, were handed up to the judge. While reading these Judge Ronald was interrupted by a foolish remark from Black to Vanderveer. Looking over his glasses the judge said:

"Every time I start to read anything, you gentlemen get into a quarrel among yourselves. I am inclined to think that the 'cats,' some of them, are here in the courtroom."

"I will plead guilty for Mr. Black, Your Honor!" said Vanderveer quickly, laughing at the reference to sabotage.

Testimony to further establish the peaceable character of the I. W. W. meetings and the rowdyism of the police and deputies was given by witnesses from Everett: Gustaf Pilz, Mrs. Leota Carr, J. E. McNair, Ed Morton, Michael Maloney, Verne C. Henry and Morial Thornburg. The statements of these disinterested parties regarding the clubbings given to the speakers and to citizens of their acquaintance proved very effective.

Attorney H .D. Cooley for the prosecution was placed upon the witness stand and Vanderveer shot the question at him:

"By whom were you employed in this case, Mr. Cooley?"

"Objected to as immaterial!" cried Veitch, instantly springing to his feet.

But the damage had been done! The refusal to allow an answer showed that there were interested parties the prosecution wished to hide from the public.

Levi Remick related the story of the deportation from Everett, and was followed on the witness stand by Edward Lavelly, James Dwyer, and Thomas Smye, who testified to different atrocities committed in Everett by McRae and the citizen deputies. Their evidence had mainly to do with the acts of piracy committed against the launch "Wanderer" and the subsequent abuse of the arrested men. A little later in the trial this testimony was fully corroborated by the statements of Captain Jack Mitten. During Mitten's examination by Black the old Captain continually referred to the fact that the life preservers and other equipment of his boat had been stolen while he was in jail. The discomfiture of the youthful prosecutor was quite evident.

J. H. Buel impeached the testimony of state's witness Judge Bell who had made the claim that a filer at the Clark-Nickerson mill had been assaulted by a member of the I. W. W. Vanderveer asked this witness:

"What was the name of the man assaulted?"

"Jimmy Cain."

"Who did it?"

"I did."

"Are you an I. W. W.?"

"No sir."

"Were you ever?"

"No sir."

Louis Skaroff followed with a detailed story of the murderous attack made upon him by Mayor Merrill in the Everett jail, his story being unshaken when he was recalled and put thru a grilling cross-examination.

William Roberts, who had been beaten and deported with Harry Feinberg, related his experience. The childish questions of Black in regard to the idea of abolishing the wages system nettled this witness and caused him to exclaim, "the trouble is that you don't understand the labor movement."

James Orr then told of having his money stolen by the officials so they might pay the fares of twenty-two deported men, and John Ovist followed with the tale of the slugging he had received upon the same occasion that Feinberg, Roberts and Henig were assaulted.

Attorneys George W. Loutitt and Robert Faussett, of Everett, stated that the reputation of McRae for sobriety was very bad. Both of these lawyers had resigned from the Commercial Club upon its adoption of an open shop policy.

Thomas O'Niel testified regarding street meetings and other matters in connection wtih the case. Cooley asked the witness how many people usually attended the meetings.

"It started in with rather small meetings," said the witness, "and then every time, as fast as they were molested by the police, the crowd kept growing until at last the meetings were between two and three thousand people."

The witness said he had read considerable about industrial unionism, and tho he was shocked at first he had come to believe in it.

"Until now you are satisfied that their doctrines taken as a whole are proper and should be promulgated and adopted by the working class?" inquired Cooley.

"In this way," answered O'Niel, "it was not the I. W. W. literature that convinced me so much as the actions of the side that was fighting them."

"That is, you believe they were right because of the actions of the people on the other side?" said Cooley.

"Yes," responded the witness, "because I think there are only two people interested in this movement, the people carrying on the propaganda and the people fighting the propaganda, and I saw the people who were fighting the propaganda use direct action, sabotage, and every power, political and industrial, they used it all to whip this organization, and then I asked myself why are they fighting this organization. And the more deeply I became interested, the more clearly I saw why they were doing it, and that made me a believer in the I. W. W."

Mrs. Louise McGuire followed this witness with testimony about injuries she had received thru the rough treatment accorded her by citizen deputies engaged in breaking up a street meeting.

W. H. Clay, Everett's Commissioner of Finance, was brought on the stand to testify that he was present and active at the conference that resulted in the formation of the citizen deputies.

John Berg then related his experiences at the time he was taken to the outskirts of Everett and deported after McRae had kicked him in the groin until a serious injury resulted. Owing to the fact that the jury was a mixed one Berg was not permitted to exhibit the rupture. This witness also told his experience on the "Wanderer" and his treatment in the jail upon his arrest.

Oscar Lindstrom then took the stand and corroborated the stories of the witnesses who had testified about the shooting up of the "Wanderer" and the beating and jailing of its pasengers. H. Sokol, better known as "Happy," also told of his experience on the "Wanderer" and gave the facts of the deportation that had taken place on August 23rd.

Irving W. Ziegaus, secretary to Governor Lister, testified that the letter concerning Everett sent from the Seattle I. W. W. had been received; Steven M. Fowler identified certain telegrams sent from Everett to Seattle officials by David Clough on November 5th; after which Chester Micklin, who had been jailed in Everett following the tragedy, corroborated parts of the story of Louis Skaroff.

The evidence of state's witness, Clyde Gibbons, was shattered at this stage of the trial by the placing of Mrs. Lawrence MacArthur on the stand. This witness, the proprietor of the Merchants Hotel in Everett, produced the hotel register for November 4th and showed that Mrs. Frennette had registered at that time and was in the city when Gibbons claimed she was holding a conversation in an apartment house on Yesler Way in Seattle.

The defense found it necessary to call witnesses who logically should have been brought forward by the prosecution on their side of the case. Among these was the famous "Governor" Clough, citizen deputy and open shop mill owner. David Clough unwillingly testified to having been present at the deportation of twenty-two I. W. W. members on August 23rd, having gone down to the dock at 8:30 that morning, and also to his interest in Joseph Schofield, the deputy who had been injured by his brother outlaws on the dock just before the Beverly Park deportations.

Mahler and Micklin were recalled for some few additional questions, and were followed on the stand by Herman Storm, who gave testimony about the brutal treatment received by himself and his fellow passengers on the launch "Wanderer." John Hainey and Joseph Reaume also gave details of this outrage.

"Sergeant" J. J. Keenan, who had become a familiar figure because of his "police" duty in the outer court corridor from the inception of the trial, then took the witness stand and recounted his experiences at Snohomish and Maltby, his every word carrying conviction that the sheriff and his deputies had acted with the utmost brutality in spite of the advanced age of their victim. John Patterson and Tom Thornton corroborated Keenan's testimony.

A surprise was sprung upon the prosecution at this juncture by the introduction on the witness stand of George Kannow, a man who had been a deputy sheriff in Everett and who had been present when many of the brutalities were going on. He told of the treatment of Berg after the "Wanderer" arrests.

"He was struck and beaten and thrown down and knocked heavily against the steel sides of the tank, his head striking on a large projecting lock. He was kicked by McRae and he hollered 'My God, you are killing me,' and McRae said he didn't give a damn whether he died or not, and kicked him again and then shoved him into the tank."

The gauntlet at the county jail was described in detail and the spirit of the free speech fighters was shown by this testimony:

"Yes, I heard some of them groan. They all took their medicine well, tho. They didn't holler out but some of them would groan; some of them would go down pretty near to their knees and then get up, then they would get sapped again as they got up. But they never made any real outcries."

The witness stated that "Governor" Clough was a regular attendant at the deportation parties and so also were W. R. Booth, Ed Hawes, T. W. Anguish, Bill Pabst, Ed Seivers, and Will Taft. He described McRae's drunken condition and told of drunken midnight revels held in the county jail. His testimony was unshaken on cross-examination.

Mrs. Fern Grant, owner of the Western Hotel and Grant's Cafe, testified that Mrs. Frennette was in her place of business in Everett on the morning of the tragedy, thus adding to the evidence that Clyde Gibbons had perjured himself in testifying for the prosecution.

A party of Christian Scientists, who had attended a lecture in Everett by Bliss Knapp, told of the frightful condition of the eight men who had taken the interurban train to Seattle following their experience at Beverly Park. Mrs. Lou Vee Siegfried, Christian Science practitioner, Thorwald Siegfried, prominent Seattle lawyer, Mrs. Anna Tenelli and Miss Dorothy Jordan were corroborated in their testimony by Ira Bellows, conductor on the interurban car that took the wounded men to Seattle.

Another break in the regular order of the trial was made at this point by the placing on the stand of Nicholas Coniaeff, member of the I. W. W., who was to leave on the following day with a party of Russians returning to their birthplace to take part in the revolution then in progress. Coniaeff stated that the first shot came from the dock. His realistic story of the conditions on the Verona moved many in the courtroom to tears. In his description Coniaeff said:

"I was wounded myself. But before I was wounded and as we were lying there three or four deep I saw a wounded man at my feet in a pool of blood. Then I saw a man with his face up, and he was badly wounded, probably he was dead. There were three or four wounded men alongside of me. The conditions were so terrible that it was hard to control one's self, and a young boy who was in one pile could not control himself any longer; he was about twenty years old and had on a brown, short, heavy coat, and he looked terrified and jumped up and went overboard into the water and I didn't see him any more."

Mrs. Edith Frennette testified to her movements on the day of the tragedy and denied the alleged threats to Sheriff McRae. Lengthy cross-examination failed to shake her story.

Members of the I. W. W. who had been injured at Beverly Park then testified. They were Edward Schwartz, Harry Hubbard, Archie Collins, C. H. Rice, John Downs, one of the defendants, Sam Rovinson and Henry Krieg. Any doubt as to the truth of their story was dispelled by the testimony of Mrs. Ruby Ketchum, her husband Roy Ketchum, and her brother-in-law Lew Ketchum, all three of whom heard the screams of the victims and witnessed part of the slugging near their home at Beverly Park. Some members of the investigation committee who viewed the scene on the morning after the outrage gave their evidence as to the finding of bits of clothing, soles of shoes, bloodstained hats and loose hatbands, and blotches of blood on the paved roadway and cattle guard. These witnesses were three ministers of the gospel of different denominations, Elbert E. Flint, Joseph P. Marlatt, and Oscar H. McGill. The last named witness also told of having interviewed Herbert Mahler, secretary of the I. W. W. in Seattle, following a conference with Everett citizens, with the object of having a large public demonstration in Everett to expose the Beverly Park affair and to prevent its repetition. It was after this interview that the call went out for the I. W. W. to hold a public meeting in Everett on Sunday, November 5th. Mahler was recalled to the stand to verify McGill's statement in the matter of the interview.

This testimony brought the case up to the events of November 5th and the defense, having proven each illegal action of the sheriff, deputies and mill owners, and disproven the accusations against the I. W. W., proceeded to open to the gaze of the public and force to the attention of the jury the actual facts concerning the massacre on the Verona.

An important witness was Charles Miller, who viewed the tragedy from a point about four hundred feet from the Verona while on the deck of his fishing boat, the "Scout." He stated that the Verona tilted as soon as the first shots came. Miller placed the model of the boat at the same relative position it had occupied as the firing started on Bloody Sunday and the prosecution could not tangle up this witness on this important point. The "identification" witnesses of the prosecution were of necessity liars if the stern of the Verona was at the angle set by Miller.

C. M. Steele, owner of apartment houses and stores in Everett, stated that he had been in a group who saw an automobile load of guns transported to the dock prior to the docking of the Verona, this auto being closely followed by a string of other machines. The witness tried to get upon the dock but was prevented by deputies who had a rope stretched clear across the entrance near the office of the American Tug Boat Company. He saw the boat tilt as the firing started and noticed that the stern swung out at the time. This testimony was demonstrated with the model. Harry Young, chauffeur, corroborated this testimony and told of rifle fire from the dock.

Mrs. Mabel Thomas, from a position on Johnson's float quite near the Verona, told of the boat listing until the lower deck was under water, almost immediately after the firing started. Mrs. Thomas testified that "one man who was facing toward the Improvement Dock, raised his hands and fell overboard from the hurricane deck as tho he were dead. His overcoat held him to the top of the water for a moment and then he went down. One jumped from the stern and then there were six or seven in the water. One got up thru the canvas and crawled back in. One man that fell in held up his hands for a moment and sank. There were bullets hitting all around him."

Mr. Carroll Thomas, husband of the preceding witness, gave the same testimony about the men in the water and stated that he saw armed men on the Improvement Dock.

The testimony of Ayrold D. Skinner, a barber in Everett at the time of the tragedy and who had been brought from California to testify, was bitterly attacked by Veitch but to no avail. When the Verona landed Skinner was so situated as to command a view of the whole proceedings. He told of the boat listing, the men falling in the water and being shot, and his testimony about a man on board the tug

"Edison" firing a rifle directly across the open space on the dock in the direction of the Verona was unshakeable. This witness also testified that about ten deputies with rifles were running back and forth in a frightened manner and were firing from behind the Klatawa slip. The witness saw Dick Hembridge, superintendent of the Canyon Lumber Company, Carl Tyre, timekeeper, Percy Ames, the boom man, and a Dr. Hedges. The last two came up to where the witness was, each bearing a rifle. Skinner stated that he said to Ames, "Percy, what is the world coming to?" and Ames broke down as tho he felt something were wrong. Then Dr. Hedges came running up from where the boat was, he was white in the face, and he cried "Don't go down there, boys; they are shooting wild, you don't know where in hell the shots are coming from."

Carl Ryan, night watchman of the Everett Shingle Company, N. C. Roberts, an Everett potter, Robert Thompson and Edward Thompson testified about the angle of the boat, as to rifles on the dock, the shooting from the tug "Edison" and from the Improvement Dock, in support of witnesses who had previously testified.

Alfred Freeman, I. W. W. member who was on the Verona, testified about the movements of those who made the trip to Everett and told of the conditions on the boat. His testimony, and that of numerous other I. W. W. witnesses, disproved the charges of conspiracy.

I. W. McDonald, barber, John Josephson, lumber piler, and T. M. Johnson, hod carrier, all of Everett, stated that the shots from the boat did not come until after there had been considerable firing from the dock. These witnesses were among the thousands of citizens who overlooked the scene from the hillside by the Great Northern depot.

On Wednesday, April 18th, the jury, accompanied by Judge Ronald, the attorneys for both sides, the defendant, Thomas Tracy, and the court stenographer, went in automobiles to Everett to inspect the various places mentioned in the court pro-

VERONA AT EVERETT DOCK,
under same tide condition as at time of Massacre.

ceedings. The party stopped on the way to Everett to look over the scene of the Beverly Park outrages of October 30th. No one spoke to the jury but Judge Ronald, who pointed out the various features at the request of the attorneys in the background.

After visiting the corner of Hewitt and Wetmore Avenues, the party went to the city dock. Both warehouses were carefully examined, the bullet-holes, tho badly whittled, being still in evidence. Bulletholes in the floor, clock-case, and in the walls still showed quite plainly that the firing from within the warehouse and waiting room had been wild. Bullets imbedded in the Klatawa slip on the side toward the Bay also gave evidence of blind firing on the part of the deputies. In the floor of the dock, between the ship and the open space near the waiting room, were several grooves made by bullets fired from the shore end of the dock. These marks indicated that the bullets had taken a course directly in line with the deputies who were in the front ranks as the Verona landed.

The party boarded the Verona and subjected the boat to a searching examination, discovering that the stairways, sides, and furnishings were riddled with shot holes. The pilot house, in particular, was found to have marks of revolver and high power rifle bullets, in addition to being closely marked with small shot holes, some of the buck-shot still being visible.

The captain swung the boat out to the same angle as it had been on November 5th, this being done at a time when it was computed that the tide would be relatively the same as on the date of the tragedy. Someone assumed the precise position at the cabin window that Tracy was alleged to have been in while firing. The jury members then took up the positions which the "identification witnesses" had marked on a diagram during their testimony. The man in the window was absolutely invisible!

A photograph was then taken from the point where "Honest" John Hogan claimed to have been when he saw Tracy firing and another view made by a second camera to show that the first photograph had been taken from the correct position. These were later introduced as evidence.

No testimony was taken in Everett but on the reopening of court in Seattle next morning Frank A. Brown, life insurance solicitor, testified that McRae dropped his hand just before the first shot was fired from somewhere to the right of the sheriff. He also identified a Mr. Thompson, engineer of the Clark-Nickerson mill, and a Mr. Scott, as being armed with guns having stocks. Mike Luney, shingle weaver, told of a fear-crazed deputy running from the dock with a bullethole in his ear and crying out that one of the deputies had shot him. Fred Bissinger, a boy of 17, told of the deputies breaking for cover as soon as they had fired a volley at the men on the boat. It was only after the heavy firing that he saw a man on the boat pull a revolver from his pocket and commence to shoot. He saw but two revolvers in action on the Verona.

One of the most dramatic and clinching blows for the defense was struck when there was introduced as a witness Fred Luke, who was a regular deputy sheriff and McRae's right-hand man. Luke's evidence of the various brutalities, given in a cold, matter-of-fact manner, was most convincing. He stated that the deputies wore white handkerchiefs around their necks so they would not be hammering each other. He contradicted McRae's testimony about Beverly Park by stating positively that the sheriff had gone out in a five passenger car, and not in a roadster as was claimed, and that they had both remained there during the entire affair. He told how he had swung at the I. W. W. men with such force that his club had broken from its leather wrist thong and disappeared into the woods. When questioned about the use of clubs in dispersing street crowds at the I. W. W. meetings he said:

"I used my sap as a club and struck them and drove them away with it."

"Why didn't you use your hands and push them out?" asked Cooley.

"I didn't think we had a right to use our hands," said the big ex-deputy.

"What do you mean by that?" said the surprised lawyer.

"Well," replied the witness, "what did they give us the saps for?"

Cooley also asked this witness why he had struck the men at Beverly Park.

"Well," replied the ex-deputy, "if you want to know, that was the idea of the Commercial Club. That was what they recommended."

Luke, who was a guard at the approach to the dock on November 5th, told of having explained the workings of a rifle to a deputy while the shooting was in progress. The state at first had contended that there were no rifles on the dock and later had made the half-hearted plea that none of the rifles which were proven to have been there were fired.

Following this important witness the defense introduced Fird Winkley, A. E. Amiott, Dr. Guy N. Ford, Charles Leo, Ed Armstrong, mate of the Verona and a witness for the state, and B. R. Watson, to corroborate the already convincing evidence that the stern of the Verona was swung quite a distance from the dock.

Robert Mills, business agent of the Everett Shingle Weavers, who had been called to the stand on several occasions to testify to minor matters, was then recalled. He testified that it was his hand which protruded from the Verona cabin window in the photographs, and that his head was resting against the window jamb on the left hand side as far out as it would be possible to get without crawling out of the window. As Mills was a familiar figure to the entire jury and was also possessed of a peculiarly unforgettable type of countenance, the state's identification of Tracy was shown to have been false.

The Chief of Police of Seattle, Charles Beckingham, corroborated previous testimony by stating that the identification and selection of I. W. W. men had been made from a dark cell by two Pinkerton men, Smith and Reese, aided by one of the defendants, I. P. McDowell, alias Charles Adams.

Malcolm McLaren was then placed upon the stand and the admission secured that he was a detective and had formerly been connected with the Burns Agency. Objection was made to a question about the employment of McLaren in the case, to which Vanderveer replied that it was the purpose of the defense to prove that the case was not being prosecuted by the State of Washington at all. In the absence of the jury Vanderveer then offered to prove that McLaren had been brought from Los Angeles and retained in the employ of certain mill owners, among them being "Governor" Clough and Mr. Moody of the First National Bank, and that McLaren had charge of the work of procuring the evidence introduced by the state. He offered to prove that Veitch and Cooley were employed by the same people. The court sustained the objection of the state to the three offers.

Testimony on various phases of the case was then given by Mrs. Fannie Jordan, proprietor of an apartment house in Seattle, Nick Shugar, Henry Luce, Paul Blakenship, Charles W. Dean, and later on by Oliver Burnett.

Captain Chauncey Wiman was called to the stand, but it happened that he had gone into hiding so soon after the boat landed that he could testify to nothing of particular importance. From his appearance on the witness stand it seemed that he was still nearly scared to death.

Another surprise for the prosecution was then sprung by placing Joseph Schofield on the witness stand. Schofield told of having been beaten up at the city dock by Joseph Irving, during the time they were lining up the forty-one I. W. W. men for deportation. The witness displayed the scar on his head that had resulted from the wound made by the gun butt, and described the drunken condition of McRae and other deputies on the occasion of his injury. And then he told that "Governor" Clough had gone to his wife just a couple of days before he took the witness stand and had given her $75.00. This deputy witness was on the dock November 5th, and he described the affair. He swore that McRae had his gun drawn before any shooting started, that there were rifles in use on the dock, that a man was firing a Winchester rifle from the tug Edison. He was handed a bolt action army rifle to use but made no use of it. Schofield voluntarily came from Oregon to testify for the defense.

Chief Beckingham resumed the stand and was asked further about McDowell, alias Adams. He said:

"We sent a man in with this man Adams, who was in constant fear that somebody might see him, and he would stand way back that he might tip this man with him and this man's fingers came out to identify the I. W. W. men who were supposed to have guns."

"What inducements were made to this man Adams?" asked Vanderveer.

"In the presence of Mr. Cooley and Mr. Webb and Captain Tennant and myself he was told that he could help the state and there would be no punishment given him. He was taken to Everett with the impression that he would be let out and taken care of."

Another ex-deputy, Fred Plymale, confirmed the statements of Fred Luke in regard to McRae's use of a five passenger car at Beverly Park and showed that it was impossible for the sheriff to have attended a dance at the hour he had claimed. The efforts of the prosecution to shake the testimony that had been given by Fred Luke was shown by this witness who testified that he had been approached by Mr. Clifford Newton, as agent for Mr. Cooley, and that at an arranged conversation McRae had tried to have him state that the runabout had been used to go to the slugging party.

Walter Mulholland, an 18 year old boy, and Henry Krieg, both of whom were members of the I. W. W. and passengers on the Verona, then testified in detail about the shattering gun fire and the wounding of men on board the boat. Mulholland told of wounds received, one bullet still being in his person at that time. Krieg, not being familiar with military terms, stated that there were many shells on the deck of the Verona after the trouble, and the prosecution thought they had scored quite a point until re-direct examination brought out the fact that Henry meant the lead bullets that had been fired from the dock.

E. Carl Pearson, Snohomish County Treasurer, rather unwillingly corroborated the testimony of ex-deputies Luke and Plymale in regard to the actions of McRae at Beverly Park.

The witness chair seemed almost to swallow the next nine witnesses who were boys averaging about twelve years in age. These lads had picked up shells on and beneath the dock to keep as mementos of the "Battle." Handfuls of shells of various sizes and description, from revolver, rifle and shotgun, intermingled with rifle clips and unfired copper-jacketed rifle cartridges, were piled upon the clerk's desk as exhibits by these youthful witnesses. After the various shells had been classified by L. B. Knowlton, an expert in charge of ammunition sales for the Whiton Hardware Company of Seattle for six years, the boys were recalled to the stand to testify to the splintered condition of the warehouses, their evidence proving that a large number of shots had been fired from the interior of the warehouses directly thru the walls. The boys who testified were Jack Warren, Palmer Strand, Rollie Jackson, William Layton, Eugene Meives, Guy Warner, Tom Wolf, Harvey Peterson, and Roy Jensen. Veitch, by this time thoroly disgusted with the turn taken by the case, excused these witnesses without even a pretense of cross-examination.

Completely clinching this link in the evidence against the citizen deputies was the testimony of Miss Lillian Goldthorpe and her mother, Hannah Goldthorpe. Miss Goldthorpe, waitress in the Commercial Club dining room, picked up some rifle shells that had fallen from the rifles stacked in the office, and also from the pocket of one of the hunting coats lying on the floor. She took these home to her mother who afterward turned them over to Attorney Moore. She also identified certain murderous looking blackjacks as being the same as those stored in the Club. It is hardly necessary to state that the open-shop advocates who continually prate about the "right of a person to work when and where they please" were not slow about taking away Lillian's right to work at the Commercial Club after she had given this truthful testimony!

James Hadley, I. W. W. member on the Verona, told how he had dived overboard to escape the murderous fire and had been the only man in the water to regain a place on the boat.

"I saw two go overboard and I didn't see them any more," said Hadley. "Then I saw another man four feet from me and he seemed to be swimming all right, and all of a sudden he went down and I never saw him any more. I was looking right at him and he just closed his eyes and sank."

Mario Marino, an 18 year old member of the I. W. W., then told of the serious wounds he had received on the boat. He was followed by Brockman B. Armstrong, another member of the union, who was close to the rail on the port side of the boat. He saw a puff of smoke slightly to the rear of McRae directly after the sound of the first shot. A rifle bullet cut a piece out of his forehead and a second went thru his cap and creased his scalp, felling him to his knees. Owen Genty was shot thru the kidney on the one side of him, and Gust Turnquist was hit in the knee on the other. As he lay in the heap of wounded men a buckshot buried itself in the side of his head near the temple. As the Verona was pulling out he tried to crawl to shelter and was just missed by a rifle bullet from the dock situated to the south.

Archie Collins, who had previously testified about Beverly Park, was then called to the stand to tell of the trip to Everett and the trouble that resulted. Prosecutor Black displayed his usual asininity by asking in regard to preparations made by Verona passengers:

"What were they taking or not taking?"

"There might be two or three million things they were not taking," cut in Judge Ronald chidingly.

Black's examination of the various witnesses was aptly described by Publicity Agent Charles Ashleigh in the Industrial Worker, as follows:

"His examinations usually act as a soporific; heads are observed nodding dully thruout the courtroom and one is led to wonder whether, if he were allowed to continue, there would not be a sort of fairy-tale scene in which the surprised visitor to the court would see audience, jury, lawyers, judge, prisoner and functionaries buried in deep slumber accompanied only by a species of hypnotic twittering which could be traced eventually to a dignified youth who was lulled to sleep by his own narcotic burblings but continued, mechanically, to utter the same question over and over again."

During this dreamy questioning Black asked about the men who were cleaning up the boat on its return trip, with a view to having the witness state that there were empty shells all over the deck. His question was:

"Did you pick anything up from the floor?"

Instantly the courtroom was galvanized into life by Collin's startling answer:

"I picked up an eye, a man's eye."

The witness had lifted from the blood-stained deck a long splinter of wood on which was impaled a human eye!

The story of Fred Savery was typical of the unrecognized empire builders who make up the migratory class. Fred was born in Russia, his folks moving to Austria and then migrating to Canada when the lad was but two years old. At the age of nine he started at farm work and at twelve he was big enough to handle logs and work in the woods. Savery took the stand in his uniform of slavery, red mackinaw shirt, stagged-off pants, caulked shoes, and a battered slouch hat in his hand. The honest simplicity of his halting French-Canadian speech carried more weight than the too smooth flowing tales told by the well drilled citizen deputies on whom the prosecution depended for conviction.

Cooley dwelt at great length on the constant travel of this witness, a feature incidental to the life of every migratory worker. Even the judge tired of these tactics and told the prosecution that there was no way to stop them from asking the interminable questions but it was merely a waste of time. But all of Cooley's dilatory tactics could not erase from the minds of the listeners the simple, earnest, sincere story Fred Savery told of the death of his fellow worker, Hugo Gerlot.

Charles Ashleigh was then placed upon the witness stand to testify to having been selected as one of the speakers to go to Everett on November 5th. He stated that he had gone over on the Interurban and had returned that afternoon at four o'clock. After the prosecution had interrogated him about certain articles published subsequent to the tragedy Ashleigh was excused.

To impeach the testimony of William Kenneth, wharfinger at the City Dock, the defense then introduced Peter Aikken of Everett. Following this witness Owen Genty, one of the I. W. W. men wounded on the Verona, gave an account of the affair and stated that the first shot came from a point just to the rear of the sheriff.

Raymond Lee, a youth of 19 years, told of having gone to Everett on the day of the Beverly Park affair in order to mail free speech pamphlets directly to a number of Everett citizens. He went to the dock at the time of the deportation, getting past the deputies on a plea of wanting to see his uncle, his youth and neat appearance not being at all in accord with the current idea of what an I. W. W. member looked like. Lee was cross-questioned at great length by Veitch. This witness told the story of the death of Abraham Rabinowitz on the Verona in these few, simple words:

View of Beverly Park, showing County Road

"Rabinowitz was lying on top of me with his head on my leg. I felt my leg getting wet and I reached back to see what it was, and when I pulled my hand away it was covered with blood. He was shot in the back of the brain."

James McRoden, I. W. W. member who was on the Verona, gave corroborative testimony about the first shot having been from the dock.

James Francis Billings, one of the free speech prisoners, testified that he was armed with a Colts 41 revolver on the Verona, and shortly after the shooting started he went to the engineer of the boat and ordered him to get the Verona away from the dock. He threw the gun overboard on the return trip to Seattle. Black tried to make light of the serious injuries this witness had received at Beverly Park by asking him if all that he received was not a little brush on the shin. The witness answered:

"No sir. I had a black eye. I was beaten over both eyes as far as that is concerned. My arms were held out by one big man on either side and I was beaten on both sides. As Sheriff McRae went past me he said 'Give it to him good,' and when I saw what was coming I dropped in order to save my face, and the man on the left hand side kicked me from the middle of my back clear down to my heels, and he kept kicking me until the fellow on the right told him to kick me no more as I was all in. My back and my hip have bothered me ever since."

Black tried to interrupt the witness and also endeavored to have his answer stricken from the testimony but the judge answered his objection by saying:

"I told you to withdraw the question and you didn't do it."

Vanderveer asked Billings the question:

"Why did you carry a gun on the fifth of November?"

"I took it for my own personal benefit," replied Billings. "I didn't intend to let anybody beat me up like I was beaten on October 30th in the condition I was in. I was in bad condition at the time."

Harvey E. Wood, an employe of the Jamison Mill Company, took the stand and told of a visit made by Jefferson Beard to the bunkhouse of the mill company on the night of November 4th and stated that at the time there were six automatic shot guns and three pump guns in the place. These were for the use of James B. Reed, Neal Jamison, Joe Hosh, Roy Hosh, Walter S. Downs, and a man named McCortell. This witness had acted as a strike-breaker up until the time he was subpoenaed.

Two of the defendants, Benjamin F. Legg and Jack Leonard, fully verified the story told by Billings.

Leland Butcher, an I. W. W. member who was on the Verona, told of how he had been shot in the leg. When asked why he had joined the I. W. W. he answered:

"I joined the I. W. W. to better my own condition and to make the conditions my father was laboring under for the last 25 years, with barely enough to keep himself and family, a thing of the past."

Another of the defendants, Ed Roth, who had been seriously wounded on the Verona, gave an unshaken story of the outrage. Roth testified that he had been shot in the abdomen at the very beginning of the trouble and because of his wounded condition and the fact that there were wounded men piled on top of him he had been unable to move until some time after the Verona had left the dock. This testimony showed the absurdity of McRae's pretended identification of the witness. Roth was a member of the International Longshoremen's Association and had joined the I. W. W. on the day before the tragedy.

John Stroka, a lad of 18, victim of the deputies at Beverly Park and a passenger on the Verona, gave testimony regarding the men wounded on the boat.

The next witness was Ernest P. Marsh, president of the State Federation of Labor, who was called for the purpose of impeaching the testimony of Mayor Merrill and also to prove that Mrs. Frennette was a visitor at the Everett Labor Temple on the morning of November 5th, this last being added confirmation of the fact that Clyde Gibbons had committed perjury on the stand.

To the ordinary mind—and certainly the minds of the prosecution lawyers were not above the ordinary—the social idealist is an inexplicable mystery. Small wonder then that they could not understand the causes that impelled the next witness, Abraham Bonnet Wimborne, one of the defendants, to answer the call for fighters to defend free speech.

Wimborne, the son of a Jewish Rabbi, told from the witness stand how he had first joined the Socialist Party, afterward coming in contact with the I. W. W., and upon hearing of the cruel beating given to James Rowan, had decided to leave Portland for Everett to fight for free speech. Arriving in Seattle on November 4th, he took passage on the steamer Verona the next day.

Prosecutor Black asked the witness what were the preparations made by the men on the boat.

"Don't misunderstand my words, Mr. Black," responded Wimborne, "when I say prepared, I mean they were armed with the spirit of determination. Determined to uphold the right of free speech with their feeble strength; that is, I never really believed it would be possible for the outrages and brutalities to come under the stars and stripes, and I didn't think it was necessary for anything else."

"Then when these men left they were determined?" inquired Black.

"Yes, determined that they would uphold the spirit of the Constitution; if not, go to jail. There were men in Everett who would refuse the right of workingmen to come and tell the workers that they had a way whereby the little children could get sufficient clothing, sufficient food, and the right of education, and other things which they can only gain—how? By organizing into industrial unions, sir, that is what I meant. We do not believe in bloodshed. Thuggery is not our method. What can a handful of workers do against the mighty forces of Maxim guns and the artillery of the capitalist class?"

"Did you consider yourself a fighting member?" questioned Black.

"If you mean am I a moral fighter? yes; but physically—why, look at me! Do I look like a fighter?" said the slightly built witness.

"Did you or did you not expect to go to jail when you left Portland?" asked the prosecutor.

"My dear Mr. Black, I didn't know and I didn't care!" responded Wimborne with a shrug of his shoulders.

Wimborne joined the I. W. W. while in the Everett County Jail.

Michael J. Reilley, another of the defendants, testified as to the firing of the first shot from the dock and also gave the story of the death of Abraham Rabinowitz. Vanderveer asked him the question:

"Do you know why you are a defendant?"

"Yes, sir," replied Reilley, "because I didn't talk to them in the city jail in Seattle. I was never picked out."

Attorney H. D. Cooley was recalled to the stand and was made to admit that he was a member of the Commercial Club and a citizen deputy on the dock November 5th. He was asked by Vanderveer:

"Did you see any guns on the dock?"

"Yes sir."

"Did you see any guns fired on the dock?"

"Yes sir."

"Did you see any guns fired on the boat?"

"No sir."

"Did you see a gun on the boat?"

"I did not."

"You were in full view of the boat?"

"I was."

Yet the ethics of the legal profession are such that this attorney could justify his actions in laboring for months in an endeavor to secure, by any and all means, the conviction of the men on the boat!

Defendant Charles Black testified that McRae

dropped his hand to his gun and pulled it just as one of the deputies fired from a point just behind the sheriff. Black ran down the deck and into the cabin, passing in front of the windows from which the deputies had sworn that heavy firing was going on.

Leonard Broman, working partner with Abraham Rabinowitz, then took the stand and told his story. When asked what were the benefits he received from having joined the I. W. W., the witness replied:

"They raised the wages and shortened the hours. Before I joined the I. W. W. the wages I received in Ellis, Kansas, was $3.00 for twelve hours and last fall the I. W. W. got $3.50 for nine hours on the same work."

Ex-deputy Charles Lawry told of various brutalities at the jail and also impeached McRae's testimony in many other particulars.

Dr. Grant Calhoun, who had attended the more seriously injured men who were taken from the Verona on its return to Seattle, told of the number and nature of the wounds that had been inflicted. On eight of the men examined he had found twenty-one serious wounds, counting the entrance and exit of the same bullet as only one wound. Veitch conducted no cross-examination of the witness.

Joe Manning, J. H. Beyers, and Harvey Hubler, all three of them defendants, gave their testimony. Manning told of having been seated in the cabin with Tracy when the firing commenced, after which he sought cover behind the smokestack and was joined by Tracy a moment later. Beyers identified Deputy Bridge as having stood just behind McRae with his revolver drawn as tho firing when the first shot was heard. This witness also corroborated the story of Billings in regard to demanding that the engineer take the boat away from the dock. Hubler verified the statements about conditions on the Verona and also told of being taken from his jail cell by force on an order signed by detective McLaren in an attempt to have him discharge the defense attorneys and accept an alleged lawyer from Los Angeles.

THOMAS H. TRACY

Harry Parker and C. C. England told of injuries sustained on the Verona, and John Riely stated there was absolutely no shooting from the cabin windows, that being impossible because the men on the boat had crowded the entire rail at that side.

Jerry L. Finch, former deputy prosecuting attorney of King County, gave impeaching testimony against Wm. Kenneth and Charles Tucker. Cooley asked this witness about his interviews with the different state's witnesses:

"If you talked with all of them, you would probably have something on all of them?"

The judge would not let Finch answer the question, but there is no doubt that Cooley had the correct idea about the character of the witnesses on his side of the case.

In detailing certain arrests Sheriff McRae had claimed that men taken from the shingleweavers' picket line were members of the I. W. W. B. Said was one of the men so mentioned. Said took the witness stand and testified that he was a member of the longshoremen's union and was not and had not been a member of the I. W. W.

J. G. Brown, president of the International Shingleweavers' Union, testified that the various men arrested on the picket line in Everett were either members of the shingle weavers' union or else were longshoremen from Seattle, none of the men named by McRae being members of the I. W. W. The testimony of Brown was also of such a nature as to be impeaching of the statements of Mayor Merrill on the witness stand.

Charles Gray, Robert Adams, and Joe Ghilezano, I. W. W. men on the Verona, then testified, Adams telling of having been shot thru the elbow, and Ghilezano giving the details of the way in which his kneecap had been shot off and other injuries received.

The murderous intentions of the deputies were further shown by the testimony of Nels Bruseth, who ran down to the shore to launch a boat and rescue the men in the water. He was stopped in this errand of mercy by the deputies.

Civil Engineer F. Whitwith, Jr., of the firm of Rutherford and Whitwith, surveyed the dock and the steamer Verona and made a report in court of his findings. His evidence clearly showed that there was rifle, shotgun and revolver fire of a wild character from the interior of the warehouses and from many points on the dock. He stated that there were one hundred and seventy-three rifle or revolver bullet marks, exclusive of the B-B and buckshot markings which were too numerous to count, on the Verona, these having come from the dock, the shore, and the Improvement Dock to the south. There were sixteen marks on the boat that appeared as tho they might have been from revolver fire proceeding from the boat itself. There were also small triangular shaped gouges in the planking of the dock, the apex of the triangles indicating that bullets had struck there and proceeded onward from the Klatawa slip to the open space on the dock where deputies had been stationed. The physical facts thus introduced were incontrovertible.

Defendant J. D. Houlihan gave positive testimony to the effect that he had not spoken privately with "Red" Doran in the I. W. W. hall on the morning of November 5th, that he had received no gun from Doran or anyone else, that he did not have the conversation which Auspos imputed to him, that he had no talk with Auspos on the return trip. All efforts to confuse this witness failed of their purpose.

In verification of the testimony about deputies firing on the Verona from the Improvement Company Dock the defense brought Percy Walker upon the stand. Walker had been cruising around the bay in a little gasoline launch and saw men armed with long guns, probably rifles or shotguns, leaning over a breastwork of steel pipes and firing in the direction of the Verona.

Lawrence Manning, Harston Peters, and Ed. J. Shapeero, defendants, told their simple straightforward stories of the "battle." Peters stated that as he lay under cover and heard the shots coming from the dock he "wished to Christ that he did have a gun." Shapeero told of the wounds he had received and of the way the uninjured men cared for the wounded persons on the boat.

Mrs. Joyce Peters testified that she had gone to Everett on the morning of November 5th in company with Mrs. Lorna Mahler. The reason she did not go on the Verona was because the trip by water had made Mrs. Mahler ill on previous occasions. She saw Mrs. Frennette in Everett only when they were on the same interurban car leaving for Seattle after the tragedy.

Albert Doninger, W. B. Montgomery and Japheth Banfield, I. W. W. men who were on the Verona, all placed the first shot as having come from the dock immediately after the sheriff had cried out "You can't land here."

N. Inscho, Chief of Police of Wenatchee, testified that during the time the I. W. W. carried on their successful fight for free speech in his city there were no incendiary fires, no property destroyed, no assaults or acts of violence committed, and no resistance to arrest.

H. W. Mullinger, lodging house proprietor, John M. Hogan, road construction contractor, Edward Case, railroad grading contractor, William Kincaid, alfalfa farmer, and John Egan, teamster, all of North Yakima and vicinity, were called as character witnesses for Tracy, the defendant having worked with or for them for a number of years.

The defense followed these witnesses with Oscar Carlson, the passenger on the Verona who had been fairly riddled with bullets. Carlson testified that he was not and never had been a member of the I. W. W., that he had gone to Everett with his working partner, Nordstrom, as a sort of an excursion trip, that he had purchased a one way ticket which was taken up by the captain after the boat had left Seattle, that he intended returning by way of the Interurban, and that the men on the boat were orderly and well behaved. He told of having gone to the very front of the boat as it pulled into Everett from which point he heard the first shot, which was fired from the dock. He fell immediately and while prostrate was struck with bullet after bullet. He then told of having entered suit against the Vashon Navigation Company for $50,000.00 on account of injuries received. Robert C. Saunders, of the law firm of Saunders and Nelson, then testified that he was handling the case for Carlson and had made out the affidavit of complaint himself and was responsible for the portion that alleged that a lawless mob were on the boat, Carlson having made no such statement to him at any time.

Charles Ashleigh was recalled to the stand to testify to having telephoned to the Seattle newspapers on November 4th, requesting them to send reporters to Everett the next day. He was followed on the stand by John T. Doran, familiarly known as "Red" on account of the color of his hair. Doran stated that he was the author of the handbill distributed in Everett prior to the attempted meeting of November 5th. He positively denied having given a gun to Houlihan or anyone else on November 5th. Upon cross-examination he said that he was in charge of the work of checking the number of men who went on the Verona to Everett, and had paid the transportation of the men in a lump sum.

As the next to the last witness on its side of the long-drawn out case the defense placed on the stand the defendant, Thomas H. Tracy. The witness told of having been one of a working class family, too large to be properly cared for and having to leave home and make his own way in the world before he was eleven years old. From that time on he had followed farming, teaming and construction work in all parts of the west, his bronzed appearance above the prison pallor giving evidence of his outdoor life.

Tracy told of having been secretary of the I. W. W. in Everett for a short time, that being the only official position he had ever held in the organization. He explained his position on the boat at the time it docked, stating that the first shot apparently came from the dock and struck close to where he was sitting. Immediately the boat listed and threw him away from the window, after which he sought a place of safety behind the smokestack. He denied having been in any way a party to a conspiracy to commit an act of violence or to kill anyone.

"You are charged here, Mr. Tracy," said Vanderveer, "with having aided and abetted an unknown man in killing Jefferson Beard. Are you guilty or not guilty?"

"I am not guilty," replied Tracy without a trace of emotion.

The cross-questioning of the defendant in this momentous case was conducted by citizen-deputy Cooley. His questions to the man whom he and his fellow conspirators on the dock had not succeeded in murdering were of the most trivial nature, clearly proving that arch-sleuth McLaren had been unable to discover or to manufacture anything that would make Tracy's record other than that of a plain, unassuming, migratory worker.

"Where did you vote last?" asked Cooley.

"I never voted." responded Tracy.

"Never voted in your life?" queried Cooley.

"No!" replied the defendant who for the time represented the entire migratory class. "I was never in one place long enough!"

Then, acting on the class theory that it is an honor to be a "globe-trotter" but a disgrace to be a "blanket-stiff," the prosecutor brought out Tracy's travels in minute detail. This examination of the railroad construction worker brought home to the listeners the truth of the little verse:

"He built the road;
With others of his class he built the road;
Now o'er its weary length he packs his load,
Chasing a Job, spurred on by Hunger's goad,
He walks and walks and walks and walks,
And wonders why in Hell he built the road!"

Then there hobbled into the court room on crutches a stripling with an empty trouser leg, his face drawn with suffering, and who was able to get into the witness chair only by obviously painful efforts with the assistance of Vanderveer and Judge Ronald. This was Harry Golden, whose entire left leg had been amputated after having been shattered by a high-power rifle bullet fired by a "law and order" deputy.

Golden stated that he had been born in Poland twenty-two years before, and had come to the United States at the age of sixteen. He was asked:

"Why did you come to this country?"

"I came to the United States," said the witness, "because it is supposed to be a free country."

"We object to that as immaterial!" cried prosecutor Veitch.

The witness described the firing of the first shot and told of his attempts to find a place of safety. He said he was wounded in the hand as he attempted to climb into a life boat. He remained on the starboard side of the starboard life boat until the Verona had backed out into the bay. Then just as he was starting to raise up a rifle bullet struck his leg, taking a course thru the limb and emerging at the knee.

"That is on your left—?"

"On my left, yes, which I ain't got; I lost it!" said the witness.

"Did I understand you to say you stood up to see something before you were shot?" asked Veitch.

"Why, sure!" replied Golden contemptuously. "I had my two legs then."

Veitch wished to learn the exact location of the witness at the time he was shot and to that end referred to the model with the remark:

"Look here. Here is the boat as it was at the dock."

"I don't like to look at it!" said Golden heatedly. "I lost my leg on that boat!"

The witness was in evident pain during the examination, having just had a hospital treatment applied to his raw stump, and was rather irritable as a consequence. He answered several questions

EVERETT from the water. To the
left G.N. Depot from where by-
standers viewed battle.

rather sharply and proceeded to explain his answers. At one of these interruptions Judge Ronald exclaimed to the witness angrily:

"When he asks you a question answer yes or no! If you want to live in this country try and live like an American!"

"I take an exception to Your Honor's remarks!" said Moore emphatically.

The judge grudgingly allowed an exception to his uncalled for statement.

In concluding his examination Veitch asked the witness:

"What is your name in Polish?"

"I am not Polish; I am a Jew," replied Golden.

"Well, what is your family name in Poland?" asked the prosecutor.

"Goldenhaul, or something like that. Now I call myself Golden. When we come to this country—."

"Never mind," interposed Veitch hurriedly.

"When we come to this country for good luck we always change the name, you know," finished Golden, and added bitterly, "I sure did have good luck!"

This ended the case in chief for the defense, the marshalling of such a mass of testimony from a host of disinterested witnesses, men, women and children, putting it on an entirely different footing from the prejudiced testimony brought forward by the prosecution.

In rebuttal of testimony produced by the defense the prosecution introduced a series of witnesses. As in their case in chief every one of the parties who testified were in some way concerned in the case as deputies, jailers, police officers, dance hall habitues, detectives, and the like. The witnesses were W. P. Bell, Dr. F. R. Hedges, E. E. Murphy, Charles Hall, Rudolph Weidaur, W. J. Britt, Percy Ames, Harry Blackburn, Reuben Westover, Harry Groger, W. M. Maloney, Albert Burke, W. R. Conner, A. E. Andrews, David D. Young, Howard Hathaway, George Leonard Mickel, Paul Hill, E. C. Mony, B. H. Bryan, all of whom were deputies, D. C. Pearson, W. H.

Bridge, and "Honest" John Hogan, all three jailers and deputies, Robert C. Hickey, city jailer, David Daniels and Adolph Miller, police officers, Charles Manning and J. T. Rogers, personal friends of McRae, Oscar Moline, dance hall musician, Albert McKay, of the Ocean Food Products Company located on the Everett Improvement Dock, T. J. McKinnon, employe of McKay, R. B. Williams, contractor, John Flynn, agent Everett Improvement Dock, W. W. Blain and F. S. Ruble, secretary and bookkeeper respectively of the Commercial Club and also deputies, A. E. Ballew, Great Northern depot agent, H. G. Keith, Great Northern detective, Charles Auspos, who was shown to be in receipt of favors as state's witness, and George Reese, Pinkerton informer and "stool pigeon."

One deputy, H. S. Groger, stated on cross-examination that he continuously fired at a man on the boat who appeared to be trying to untie the spring line. Outside of this evidence of a desire for wholesale slaughter nothing developed of sufficient importance to warrant the production of sur-rebuttal witnesses, except in the testimony of Auspos and Reese.

Auspos testified that defendant Billings in the presence of John Rawlings had stated in the Everett County jail that he had a gun that made a noise like a cannon. This was intended to controvert the testimony of Billings.

Reese related a conversation that Tracy was alleged to have carried on in his presence on the Verona as it was bound for Everett. He stated that a launch was seen approaching and someone remarked that it was probably coming to head them off, to which Tracy replied "Let them come; they will find we are ready for them, and we will give them something they are not looking for." This was intended as impeachment of Tracy.

Cross-examination of this informer brought out the fact that he was a Pinkerton agent at the time he was holding the office of delegate to the Central Labor Council of the American Federation of Labor.

Reese stated that he was employed on the waterfront during the longshoremen's strike with instructions to "look for everybody who was pulling the rough stuff, such as threatening to burn or attempting to burn warehouses, and shooting up non-union workers, and beating them up and so forth." He had been in the employ of the Pinkerton Agency for six weeks this last time before he was ordered to go down and join the I. W. W. He stated in answer to a question by Vanderveer:

"I was instructed to go down there and find out who these fellows were that was handling this phosphorus and pulling off this sabotage and the only way I could find out was to get a card and get in and get acquainted with them."

Attorney Moore in the absence of the jury offered to prove that Reese had practically manufactured this job for himself by promoting the very things he was supposed to discover. Moore stated some of the things he would prove if permitted by the court:

"That on or about August 1st Reese went to one J. M. Wilson, an official of the longshoremen's union, and endeavored to get $10.00 with which to buy dynamite to blow up a certain city dock; that on September 20th the witness gave Percy May, a member of the longshoremen's union, a bottle of phosphorus with instructions to start a fire at Pier 5; that in the month of July the witness opposed a settlement of the longshoremen's strike and when members of the union argued that they could remain out no longer as they had no money, Reese clapped his pockets and said, 'you fellows wouldn't be starving if you had the nerve that I have got. Why don't you go out and get it, take it off the scabs the way I do;' that in September Feinberg had to make Reese leave the speaker's stand in Everett because he was talking on matters harmful to industrial union propaganda; that on November 4th the witness went to the place where Feinberg was employed and left a suit of clothes to be pressed, saying to Feinberg, after he had ascertained that Feinberg was thinking of going to Everett on the following day, "mark the bill 'paid' so I will have a receipt if you don't come back;" that on August 16th, the day before the big dock fire in Seattle, Reese went to the down-town office of the same dye works in which Walker C. Smith was manager and in charge of the purchase of chemicals and tried to get Smith to purchase for him some carbon disulphide to be used in connection with phosphorus; that in the month of November in the Labor Temple, in the presence of Sam Sadler, Reese had said to Albert Brilliant that if the longshoremen had any guts they would go out with guns and clean up the scabs on the waterfront; and that Reese tried to get other men to co-operate with him in a scheme to capture a Government boat lying in the Sound during the progress of the longshoremen's strike."

The court refused to allow the defense to go into these matters so the only showing of the true character of Reese was confined to examination as to the perjury he had committed in his initial sworn statement to the defense.

The sur-rebuttal of the defense occupied but a few minutes. It was admitted that Mr. Garver, the court reporter, would swear that Reese had made an initial statement to the defense counsel and that the same had been taken down stenographically and sworn to. Charles Tennant, captain of the detective force of the Seattle police department, testified to having telephoned to the sheriff's office in Everett on November 5th to give the information that a boatload of I. W. W. men had left for Everett. He did not describe the body of men in any way and had not said that they were armed. This was for the purpose of showing that somewhere between the time that Jefferson Beard received the message and the time it was transmitted to the deputies some one had insterted the statement that the men on the boat were heavily armed. John Rawlings, defendant, testified that no such conversation as that related by Auspos had occured in the presence of defendant Billings. Thomas H. Tracy denied making the threats ascribed to him by Reese, and this closed the hearing of evidence in the case.

Outside the courtroom on the day the last of the evidence was introduced there was in progress one of the largest demonstrations of Labor ever held in the Pacific Northwest. The date was May first, and International Labor Day was celebrated by the united radicals of the entire city and surrounding district. Meeting at the I. W. W. hall at 10:30 in the morning, thousands of men and women fell into a marching line of fours, a committee pinning a red rose or carnation on each marcher. Fifteen solid blocks of these marchers, headed by Wagner's Band, then wended their way thru the streets to Mount Pleasant Cemetery and grouped themselves around the graves of Baran, Gerlot and Looney—Labor's martyred dead.

There, upon the hillside, in accordance with his final wishes, the ashes of Joe Hill were scattered to the breeze, and with them were cast upon the air and on the graves beneath, the ashes of Jessie Lloyd and Patrick Brennan, two loyal fighters in the class struggle who had died during the year just passed.

A fitting song service, with a few simple words by speakers in English, Russian, Swedish, Hungarian and Italian, in commemoration of those who had passed away, completed the tribute to the dead.

Nor were the living forgotten! The great crowd drifted from the graveside, but hundreds of them reassembled almost automatically and marched to the King County jail. Standing there, just outside of the very heart of the great city, the crowd, led by the I. W. W. choir, sang song after song from the revolutionary hymnal—the little red song book, each song being answered by one from the free speech prisoners confined in the jail. The service lasted until late in the day and, to complete the one labor day that is as broad as the world itself, a meeting was held in one of the largest halls of the city. At this meeting the final collection for the Everett Prisoners' Defense was taken and at the request of the imprisoned men one half of the proceeds was sent to aid in the liberation of Tom Mooney and his fellow victims of the Merchants' and Manufacturers' Association in San Francisco.

There remained but the reading of the instructions of the court and the addresses by the counsel for either side to complete this epoch making case and place it in the hands of the jury for their final verdict.

CHAPTER VIII.

PLEADINGS AND THE VERDICT

The instructions of the court, carefully prepared by Judge J. T. Ronald, required sixty-five minutes in the reading. These instructions were divided into twenty-three sections, each section representing a different phase of the case. Herewith is presented the first section in its entirety and a summary of the remaining portion:

"Ladies and Gentlemen of the Jury:

"My responsibility is to decide all questions of law in this case; yours to decide one question of fact. With these instructions my responsibility practically ends, your commences. You have taken a solemn oath that 'you will well and truly try and true delivery make between the State of Washington and the prisoner at the bar, whom you have in charge, according to the evidence.'

"There is no escape from the responsibility which has come to you, save in the faithful effort to render a true verdict. Any verdict other than one based upon pure conscience will be an injustice. An honest juror yields to no friendship, nor bears any enmity. He is moved by no sympathy, nor influenced by any prejudice. He seeks the approval of no one, nor fears the condemnation of anyone—save that one unerring, silent monitor, his own conscience. Disregard this whispering voice in yourself and you may fool the public, you may fool the defendant, you may, hereafter, with some effort, even close your own soul to her whispering reproaches and enjoy the ill-earned plaudits of the selfish or biased friend or interest whom you sought to please, but be assured you will not change the truth, you will not deceive justice which, at some time, and in some way, will collect from you the penalty which is always sooner or later exacted from those who betray the truth.

"So let me urge that in deciding the issue of facts which is now your responsibility you be guided by these instructions which you have sworn to follow, and by their conscientious application to the evidence in this case.

"Do not permit yourselves to be swayed by sympathy, influenced by prejudice, or moved in the least by a consideration of what might or might not meet the approval or the condemnation of any person or class or persons, or of interest whatever. To do so will be an act alike dishonest, violative of your oath, substituting for a fair and impartial trial an unfair and a partial one. This is an epoch in your lives to which you will ever look back. Be sure that when you do you may face the smiling approval of your conscience rather than its stinging reproach.

"The guilt or innocence of this defendant is a single question of fact to be determined by the evidence alone. If this evidence shows defendant to be guilty, then no sympathy, no desire for approval, no fear of condemnation, can make him innocent; if the evidence fails to show him guilty, then no prejudice, no desire for approval, no fear of condemnation, can make him guilty. The issue is a momentous one, not only to the defendant, who, if innocent, deserves the deepest sympathy, for the accusation made against him is a serious one; but likewise to the public and to society at large, and the tranquility and security of our different communities.

"A false verdict against the defendant conflicts with the purpose and the laws of the State as effectively as a false verdict in his favor. The State has no higher duty or interest than to preserve all its citizens from suffering under unfounded accusations. If, on the other hand, the guilt of the defendant has been shown, a false verdict of acquittal would not only be a breach of your oaths, but it would inflict a grievous wrong upon the State. If a true verdict calls for conviction, the misfortune to the defendant is not in the verdict, nor in the penalty, but in the fact it was his conduct which makes the verdict true. You alone of all the world, and who now possess all the facts, are therefore responsible for the verdict in this case. The law is not concerned about conviction merely—but it is concerned, deeply concerned, that juries shall conscientiously and fearlessly declare the truth. Whether it be conviction, or whether it be acquittal, a true verdict is justice—a false is injustice."

Judge Ronald followed this lecture on civic righteousness and personal duty with more specific instructions to the jury, of which the following are excerpts.

"In this case you must answer the question—Is this defendant guilty or innocent? * * * Keep constantly in mind this issue and do not go astray to discuss any other of the many issues that may be suggested by or may lay hidden among the great mass of evidence in this case. Whether the Industrial Workers of the World shall or shall not speak at a certain place in the City of Everett is not an issue here. * * * Whether the open or the closed shop shall prevail is not a subject for your consideration.

"Every defendant in a criminal case is presumed to be innocent. * * * You must be satisfied beyond a reasonable doubt of the facts necessary to show guilt before you can convict. * * * You should give the phrase 'proof beyond a reasonable doubt' its full meaning and weight as explained and defined to you in these instructions. On the other hand, you should not magnify nor exaggerate its force and fail to return a verdict of guilty simply because the evidence does not satisfy you of guilt to an absolute certainty. No crime can be proved to an absolute certainty.

"It does not follow because every one of the facts which are disputed between the parties may not be established beyond a reasonable doubt, that there cannot be a conviction. At the same time you will bear carefully in mind that all facts which are necessary to establish the conclusion of guilt must be proved beyond a reasonable doubt.

"There are two facts necessary to convict this defendant:

(1) That some person on the boat unlawfully killed Jefferson Beard.

(2) That this defendant aided, incited or encouraged such shooting.

"If you are satisfied beyond a reasonable doubt of these two facts, then you must convict, no matter what may be your belief concerning any other question in dispute in this case; if you have a reasonable doubt as to either of these two facts, then you must acquit."

The instructions then went into detail as to the rights of the workers to organize, to bargain in regard to compensation, hours of labor and conditions of work generally, to go on strike, to persuade or entice their fellow workers by peaceful means from taking the positions which they have left, to assemble at public places where such meetings are not prohibited by law and ordinance, and "no person, either private citizen or public official, has any right to deny, abridge or in any manner interfere with the full and free enjoyment of those privileges and any person who attempts to do so is himself guilty of an unlawful act."

After reciting such acts attributed to the workers in this case as were in violation of law, the instructions went on to state that "a sheriff has no authority to arrest any person without a warrant except upon probable cause for believing such person has violated a law of the state; nor has he authority after making such arrest to hold his prisoner in custody for a longer time than is reasonably necessary to cause proper complaint to be filed, and an opportunity given for bail. * * * A sheriff has no right or authority to interfere with or prevent any person from violating a city ordinance, nor has he the right or authority to arrest for violations of city ordinances" unless "the act threatened, or the act done, in violation of such ordinance be at the same time violation of a state law."

The instructions then outlined the scope of criminal conspiracy, stating that it was unnecessary for one conspirator to know all of the other conspirators but that common design is the essence of the charge of conspiracy. The acts of one conspirator become the acts of any and all conspirators. In the eyes of the law the sheriff and the deputies also consituted in this case but one personality, the sheriff being bound by the acts of his deputies and the deputies being authorized by the powers of the sheriff. Also the ordinance dated September 21st, 1916, was held to be a valid one.

"Now whether any of the Industrial Workers of the World have been, prior to November 5, 1916, guilty of encouraging disrespect for law, or of unlawful assemblage, or of riot, is not the question on trial here. They could all be guilty of all the acts or offenses heretofore mentioned, and still this defendant be innocent of this particular crime charged on November 5th, or they could all be innocent of all the acts mentioned, and defendant still be guilty of the main charge here.

"Again, whether the sheriff or any of his assistants have been guilty of any of the acts charged against them is not on trial here. They could all be guilty of all the acts charged and still be the victims of unjustifiable shooting from that boat, or they could all be innocent of any offense, and still be the aggressors and cause of that shooting on the dock wherein Jefferson Beard lost his life.

"One of the questions in this case is the question—Which side was the aggressor on that occasion?

"In determining who was the aggressor it is your duty to consider all the facts and circumstances surrounding the situation, the relations of the parties to each other, their intentions toward each other, and all the things they did. You will also consider the past conduct of all the parties, any acts of violence or other assaults that may have been com-

Victims at Morgue.

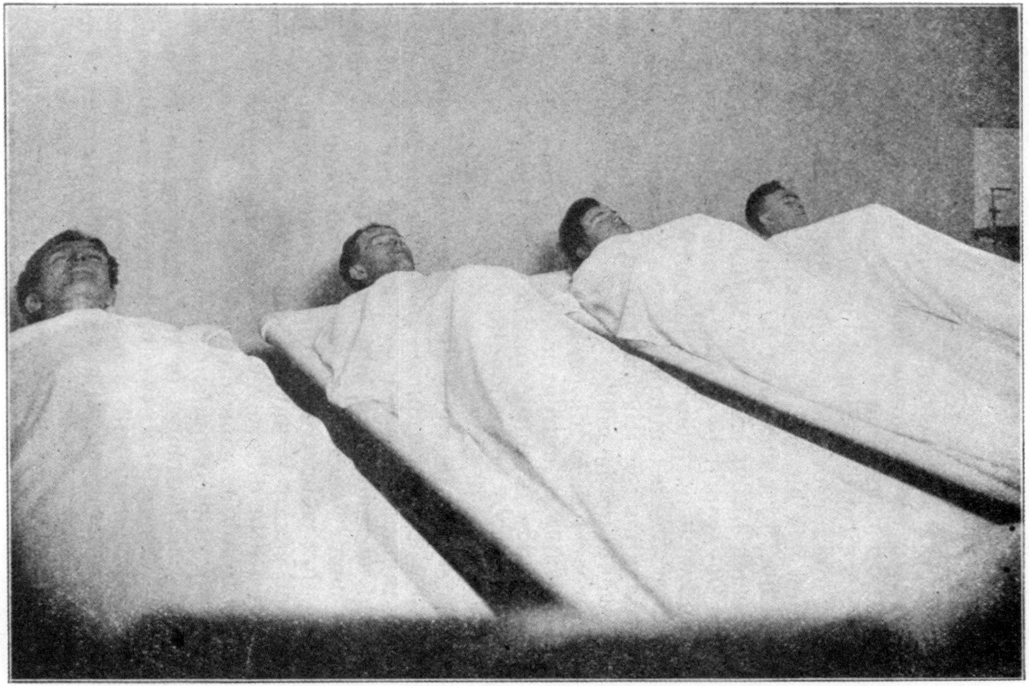

John Looney Hugo Gerlot, Felix Baran Abe Rabinowitz

mitted, and any threats that may have been made, and the character as known and understood by each other.

"Therefore, simplify your deliberations and determine first the question: Did somebody on the boat unlawfully kill Jefferson Beard? If somebody on the boat did not kill Beard, then of course Tracy could not be guilty of aiding John Doe to do something which John Doe did not do. But if the State has satisfied you beyond a reasonable doubt that Beard was killed by a shot fired by somebody on the boat, then such killing is either unlawful, in which case John Doe would be guilty of one of three degrees of unlawful or felonious homicide, viz., murder in the first degree, murder in the second degree, or manslaughter; or it is justifiable in which case John Doe would not be guilty. Hence you will render one of four verdicts in this case—

1. Guilty of murder in the first degree, or
2. Guilty of murder in the second degree, or
3. Guilty of manslaughter, or
4. Not guilty.

"It is very desirable that you reach a verdict in this case. The law requires that your conclusion shall be unanimous. It is not required that any one of you should surrender his individual freedom of judgement, but it is well that each of you should have in mind that your true verdict cannot ordinarily be reached except by mutual consideration and discussion of all the different views that may suggest themselves to any of your number. The jury room is no place for pride of opinion. A verdict which is the result of real harmony, or that growing out of open-minded discussion between jurors, and a willingness to be convinced, with a proper regard for the opinions of others, and with a reasonable distrust of individual views not shared by their fellows, is a fair yielding of one reason to a stronger one; such, having in mind the great desirability of unanimity, is not open to criticism. The law contemplates that jurors shall, by their discussions, harmonize their views if possible, but not that they shall compromise and yield for the mere purpose of agreement. One should not surrender his conscientious convictions.

"And now, ladies and gentlemen of the jury, I commit the case to your hands. Listen to the arguments. Regardless of what may be counsel's recollection of testimony, you must take and follow your own recollection. You are not required to adopt any view which counsel may suggest in argument, but you should give close attention to all they say. Take up your task fearlessly, with but one single aim—to discharge the obligations of your oaths. You have no class to satisfy—simply the dictates of your own conscience."

Taken as a whole the instructions were distinctly unfavorable to the defendant, not because of any particular bias of the judge whose political ambitions might have made him desirous of establishing a record for fairness, but by reason of the fact that the law itself on the question of criminal conspiracy is archaic and absurd, being based upon precedents established when the use of electricity and steam power were unknown, when the stage coach was the fastest means of locomotion and the tallow dip the principal form of illumination. This law, like all other statute law, was created thru the desire of the ruling class to protect property, therefore it contained no element of justice when applied to the modern proletariat, the twentieth century worker stripped of everything but his power to labor.

Following the reading of the court's instructions prosecutor Black made his argument, Vanderveer and Moore for the defense addressing the jury in turn, and Cooley making the concluding plea for the state. This arrangement gave Veitch no chance to turn loose his oratorical fireworks, much to the chagrin of the gentleman who had been so kindly loaned to the prosecution by the Merchants' and Manufacturers' Association.

Black's lengthy address was a whine for pity because of his youth and a prayer for relief from the dire straits and legal bankrupcy into which Snohomish County had fallen. It is summarized in the following:

"We are at the close of a great trial. A great deal of evidence has been introduced; practically two million five hundred words. From the standpoint of the attorneys who have tried this case the evidence has been very complicated because it had in it a great mass of evidence that was only remotely connected with the real issue at bar. You as jurors have a very simple question to decide in this case.

"Thomas H. Tracy is charged with the crime of murder in the first degree, not that he himself killed Jefferson Beard, but that he, Thomas H. Tracy, aided, incited and encouraged some unknown one to kill Jefferson Beard of Everett, on last November 5th.

"I repeat first that some person on the boat unlawfully killed Jefferson Beard; secondly that this defendant, aided, incited and encouraged such shooting.

"I come before you as the prosecuting attorney of Snohomish County. Owing to the exigencies of politics I was elected to office a few days after November 5th, the time of this catastrophe. Two months and a few days after, I took office and found a man charged with a crime that I did not have the power of prosecution over up to that time. Mr. Webb, then prosecuting attorney, who had started the action and initiated and seen fit to collect some of the evidence, was not able to complete the prosecution on account of the size of the trial.

"I am a young man without the experience that any man ought to have in the prosecuting of a case like this, a case the size of which has never been experienced in the State of Washington, and in many ways an absolutely pioneer case in criminal trials the world over.

"So the State has been hampered in that at the outset a young man, a new prosecuting attorney, has come into office and to him there has come a case that no man could read up concerning, and a large piece of battle—it is the State's contention, a battle between hundreds of men on the boat and a large number of deputies on the dock, a battle absolutely and surely initiated by firing from the boat, but still a battle;—a case without parallel in the criminal history of this State or of the United States.

"It happens that fortunately the State has had assistance in this case. The State of Washington, thru its county commissioners, requested the assistance in this case of Mr. Cooley, whom you have all grown to know, a man who formerly for four years was prosecuting attorney of Snohomish County, and who since that time has been associated as assistant counsel in practically all the criminal prosecutions of Snohomish County that have required assistance.

"And in addition to this the State has been fortunate in having, at the request of the county commissioners, the assistance of Mr. Veitch, a young man it is true, but one who thru years of service in the district attorney's office in Los Angeles County had experience in criminal trials, and especially because of his connection with what are known as the conspiracy murder trials in Los Angeles County, and also in assisting the federal prosecution at Indianapolis. It has been necessary in this kind of a case for the State to have assistance.

"Now I told you my friends that I came here as prosecuting attorney of Snohomish County. I am also a deputy prosecuting attorney of King County under Mr. Lundin. After I was appointed I was very unpleasantly surprised by one statement. A little phrase, 'without pay,' so that I don't know whether really I am a deputy prosecuting attorney or not, because I found that in public office a man always likes to see the warrant come at the end of the month!

"You are a jury in this case from King County because the defendant and the other defendants filed an affidavit to the effect that they didn't expect that a jury selected in Snohomish County would give the defendant a fair trial. The State is happy in your selection and knows that you will follow the dictates of your conscience and is likewise confident that you cannot help but believe that Jefferson Beard was killed by someone shooting from the Verona, and that Thomas H. Tracy, alias George Martin, incited, aided and encouraged in that shooting.

"Now, the witnesses on the dock are men of Everett, men of family, men who are laborers, but with families; men who are clerks, with interests in Snohomish County; men who hold some important positions, as lawyers; people with families, people who by residence have established reputation for truth and veracity; men who have established themselves, have made themselves successful, sometimes in merely that they have established a small home, or who have lived in Everett and have made friends and acquaintances. That is the class of men that were on the dock.

"There are only two classes of people who know anything about the shooting. The people on the dock are one set, and the people on the boat are the other.

The people on the boat, with but one or two exceptions, are men who have established no reputation for truth and veracity, have been successful in the world in no way, even from the standpoint of stable friends, living here and there, unfortunately; perchance, with some of them it is due to unfortunate circumstances and environments, and they have been unlucky, but still they haven't established stable friends in any community.

"Then there are the three boatmen on the boat— and those three men, unprejudiced, unbiased, not deputies and not Commercal Club members, but merely laborers, they know where the first shot came from, and they tell, and their testimony absolutely and entirely contradicts the testimony of the defense in this case from start to finish.

"And when you look at that red face and red hair and that honest expression of big Jack Hogan John Hogan here, and his honest blue eyes, it doesn't seem to me that you can have any more doubt than I have that Jack Hogan saw Tracy.

"Now, these men that come on the stand all confess they had a common design. Their common design they say, was that about two o'clock in Everett they were going to speak at the corner of Wetmore and Hewitt Avenues, that is their common design.

"The court tells you that the purpose that they admit was unlawful, so Tracy, by the testimony adduced in his favor, was one of the men having a common design for an unlawful purpose. Tracy, regardless of his location, regardless of whether he fired or not, is guilty.

"The sheriff and his deputies could have been guilty of everything claimed against them previous to this and the defendant still be guilty of helping and encouraging someone else to unjustifiably kill Jefferson Beard.

"Under the Court's instructions there were acts done at Beverly Park that were unlawful. There is no question about that. Instead of this being a weakness on the State's part, it seems to me that it is an added strength. Because the I. W. W. used Beverly Park for what purpose? They jumped on it with desire, deeming it a fortunate circumstance because they wanted to inflame men to invade Everett. They jumped on this, the men at the head of the conspiracy, they jumped on Beverly Park because they could use it to inflame their members. How do we know? Their own statements! Their telegrams! 'Advertise conditions and send volunteers.' Volunteers for what? Volunteers for what? When a man represents things and so helps to make men mad he wants these men up there as volunteers for retaliation. And the Court has instructed you that if these men went up there with the purpose of retaliating, they are guilty. Tracy having been one of a common design makes it central, vital, in good conscience as citizens, that you return your verdict asked by the state.

"Any time a murder is committed it is important that prosecution be had and conviction secured. That is always vital from the standpoint of protection to society. The police, the sheriff's office, and the officials of all cities and states of the United

States sometimes forget themselves, I take it, sometimes do things they shouldn't do, sometimes do things they should be censured for, but the fact that they had is no reason that murder is to be excused or justified, because if you did, we would have no society. That is true in an ordinary murder case. That is overwhelmingly true in this case.

"The I. W. W. is an organization that realizes the great truth in combating government. They have stumbled upon an overwhelmingly successful instrument in fighting society. What is that? To commit a violation of the law in numbers, to violate the law by so many people that only a few can be prosecuted and even if they are convicted, the great majority go scott free. They built better than they knew when they stumbled upon the great secret that the violation of a law in great numbers would protect practically all of the violators. And this trial itself is proof of that.

"Snohomish County can ill afford the expense of this one trial; can ill afford the expense of two or three trials after this; would be overwhelmed with debt to convict all the men who are in this conspiracy, if there were a conspiracy it can't do it; most of them are safe from prosecution and they know it; and the only protection that Snohomish County has, and King County has, and the State of Washington has, and the United States has, is that when something happens like this a conviction be secured against a man who is guilty, not because you are convicting all, because you can't, you are helpless—but because that at least is the voice of warning to the men that if you lead an attempt you may be the one of the great number that will be caught. It is important from the standpoint of citizens of the State of Washington to establish the principle that crimes cannot be committed by numbers with impunity, that while it is fairly safe, it won't be absolutely safe. We have no protection. That is the vital part of this case. We have no protection.

"If this case were just that of murder committed by one man acting alone, the importance of your

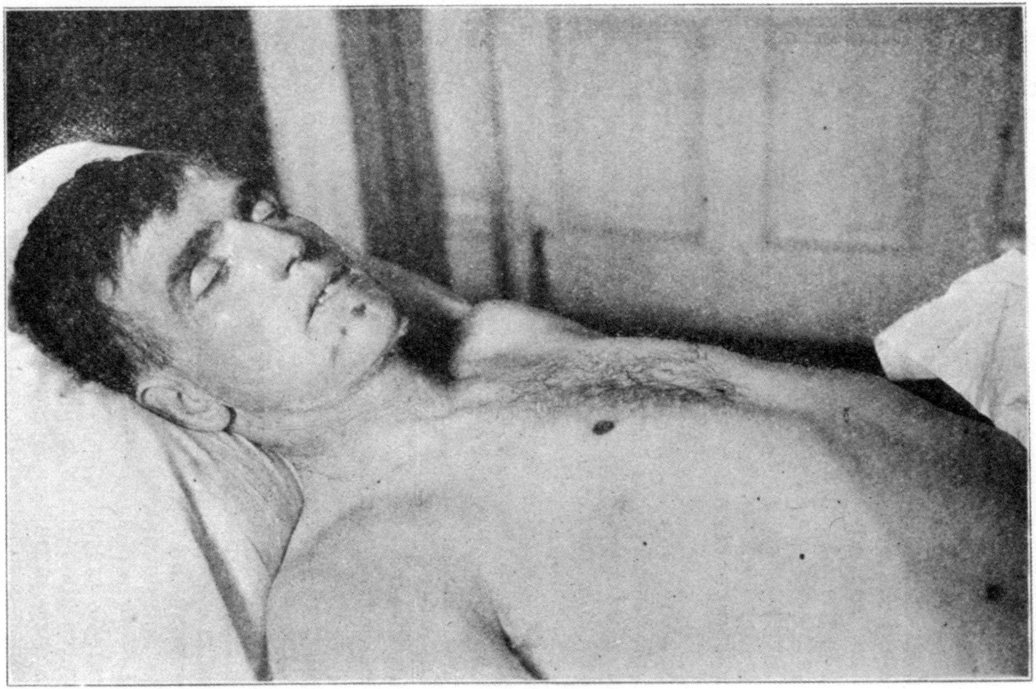

JOHN LOONEY

verdict would be of small significance, compared with the importance of your verdict in a criminal case where the members are part of an organization. True, the society has no doubt a great many aims that are desirable to improve the welfare of the workingman. But it has one aim, one vital aim, in its platform to bring upon it the condemnation of thinking, sober men and women residing permanently in the State of Washington, and that is sabotage.

"We are not claiming that the killing of Jefferson Beard was in the exercise of sabotage. We are saying that sabotage along with the conscious withdrawal of efficiency, sabotage along with the destruction of property, may also mean crime.

"The I. W. W. members did not come to Everett for the purpose of employment; they were men who were wanderers upon the face of the earth, who desired to establish themselves nowhere, and none of them, as far as this witness stand is concerned, expected to work in Everett or to put sabotage in effect in Everett by working slow. The only way they could use sabotage in Everett was by the destruction of property. The mayor became alarmed, and the sheriff, after their repeated threats in their papers. But whether you believe sabotage to be good, bad, or indifferent, really is not vital in this case except as a circumstance.

"Now, the Wanderer. The Wanderer did not happen the way they said it happened. The sheriff did shoot after they refused to stop. The sheriff did hit some of them with the butt of his gun. The sheriff brought them into Everett because they constituted an unlawful assemblage. The sheriff did the only thing he could do. He filed charges against them and they were arraigned in court. Twenty-three men cannot be tried quickly when each one demands a separate trial by jury. Twenty-three trials would stop the judicial machinery for three months. They could not be tried and so the sheriff turned them loose. Maybe he did hit them harder than he should have. Policemen do that! Sheriff do that! Lots of time they hit men when it is not necessary. Hit them too hard, sometimes. They don't always understand exactly what they are supposed to do. But the I. W. W. exaggerated the matter and used it to incite retaliation on the fifth. So the Beverly Park incident, and all other incidents, if true to the last syllable of the defense testimony, merely in this case extenuated the motive on November 5th.

"Now then, why did the State select Tracy? The State's evidence was to the effect that Tracy was not only a member of the conspiracy, but was firing. Several State's witnesses recognized Tracy. There was another reason. What was that? Some of these men, some of these boys, flitting here and there from job to job, with never more than a dollar or two in their pockets, were inflamed intentionally by people who misrepresented conditions. They did not have any right to be inflamed; they did not have any right to go to Everett and they are guilty of murder if they went up there to retaliate for any wrong, actual or conceived. But the State has preferred to put on first a man who was in the forefront of the conspiracy; the man that appeared to be an important cog of that conspiracy, and that man is Tracy.

"Tracy knew that a great many people of Everett were alarmed and disturbed. Tracy knew that the I. W. W. did not want anything in Everett, had no interests there, no friends there except as they were disturbing conditions. Tracy knew the purposes and Tracy went back to Seattle so he could lead this excursion to Everett. Tracy is a man of determination. He knew the situation and he was prominent enough to be selected by the organization as a stationary delegate. And if any man knew what they intended to do in Everett, it undoubtedly was Tracy. So, regardless of whether he fired or not, Tracy was one of the men who were on the inside. Tracy is a part of the conspiracy that happened. But no man, my friends, on that boat, that went up there with a common design to break the ordinance has been sinned against because he is in jail.

"Now, my friends, you want in good faith to follow the instructions of the court. It seems to me that the only question you have to decide is the one the court told you to decide—Was Beard killed unlawfully by a shot from the boat, and did Tracy aid, encourage or incite that killing?

"The murder of Jefferson Beard was a premeditated murder. Following the instructions of the court, separating the wheat from the chaff, and deciding that one question, we of the State are confident that you as jurors and good citizens, as honest, sincere and conscientious citizens, will protect Snohomish County—we believe that your verdict will say 'We are convinced, beyond a reasonable doubt, that Tracy is guilty, and, being so convinced, we are going to protect Snohomish County as we would our own.' I thank you!"

Vanderveer handled the case from two different viewpoints—that of a first degree murder trial and also as a section of the class struggle. His address was a masterly array of invincible logic and satire. Omitting his readings from the transcript of evidence, his speech was substantially as follows:

"This cause is, as the counsel for the state has told you, one of momentous importance not only to the defendant but to a class—a large class of people of whom today he stands merely as an unfortunate single member, fighting their battle.

"We do not ask in this case for mercy, we do not ask for sympathy, but it is essential, absolutely essential that we should have cold, stern justice; justice for the defendant, justice for those who have oppressed him, those who have denied him his rights. We hope this case is the beginning of a line of prosecution which will see that justice is done in the Everett situation.

"It is not the defense who outlined the issues in this case, it was the State who determined that. They have chosen their fighting ground, and we had to meet them on that battle. In the beginning of this case the State, thru Mr. Black, told you that it would prove a conspiracy of very formidable proportions, a conspiracy in the first place to commit acts of violence and to incite acts of violence, a conspiracy to commit arson, a conspiracy to overrun all law and order in Everett and bring on a condition of chaos. The claim was a very formidable one. The evidence has been very silly. The State ought to apologize, in common decency, for ever having suggested these things.

"What is the evidence about the fires? The fire marshall's report, made by a man who would naturally try to enlarge the performance of his duties and impress upon the public the manner in which he discharged them, reports only four fires of incendiary origin for the entire year. Every one of these were discovered before they did five cents worth of damage. Who had notice of them? Was it the I. W. W. who set them or was it Reese or some paid employe of the Pinkerton Agency? Can you conceive that an organization embracing as many members as this does, bent upon the destruction of Everett, could not set one fire at least that would do some damage. It is nothing but a hoax!

"As to force and violence, who did they put on to prove it? Young Howard Hathaway, a mere boy, whose father represents some mill companies in Everett. Then Sheriff McRae, and McRae couldn't tell you one thing that he heard at the street meetings. Then they put on Ed Hawes, the big brute that out at Beverly called the little boy a coward, a baby, because he wouldn't stand there and be slugged with guns and clubs. And what did Hawes say? That he looked up sabotage in the International Dictionary! And you can search that book until you are black in the face and you won't find a word in there about sabotage. Why, if sabotage is such a terrible thing, did Hawes, having heard all about it at the street meeting, have to go home to look it up at all?

"At these meetings there was not one thing said that could invite criticism, there was not one thing said that could justify or invite censure or abuse; there was not one disorderly thing done but was done by the officers of the law themselves, and they went in recklessly, without excuse, without right, they clubbed Henig, they clubbed Carr, a former member of the council, and they roughed women around and knocked them down. Why? Because these people were mill owners, their hirelings and their representatives, who had been instructed in the propaganda of the open shop by employes, aides and emissaries of the Merchants' and Manufacturers' Association.

"A lot of people went to the jail one night, a thousand, maybe. They hooted, they cat-called, and they hissed. Is it any wonder they did? Ladies and gentlemen, I want to tell you there is no surer verdict on earth than the verdict of a crowd; and the verdict of that crowd condemned what the deputies had done.

"Finally they say there was a conspiracy on the 5th of November to go to Everett and to hold their meeting at all hazard, to brook no opposition, to ride rough-shod over it, to oppose everyone and anything that stood in the way of accomplishing their purpose. I ask you to think just for a moment how foreign that is to everything you know about the I. W. W. and their operations and behavior in Everett. Not one witness for the state could tell you an incident where one of them resisted arrest, could tell you an occasion where one of them had advocated violence, could tell you one occasion where any one of them had committed any acts of violence.

"These people wrote to Governor Lister calling his attention to the violations of the law on the part of the officers of Everett; they wrote to Mayor Merrill, enclosing a copy of that letter and calling on him to restore the order that had been violated by the officers of the law; they scattered handbills all over Everett, among its best homes and in its business streets, calling upon the good citizens to come to their meeting on November 5th at Wetmore and Hewitt, to come and help maintain your own and our constitutional privileges; they mailed to the citizens of Everett on October 30th, seven or eight hundred copies of a little pamphlet calling upon them to intervene and stop the brutality of officers of the law; they questioned Governor Lister at a public meeting and again called his attention to the conditions in Everett; they called in the reporters, called the newspapers and notified the editors that they were going to Everett and asked them to have representatives present. Are these the acts of conspirators?

"You know how that meeting was called and why it was called. You know it from ministers of the gospel, you know it from the lips of those whom you cannot help but believe. And it was called for Sunday, the day when people ordinarily resent disorders of the kind that had occurred there. It was called for the daytime, when ordinarily abuse and violence are not attempted. And this big crowd went up there on this fine Sunday afternoon because in number there is strength and in numbers there is protection against brutality.

"At first the deputies had taken out one or two and abused and beaten them; then they had taken five or six; they had taken eighteen; finally they had taken forty-one. But I ask you, would you believe it possible that they could take two hundred or three hundred people in broad daylight and do to them what had been done to the others? Yet the evidence in this case shows convincingly and conclusively they intended to do substantially that thing. They intended to run those men into a warehouse; they didn't intend to let one of them get away. And had they gotten them into that warehouse you don't know, I don't know, nobody knows what would have happened!

"That is the evidence of conspiracy in this case. They have claimed no other conspiracy; they have offered no other evidence of conspiracy, either to set fires or to incite violence, or to override all opposition on November 5th. Their evidence doesn't stand even if unanswered—and no evidence could be more successfully answered.

"What evidence is there that Tom Tracy had anything to do with such a conspiracy, if there were one? Their most willing tools, Auspos and Reese, don't say a word about Tracy.

"What does the identification by McRae amount to? He identifies Tracy as the man who leaned out of the window and shot at him. Now at the time this shot was fired McRae had his back turned to the man who shot it. He says himself he did, and he was shot thru the heel, which seems to prove it. That, by the way, suggests to me that it was not an I. W. W. who shot McRae. The man who shot him must have thought McRae a hero, like the gentleman of mythological fame who was killed by an arrow thru the heel which no I. W. W. does, I assure you. Or else he thought that McRae wore his brains there.

"But I am not going to discuss McRae at great length either now or at any other stage of this case, because the greatest kindness I can do him is to forget him. The man is a perjurer! He lied! He was not mistaken. He deliberately, cold-bloodedly lied about almost everything in this case wherein his conduct as an officer was questioned. He lied about 'Sergeant' Keenan! He lied about shooting at the "Wanderer," and you saw the bullet holes. He lied about Berg and about Mitten, and finally, and last of all lied, and we have proven it conclusively, about being out to Beverly Park.

"Bridge's identification of Tracy does not agree with that of Smith, and Bridge does not even agree with his own testimony given at the coroner's inquest. Smith picked out a photograph and said it was Tracy and that picture resembles Tracy about as much as I do some of you jurors. Bridge and Smith say that Tracy fired three shots, and Hogan says he fired only one. And you know, ladies and gentlemen, that Hogan did not see this man at all. You know that he did not even see the window at which he pretends this man was sitting when the shot was fired. You know it because you went there to the dock and you saw the boat lined up to a mathematical certainty by the shot marks, and you saw a photograph taken with the camera placed by

John Hogan exactly where he said he was standing himself. And there wasn't a one of you who could identify Bob Mills, with his long nose and angular features, with everything that makes identification easy, when he was in the position attributed to Tracy. And when you came around from there to where you could look directly at the place, the reflected glare of the sunshine left nothing but a blank background.

"There were one hundred and forty deputies looking toward the place where the first shot was supposed to have been fired. They have produced on the witness stand only about one in ten. We challenged them to bring them all on, we dared them to do it, and Mr. Cooley said 'I accept that dare!'—look it up Mr. Cooley on page 1802 of the transcript—but he did not dare accept that dare. Mr. Cooley knows what those nine-tenths would testify to. Twelve out of their sixteen witnesses who testified about the first shots said that their brother deputies were mistaken as to even the place on the boat where the first three shots came from.

"I venture, ladies and gentlemen, that with a bit of the kind of work the State has employed in this case, a little bit of the same zeal that was employed on Auspos, a little bit of the same zeal that was employed with Reese, a little bit of the help of McLaren of Los Angeles, I can take these one hundred and forty-five men and pick out four men who will honestly and truthfully testify that they saw anything, and I say that with no reflection on their honesty either, because the power of suggestion is enormous. It is not surprising that four people have come here to say they saw Tracy. It is not surprising that three out of the four should have been proven, conclusively, convincingly and absolutely, not to know what they were talking about.

"The court has told you that in this case it is not a question of who shot first, not a question of which side shot first, it is a question of who was the aggressor, who made the first aggressive movement,

FELIX BARAN

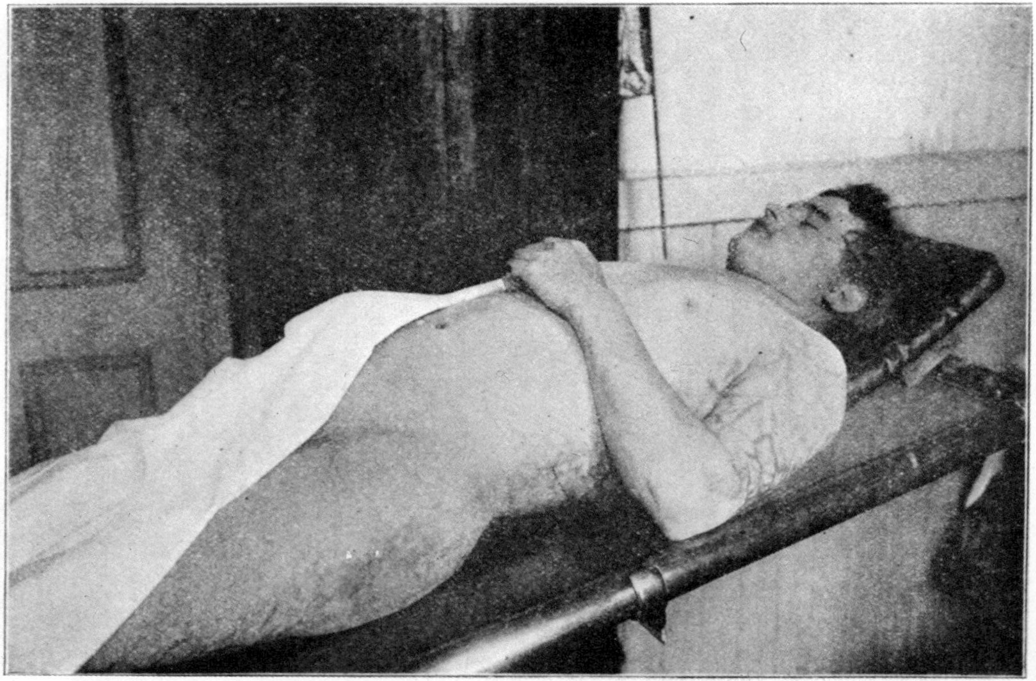

Dark lines on body caused by internal hemorrhage; Portland doctor said life might have been saved by operation.

who did the first hostile thing. The man who did a thing to excite fear was the aggressor, and that man was McRae when he pulled his gun. McRae clearly did that before there was any shooting.

"In determining who the agressor was, you are entitled—not only entitled but must take into account the past behavior of all parties. And what does that show you? Was it the I. W. W.'s who had never offered violence, who had never done an act of violence, who had decried and deplored violence, as members of their audiences told you, and advised caution against it? Or was it McRae and his deputies?

"It is only formally correct to refer to these as deputies. They had commissions, but in nothing else in the world did they bear the remotest resemblance to officers of the law, not in their conduct, not in their training, not in their purposes, not in anything. They were the hirelings of either the mill owners of Everett or the Commercial Club. Did you ever in your life before hear of officials taking their instructions from representatives of an industrial movement? Did you ever before hear of deputy sheriffs being instructed in the propaganda of the open shop, being instructed in the methods employed at Minot unlawfully to prevent street speaking? That is where the first mistake in this case was made. First in the selection of that kind of men; second in the deliberate attempts which were made to color their actions, to prevert them, to make them the tools of the employers.

"That is the reason Henig and Carr were beaten, that is the reason Feinberg and Roberts were beaten, that is the reason men and women were knocked down in the crowds, that is the reason that this boy, Schwartz, was taken out by McRae and chased zigzag down the road in mortal terror of being run down by the sheriff's automobile, that is the reason 'Sergeant' Keenan was hit over the head with a gun, that is the reason James Rowan was taken out and beaten black and blue. How do you suppose Rowan got those marks on his back? Did he put them there for fun, or were they put there by somebody else's rotten, dirty brutality? If you didn't know a thing about him except what you know about Beverly and these other incidents, and it was deep darkness where this happened, I venture you would all say off-hand, 'It must have happened at Everett, anyway. There is no place else that I know of where they do such things.'

"Black says the "Wanderer" has been greatly misrepresented to you, that the things we claim happened did not happen there at all. Well, there is a lot of evidence that they did happen. There are a lot of people who could have denied it. There are a whole crew of deputies who could have come up here and denied it. Why didn't they? Because they were ashamed of it and they knew they could not stand the grilling that was awaiting them in the court room. It is true, certainly! And I say here that nothing but providential intervention prevented McRae on that day from being a cold-blooded murderer! That is the manner of man you are considering. You are considering whether he was the aggressor, he or the people he shot at.

"Counsel says that Louis Skaroff lied. Now I am very frank to confess that when we produced that story on the witness stand I feared you would not believe it, not because I doubted the truthfulness of his statement but because the story itself is so brutal and inhuman that I questioned whether there could be found anywhere in the county twelve persons who would think such things could possibly happen just thirty miles away. But when one of their own witnesses went on the stand here, in rebuttal, and told you that Louis Skaroff came out of that room with his arms above his head, crying, with the blood running from his finger tips, I knew that you knew that Louis Skaroff had told the truth.

"The state has been very reluctant in this case to admit that there were rifles on the dock, because if the deputies went there with rifles there was a reason for it. You could not find a rifle on that dock until we proved—what? That rifle shells were around the dock in great numbers; we proved it by innocent, clean little boys who picked up the shells; until we proved by witnesses that the rifles were there and were being shot; until we proved by a rifle bullet with human blood and a man's hair on it that the use made of the rifles was a deadly one.

"Who was the aggressor? Even now the State doesn't like to admit, because the State knows it is fatal to their case to admit, and notwithstanding hopeless to deny, that there were helpless men in the water being shot at. They do not like to admit that a man was so impressed with the inhumanity of the thing that he ran from the depot to the boat house hoping to effect a rescue of the men and was stopped by the armed deputies. The State does not like to admit the evidence of their own deputy witness, Groger,—whose actions I want the counsel for the state to explain and justify is he can—who repeatedly fired at a man who was trying to untie the boat so the unarmed men could escape.

"Counsel said that if there was any intention to start trouble men would not have lined up as they were on the dock in an exposed position. And I ask you, if there was not an intention to start trouble why were they kept in the warehouse until the boat had almost tied up? If that was not an ambuscade, what on earth was it? If they did not intend to start trouble why was it McRae waited until the line was out and made fast. Why was it, then, he did not say to the captain, 'Take your boat out?' He said he was afraid they would go somewhere else. Well, when he told those boys they could not land he expected them to go away. Or did he expect them to go away? Which was it?

"The manner in which McRae handled this thing indicates nothing so much as that he intended to get them there and administer to them another of the things that he calls a lesson, another of the things that other people call infamous, damnable brutality.

"Counsel says there have been mistakes made. He doesn't want to apologize for them, but clearly he doesn't want to be held responsible for them.

There were mistakes made. Beverly was one! The "Wanderer" was one! From the beginning to the end of all their operations in Everett everything has been a mistake—a mistake because the ordinary processes of law and the rights of other people were ignored. There was no ordinance prohibiting speaking. The boys were yielding implicit, careful obedience to such law as there was. McRae unblushingly tells you that the reason he made arrests was because there were labor troubles in Everett and the shingle mill owners didn't want things embarrassed by the truth, by the disclosures contained in this little report of the Industrial Relations Commission.

"They were not afraid of the I. W. W.'s going up there to incite violence, to advise disorder, to invoke a reign of terror. Reigns of terror are the employers' specialty! They were afraid of cold fact. Never a man went up there to speak on the street and used that little Industrial Relations report but was thrown in jail for it—Thompson, Rowan, Feinberg, Roberts, all.

"It's nice to enjoy the powers, the position and authority of a dictator who can repeal, amend and modify, ignore, disregard laws when it suits his fancy, but it's kind of tough on other people. That's what McRae did!

"On the 5th of March, nearly nine weeks ago, His Honor called this case from his bench 'State versus Thomas H. Tracy,' and my friend Mr. Cooley rose from his chair and said 'Your Honor, the State is ready.' I say to you, Mr. Cooley, you slandered the fair name of your state! What has the State of Washington to do with this thing? The name of the State of Washington in such a case as this should stand for law and order and decency. The State is supposed to protect the innocent against abuse and injustice and you who are now running this case do not now maintain these things, or if you do, you protect them only when convenience requires it.

"It is not the State of Washington versus Thomas H. Tracy at all, and if the decent people of Everett who know the facts could decide what course this action should take it would never be here. Even the title of the case is a mistake. It is the case of the Commercial Club of Everett, the mill owners of Everett, against Labor. This is an attempt, just as all the actions for months have been an attempt, to keep Labor out of its rights in Everett. The same people who took possession of the machinery of law in Everett, who took possession of the sheriff and furnished him with guns and clubs and murderous things like that and instructed him how to act, the same people who employed detectives to set fires in order that they might manufacture evidence and public sentiment against these boys, those same people are today prosecuting this case.

"I don't know where Governor Clough was on November 5th. I suspect he was not anywhere where there was any danger, but I know the smoke had not left the decks of the Verona before he was hot-footing it to the telegraph office,—Governor Clough, not the prosecuting attorney, not the sheriff, nobody but Clough and Joe Irving, the man who was so drunk that he beat up Schofield,—to send a telegram to Judge Burke of the Chamber of Commerce of Seattle, to the Mayor of this City and to the Chief of Police of this City to arrest the whole bunch of them.

"Then right away they got their other emissaries at work, Reese and Smith, down here with two fingers out of the door of a darkened cell, deciding for the State of Washington who should be prosecuted in this case, and H. D. Cooley, who surely then was not a prosecuting attorney, giving them legal counsel and directing their energy, taking out the men, preparing statements, and getting ready for the work he was going to do in this case, because his employers wanted it.

"There is a conspiracy in this case, a conspiracy supported by evidence, a conspiracy of men in the Commercial Club to take over the machinery of government, and by it club these fellows out of their rights, club them out of Everett, club them out of all contact with the workers in order that they might not bring to them the gospel of their organization.

"But I say to you, ladies and gentlemen of the jury, that this struggle, the struggle of Capital against Labor, the struggle of the Commercial Club against the I. W. W., which is just one phase of the bigger one, this struggle is going on in spite of Cooley, this struggle is going on in spite of McLaren, this struggle is going on in spite of Arthur L. Veitch of the Merchants' and Manufacturers' Association, this struggle is going on in spite of McRae, this struggle is going on in spite of the Commercial Club, because it is founded on a principle so big, so wholesome, and so decent, so righteous, that it must live. And it will go on until in this country we have industrially that which we have struggled so long and hard for and finally won politically; until we have democracy.

"There is nothing in revolution, gentlemen, that is wrong. We came to the condition in which we now find ourselves by revolution; first the grand American revolution and then the revolution against chattel slavery. It was nothing more nor less than revolution, because slavery was then entrenched under the highest law of the land, the decision of the Supreme Court in the Dred Scott case. We took it out of the courts and slavery was wiped out. Slavery again will be wiped out!

"The thing about this case which makes it of most serious importance, the thing about this case which makes it of public interest, the thing about this case which has so enlisted the sympathy of every one connected with it, which makes us feel the importance of a just verdict, is that it is not merely the liberty of a man that is at stake, but in a larger measure than you know there is at stake in your verdict in this case the rights of the working people, their right to organize, their right to protect themselves, their right to receive and enjoy the fruits of their labor.

"There is involved the question of whether or not the working people shall receive justice or forever must be victimized by organized capitalists. There is involved the question of whether or not such things as have gone on in Everett for the last six months may continue forever with the endorsement of the jury or whether the working people on the other hand may go and discuss their wrongs and grievances and strive for their rights.

"As I have confidence in the righteousness of this cause and the integrity of this purpose, so I have confidence that your verdict will be not guilty."

Attorney Fred Moore closed the case for the defense with one of the greatest speeches ever delivered in a court room, a speech that seered its way to the minds and hearts of the jurors. Far more than a defense of Thomas H. Tracy it was an explanation of the industrial problems underlying society, the class warfare rooted in industry and manifesting itself on November 5th. It was a sustained and definite statement of the aims and objects of the I. W. W. and Moore showed, not only a great knowledge of the problems of the working class, but a wonderful command of satire and irony. Following is an abridgement of Moore's speech to the jury:

"May it please the court, and ladies and gentlemen of the jury; For a period of something like five hundred years the Anglo-Saxon has seen fit to place the final adjustment of the question of justice in the hands of twelve men. In the evolution of the law, that number has been increased until now in this state we have fourteen. Likewise, in the evolution of the law and in the face of the vast amount of public protest, and in the face of the most reluctant world, we have enlarged the term jurors to include women jurors. This is the first time that I personally have ever tried a lawsuit in which ladies sat in the jury.

"The state has told you why this case is one of grave responsibility for them. Allow me to tell you why this is one of grave responsibility for you. One hundred and ninety-six witnesses have appeared for the defendant in this case. Yesterday, counsel brought home the fact that many of these witnesses

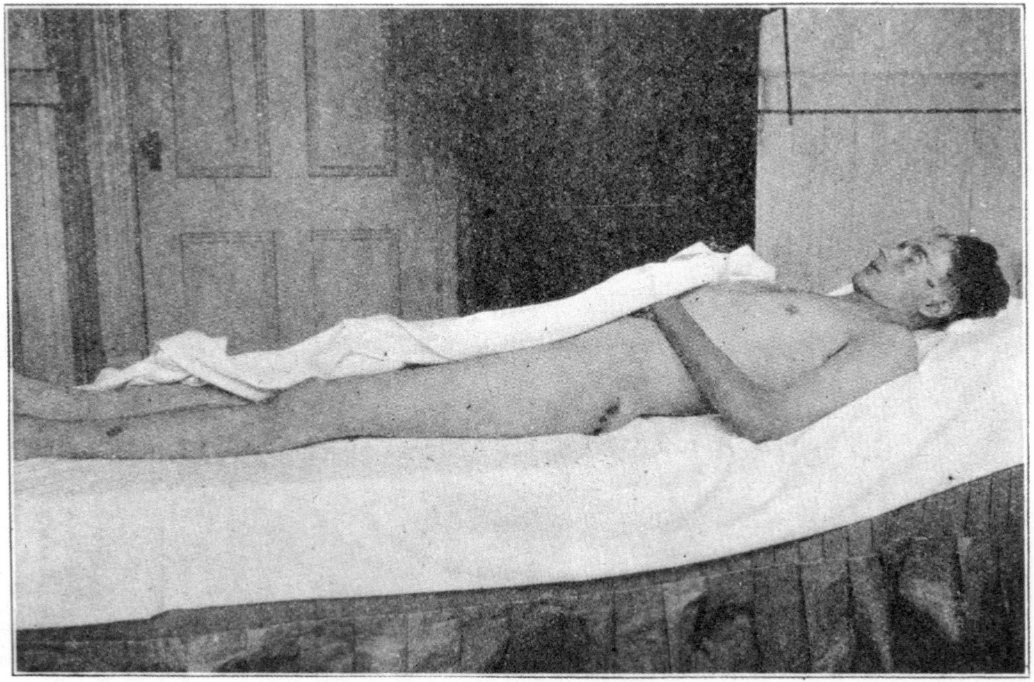

HUGO GERLOT

were not residents of this community, were without homes, without any permanent places of abode. All true. The responsibility that you have in this case is commensurate with the fact that the case reveals to you, as it were, a cross-section of our lives. You who are property-qualified have a responsibility to pass upon the liberties and the lives of a body of men who are propertyless. If there is any change in men's thoughts and views as they acquire a home, as they settle down, as they marry, as they bring into the world children, then I ask you in all fairness to attempt to put yourselves in the places of this defendant and of this defendant's witnesses who have taken the stand, and to realize that your responsibility here is commensurate with the fact that the testimony reveals, as it were, a most deplorable condition of modern life. In other words, your responsibility here is that of measuring out absolute and complete justice between warring elements in our modern life, not for one moment allowing your judgment to be swerved by the fact that one class of witnesses here are witnesses of social position, are witnesses of property qualifications, are witnesses with homes, while, on the other hand, the witnesses called by the defense were witnesses from the four parts of the earth, witnesses whose only claim to your consideration is that they have built the railroads, that they have laid the ties, that they have dug the tunnels, that they have harvested the crops, that they have worked from one end of the country to the other, in season and out, floating from job to job.

"In most jurisdictions, the defendant has the opportunity of either a grand jury investigation or of a preliminary; in other words, he is in some degree advised of what evidence he is going to be called upon to meet. In this case, we came in here on the 5th day of March with no information whatsoever relative to the State's case other than that given us from the four corners of the instrument on file here, known as the information, together with the fact that on that information there were the names of some three hundred or more witnesses. That was all we had. We were further handicapped in view of the fact that we did not have behind us all the resources of the State of Washington and the county of Snohomish, neither did we have behind us all of the resources of various business interests, neither did we have behind us all the resources of allied business on this west coast, as represented by Mr. Veitch."

Mr. Veitch: To which I take an exception, if the court please.

The Court: Exception allowed.

Mr. Veitch: On a matter of personal privilege, I have a right to characterize that statement as a deliberate misstatement of the fact.

Mr. Moore: Mr. Veitch has not seen fit to explain why he was here.

Mr. Veitch: I am employed by friends of Mr. Jefferson Beard. If that is not enough—

Mr. Moore: That is outside of the record.

The Court: Both of you are outside of the record. Proceed Mr. Moore.

"Suffice it to say that we are here as the frank and honest representatives of the defendant and of the defendant's organization. We do not have behind us the power of the State, or the power of any interest other than the defendant himself and of his organization.

Mr. Black complained that the State had been hampered in this cause. Is it fair to say that the state has been hampered when on the fatal November the 5th. Judge Bell and Mr. Cooley were both on the dock? Judge Bell would have us believe that he was unarmed, and so far as we know Mr. Cooley was unarmed. Then why were they on the dock? Judge Bell was there as the representative, as he himself has testified, of a number of lumber mills, and Mr. Cooley was there likewise; both citizen deputies; both there; both unarmed if their testimony is to be believed. Again Mr. Cooley was, in the matter of a few hours, down here at the Seattle jail. Certainly he was not there to represent the defendant Tracy. Who was he there to represent? He was either there in a private capacity, representing private clients, or he was there in a public capacity representing a public client, namely, Snohomish County. Wherein do you find the evidence of the State being hampered, sir? From the beginning to the end the State has moved majestically, exercising all the power that it had. Mr. Black has had able assistance in this cause, the able assistance of Mr. Cooley, the able assistance of Mr. Veitch, the able assistance of the man behind Mr. Cooley and Mr. Veitch, Mr. McLaren. Yet, all the resources of the State have failed to produce one scintilla of evidence against the defendant Tracy here so far as tending to indicate that he did counsel, aid, incite, abet, or encourage anyone to fire any shot, except the testimony of George Reese produced at the eleventh hour on rebuttal. I intend to treat of our friend Mr. Reese later.

"It is significant that out of all that mass of testimony that has been introduced in this case up to this time not one single bit of testimony has been introduced or any argument had upon that testimony dealing with the object and principles and purpose of the Industrial Workers of the World. Mr. Black did not refer to it. Mr. Cooley has the final say. I anticipate his argument for the State. They have that old reliance, that old faith, if you will, in the trial of a case of this character, namely conspiracy; hallowed by age.

"Way back in the sixteenth century the tub women on the banks of the river Thames were indicted for conspiracy in attempting to raise wages. The chandlers in London were likewise later indicted. The stonebreakers in New York, the carpenters in Boston. From time immemorial the charge of conspiracy has been leveled against the ranks of labor. Indeed, it was only in the reign of Queen Victoria that labor unions became other than simple conspiracies. Up to that time labor unions were within a classification themselves of criminal conspiracy.

"Knowing that under the charge contained in the information we might be called upon to meet evidence of conspiracy, we then commenced a careful survey of all the facts in connection with the Everett

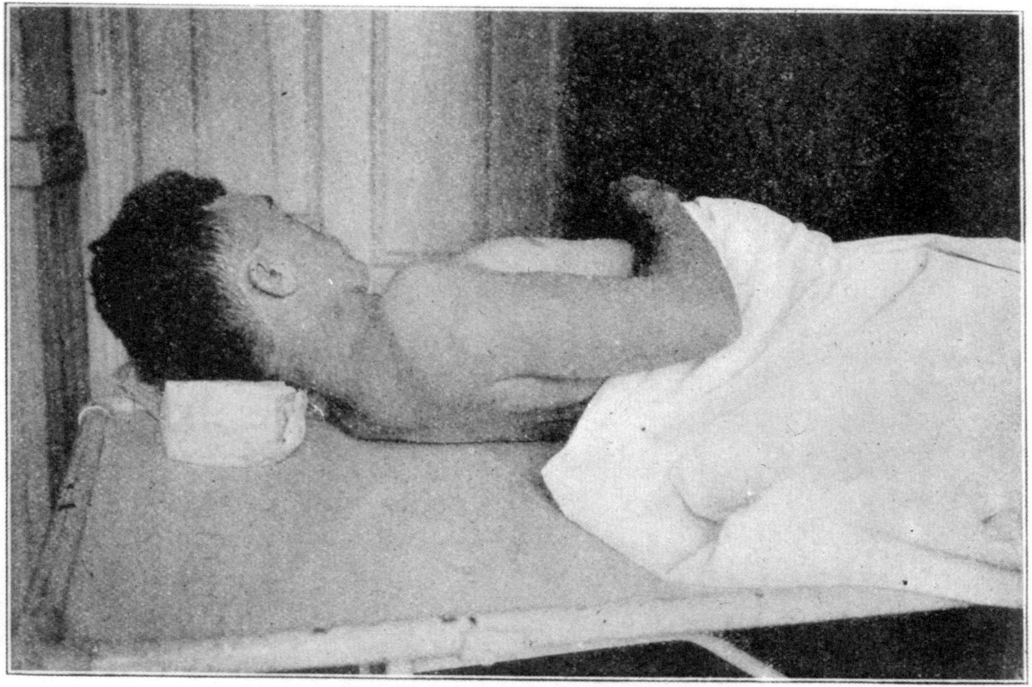

Dead body of Abraham Rabinowitz.

tragedy. And what did we find? We found not a hint of conspiracy!

"James Rowan had come into Everett without knowledge at the time that there was any trouble there. He had not been advised that there was any possibility of trouble. From all the prior history of Everett he had no reason to anticipate trouble. Thompson had spoken there and many others had spoken there. Rowan was charged with a violation of the peddling ordinance. He had been given an arbitrary floater out of town and had exercised his right to come back, was seized again and taken to the city jail; the sheriff goes there and arbitrarily demands Rowan from the Chief of Police. These things happened prior to any acts that by any remote possibility could be charged to us. There was no literature in the town at that time other than the Industrial Relations report. What at that time did we have to conspire about? We had no object.

"And as with Rowan so it was with Thompson, Remick and others. If there was a conspiracy to violate a city ordinance why did not the city officials make arrests and charge the men with such violations? The record is silent. Why wait until Tom Tracy is on trial for murder, and then at the eleventh hour spring this delightfully specious argument?

"I can almost hear ringing in my ears the impassioned plea of Mr. Cooley in closing this case. He is going to read this,'The question of 'right' and 'wrong' does not concern us.' He is going to say that is the I. W. W. philosophy. My God, did it ever concern the sheriff of Snohomish County? Does it seem very much to concern others who are attempting this prosecution?

"We were told in connection with the argument of counsel that Hickey was not on trial. They might have said that sheriff McRae was not on trial; they might have said that Bill Pabst was not on trial; they might have said that Joe Irving was not on trial; they might have said that the Commercial Club was not on trial; they might have said that all the men that have been guilty of all the brutality in that

County during the months of August, September and October were not on trial. We know it! Why are they not on trail?

"Deprivation of due process of law and confiscation of property! And yet Mr. Cooley is going to urge that the I. W. W. does not believe in government; he is going to urge that the I. W. W. does not respect the law. That kind of law never gets the respect of anyone. I hang my head in shame before such a history of usurpation and seizure of public authority as has been shown in this case.

"Are you going to give the stamp of your approval to this sort of thing? When you bring in a verdict in this case for the State you give your approval to Donald McRae. I beg of you to not put the seal of your approval upon lawlessness, official lawlessness, the kind of lawlessness that is worse, tenfold worse, than any private lawlessness.

"You are asked to stamp with your endorsement, to give your approval, to a man; a public official, the chief executive officer of a municipality, Mayor Merrill, who admits on the witness stand that he allowed a little group of members of the Commercial Club to take the power of the police department out of his office and turn it over to the sheriff of the county.

"Had the State put on Governor Clough and others on their side of the case we might have wrung from their reluctant lips the evidence of what occurred at the meeting on August 30th at the Commercial Club. But the State was careful not to put him on. Indeed, the most significant and outstanding thing in all this case is not who they put on, but who they did not put on. Neil Jamison did not testify in this case for the State; Governor Clough did not testify in this case for the State; Joe Irving did not testify in this case; Colonel Hartley did not testify in this case; Captain Ramwell did not testify. Why didn't Kelly, Chief of Police, take the stand? You might go down the line and you will find that the assets of all the witnesses for the State combined would total but a few thousand dollars, while you could take the remaining witnesses for the State who did not testify and you could build up an enormous fortune, running into the hundreds of thousands of dollars. We didn't call them because we cannot cross-examine our own witnesses.

"Is the administration of the law to be made a farce? Shall the State be allowed to blow hot and cold; one minute hot on the enforcement of the law, the next minute cold when the shoe pinches, and then hot again when they can use the law for the advancement of the interests of their prosecution? They say McRae and Hickey are not on trial; there is no promise that they shall ever be on trial!

"Let me say to you that no one violates the law, I care not who it is, just for the fun of violating the law. Jails are not pleasant places to abide in. People who violate the law and go to jail do so either because they are deliberately criminal or because they want to focus attention on some public issue. However, Mr. Black is too kind and considerate when he gives all this credit to the I. W. W.

"The facts are, if you go back into the history of the Revolutionary Days, that our forefathers urged and banded together and combined and federated, and if you will, conspired to violate the Stamp Act of the British Government, and were willing to go to jail if necessary. They went even further! They threw the British tea into Boston Harbor. Violation of the law? Yes, if you want to call it such, but the indignant protest of a people as against the enforcement of an unjust law.

"I might urge upon you that the State at that time wanted to absolutely suppress any speech whatsoever, because they had constituted the chief of police, the sheriff, the arresting officer, as the executive, the legislative and the judicial department of our government. The sheriff executed the law in person, the sheriff declared the question of guilt himself, the sheriff ordered deportations, and the sheriff took physical charge of the deportations. Isn't it impossible to avoid a fight when someone usurps unlawfully and illegally the legislative and judicial functions of government? Isn't it time to fight? If it isn't then we may as well cease any attempt to administrate the law!

"In the phraseology of these boys 'Fight' means a moral adherence to principle, a firm determination to face the authorities in the administration of the law, and if necessary to be arrested. But the State would have you put into it now a more sinister meaning, entirely new and foreign to its former use.

"The State brought in the death of Sullivan of Spokane in their opening and abandoned it in their close. One of the exploded hopes of the State! They counted on North Yakima and Wenatchee to show violence and arson, and they failed most miserably. They have failed in their identification of the defendant. Now, their folorn and bankrupt plea here is the charge of conspiracy.

"The court has told you that this is a murder case. Why then has the State cumbered the record with the I. W. W. preamble and constitution? Why with two pamphlets on sabotage? Why with an I. W. W. song book and such matters? Why?

"Because out of some of the phraseology here, phraseology far removed from you and me, they may build up a condition of prejudice which may result in your returning a conviction on a smaller degree of evidence than you would otherwise require. Mr. Cooley is going to stand here and read little, short, listed extracts from the context of the whole. The pamphlets he has introduced on the question of patriotism and the worker is the foundation from which Mr. Cooley will appeal to your prejudices and passions.

"We are not afraid of the evidence. We are afraid of this deep-grained interest that goes down into men's conscience and that reached back a thousand years.

"Remember that behind this case are many women and children whose cause these boys represent; whose cause these boys are attempting to fight for. They fight because they must! They fight because to do anything else is suicide. You could not have stopped the American Revolution with all the powers of the British government. Since this jury was empaneled you have had the collapse of one of the greatest powers of modern times. I refer to Russia. It has passed from an absolute monarchy to a stage of a republic.

"The trial of this cause is the presentation of a great social issue, the greatest issue of modern times, namely, what are we going to do today with the migratory and occasional workers? These migratories, they are the boys who have told their story on the stand.

"If there is one principle that is ground into Angle-Saxon thought it is that of liberty of the press and freedom of speech. Those two things stand as the bulwark of our liberty. They are the things for which the Anglo-Saxon has fought from time immemorial. Away back in the eighteenth century Charles Erskine, a member of the British bar, defended Thomas Paine for having written the 'Rights of Man'. Case after case was fought out during that period when English thought was budding into fruition; when English thought was being tremendously influenced by the French Revolution and when those thoughts were bearing fruit in England. Time and time again the British crown attempted to throttle freedom of speech and liberty of the press. Time and time again Charles Erskine's voice was raised in the House of Lords in protest. Time and time again the British courts and finally the British jurors, gave voice to the doctrine that freedom of speech and liberty of the press may not be invaded except insofar as that subject, that document, is accompanied with acts; that you may not convict men for what they think; you may convict men only for what they do. Freedom of discussion thru the press and thru the public forum are the mainstay and the backbone of social development and social evolution. Only in that way, thru freedom of thought and freedom of discussion, may you fan the wheat from the chaff.

"Why, if this I. W. W. literature is all the State claims it is, why doesn't the State act in the way the law says they should act, prefer charges, arrest someone, bring the literature before a duly qualified body, a court with jurisdiction, and try the matter out? The State has not done that; the State will not do that; and we are in the position of a man fighting in the dark, without knowledge of what character of argument the State proposes to make.

"I do know that the name of Joe Hill is going to be paraded in front of this jury. The I. W. W. song book dedicated to Joe Hill, with the inscription 'Murdered by the authorities of the State of Utah, November 19th, 1915.' I cannot go into the conditions that surround that tragedy, but I can call your attention to one or two things that bear upon the question of the type of the man. Before he died, written in his cell on the eve of the execution, was Joe Hill's last will:

My will is easy to decide,
For there is nothing to divide.
My kin don't need to fuss and moan—
Moss does not cling to a rolling stone.

My body? Ah, if I could choose,
I would to ashes it reduce,
And let the merry breezes blow
My dust to where some flowers grow.

Perhaps some fading flower then
Would come to life and bloom again.
This is my last and final will.
Good luck to all of you, JOE HILL.

"This is the type of man you are asked, because he was honored, because some odd hundred thousand workers who suffer and who wander and who live in the jungles of labor as he did, and because he wrote songs that they understood, songs that because their songs, to judge as the author of the songs and bring in a verdict against Tom Tracy. Mr. Cooley will parade the songs one by one. Remember that behind any words he voices, any thought he expresses, behind it all was a human soul, a human soul passed, a human soul that lived as you and I. a human soul that had rights that had been trampled upon, and who attempted to voice those things.

"With all the oratory he can display Mr. Cooley will read the song, 'Christians at War.' A song that Mr. Thompson designated as a satire. You recollect that when the European war broke out both parties in that conflict called to their aid and said they were acting under divine guidance; that the Kaiser was fighting under the name of God, and that the British and French governments were allied with the Almighty. It is not for me to attempt a settlement of that dispute. History will say that of all the tragedies of the Twentieth Century, the most tragic thing of our modern life is that we of different nationalities, but bound together by all other ties, should be engaged in a death grapple. But that is not the issue here. But I cannot at this time anticipate wherein and how this literature presented by the State helps you to decide the question of who was the aggressor on November 5th.

"Who was the aggressor on July 31st when James Rowan was arrested and brought into the city court? McRae comes in and tells him to get out of town. An intervening series of events and Levi Remick is run out of town. Who was the aggressor? Sheriff McRae! On August 22nd Rowan and Remick were both in the union hall. McRae comes in and orders them out of town. Who was the aggressor? That night Thompson and others came up to Everett—who was the aggressor then? Next morning, with Kelly treating them half way white, along comes McRae and takes away one of the boy's money. Who was the aggresser? We come now to the deputies meeting at the Commercial Club on August 30th. Who was the aggressor? Had any of their members been beaten up? Had anything happened to their members whatsoever? Not at all! Yet murderous blackjacks were put into the hands of the membership of the club. Was James Rowan the aggressor when he was railroaded out of town and beaten? Who was the aggressor at the time of the 'Wanderer' outrage? Old Capt. Mitten, old John Berg, Edith

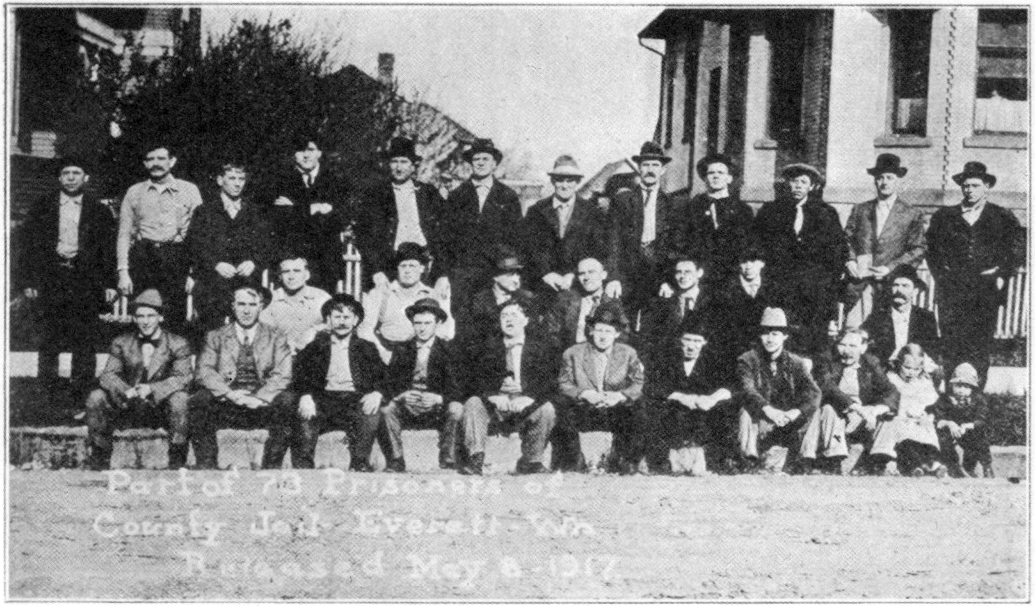
Part of 73 Prisoners of
County Jail Everett Wn
Released May 8 1917

Frenette? Who was the aggressor with Henig? With Feinberg? With Roberts? You have the testimony of Cannow, you have the testimony of Schofield, you have testimony showing the instructions given to the deputies. No one denies it Here is a series of acts leading up to October 30th, in which on each and every occasion McRae and his deputies, either regular or citizen deputies, were the aggressors. I said, who were the aggressors? Is there any question in your mind who was the aggressor up to Beverly Park? Any question in God's world who had done the dirty work up to that time? The State would have you believe that the I. W. W., with its membership coming from the four corners of the country, changed complexion practically over night, changed their whole ideas and their methods. I do not believe it and you do not believe it.

"The excuse the State gives for the actions of the deputies is that in the case of large numbers they could not give due process of law. Gentlemen, I refuse to believe that the Government is bankrupt in its capacity to protect itself thru legal and lawful measures of law enforcement. I have yet to sit in a court room and hear a plea on social and governmental bankrupcy such as is the plea of counsel for the State.

"The machinery of the government was there but it was not the kind of machinery that McRae wanted to use. It was not the kind Clough wanted to use. It was not the kind of machinery the executive committee, whoever they were, sitting behind the closed doors of the Commercial Club, wanted to use.

"And these members and leaders of the Commercial Club passed resolutions stigmatizing their own citizens, member of their own community, property owners in their own town, as well as the I. W. W., when they declared for an open shop. How do they stigmatize them? 'Professional agitators!' Yes. Lloyd Garrison was a professional agitator. Wendell Phillips was a professional agitator. The men who fought the battle that lay the ground work that made Abraham Lincoln possible, the men who are at work to better American politics, those men have all been professional agitators.

"Now on the boat they were ninety-nine percent I. W. W.'s, just a few passengers had bought their passage before. On the dock they were all citizen deputies, persons interested therein, and persons satisfactory to the men who had been stationed there to see that nobody but the right ones got on the dock. That means that as far as the first shot was concerned the two classes of witnesses are in some degree interested parties. The State put on a total of twenty-two witnesses, one of them not a deputy, all of whom testified that the shot came, or they thought it came from the dock, and of that number thirty-seven were I. W. W.'s, and twenty-four were not members at all but were Everett people from all walks of life.

"Now counsel is going to discount the value of the testimony of these citizens. Well, Mr. Cooley, we used the only kind of witnesses that you, in all of your care exercised in advance on November 5th, left for us. In the exercise of the hightest degree of judicial advance knowledge they saw to it that nobody got any closer to the end of the dock than the landing. We could not help that. You barred us from the dock; you barred us from access to the facts. We did all we could to get the facts, and if we couldn't get any closer it was not our fault. And the man who barred us from access to the facts is the man who is least qualified to come into court now and urge that our witnesses are disqualified in the face of the evidence that they disqualified them. But those witnesses could testify, and they did testify, to the very definite and specific facts—the first tipping of the boat, the rushing of the men, the volley firing, all of those matters.

"At the eleventh hour there came into this case a man by the name of Reese, a member, if you will, of the I. W. W. Back in the Chicago stockyards they have a large pen where they keep the cattle which are to be driven to slaughter. In that place they have had for years a steer that has performed the function of going into the big pen where all the cattle are, and, after mingling with them, then walking out thru a gate. He is trained to do it, he is skilled at it, this steer—and after walking around with the poor peaceful cattle that don't know they are about to be killed, this steer then goes up an incline, the gate is opened and the other cattle follow, and when he gets to the top of the incline there is a door and he turns to the right thru this door to safety and his followers turn to the left to death. That's George Reese! Proud of him? George Reese, the man who reported day by day with his confederates! To whom? During one period to the Pinkerton agency in regard to the longshormen's union; during another period on behalf of the Pinkerton Agency to the Commercial Club in Everett. George Reese! A man who doesn't even come under the approximately dignified title of a detective; a man whom Ahern, of his own agency says, "Well, he wasn't a detective, we used him as an informer.' Informer! A human being that has lost its human color.

"In connection with the testimony of Reese let me call your attention to the Industrial Relations Commission Report, a report that our friends of the Commercial Club had read and knew all about:

" 'Spies in the Union: If the secret agents of employers, working as members of labor unions, do not always instigate acts of violence, they frequently encourage them. If they did not they would not be performing the duties for which they are paid. If they find that labor unions never discuss acts of violence they have nothing to report to those employing them. If they do not report matters which the detective agencies employing them can use to frighten the corporation to cause their employment, they cannot continue long as spies. Either they must make reports that are false, in which case discovery would be inevitable, or they must create a basis on which to make a truthful report. The union spy is not in business to protect the community. He has little respect for the law, civil or moral. Men of character do not engage in such work, and it follows that the men who do are, as a rule, devoid of principle and ready to go to almost any extreme to please those who employ them.'

"That is the descriptive adjective, definition and analysis of the character of union informants made by the National Industrial Commission, appointed by President Wilson, and composed of nine men, all men of national standing, three representatives of labor, three representatives of capital and three representatives of the general public. That is their definition, description and classification of that character of testimony.

"Mr. Vanderveer closed yesterday by saying that this struggle, whatever your verdict is, will win. If yours is a verdict of 'not guilty,' Tom Tracy must take up again the job of finding a job, the endless tragedy of marching from job to job, without home, wife or kindred. His offense consists of being a migratory worker. I beg of you to render a verdict that has due regard and consideration for the tragedy of our twentieth century civilization that does not as yet measure out economic justice.

"Your verdict means much. The wires tonight will carry the word all over this land, into Australia, New Zealand and thruout the world. Your verdict means much to the workers, their mothers, their children, who are interested in this great struggle. We are not in this courtroom as the representatives of one person, two persons or three persons; our clients run into five or six hundred thousand. We are here as the mouthpiece of the workers of America, organized and unorganized, and they are all behind our voices.

"Tom Tracy stands here in your control. Your are the ones to determine whether or not he shall walk out free, whether or not he shall be branded for all times with the most serious felony known to the law, namely, that of a murderer. Can you find it in the evidence to bring in a verdict of guilty in this case?

"In conclusion, ladies and gentlemen, we want no compromise here. When you retire to your jury room I beg of you not to compromise with any ver-

Singing to the Prisoners.

dict other than not guilty. We don't want manslaughter in this case, we don't want second degree murder in this case; it is either first degree murder or an acquittal, one or the other. Allow none of those arguments that we, as lawyers, know are made in the juryroom to influence your honest verdict in this case. We ask at your hands, and we believe with all the sincerity of our souls, that the evidence warrants it, we ask a verdict of not guilty for the defendant, Thomas H. Tracy!"

If the speech of prosecutor Black was a whine, that of prosecutor Cooley was a yelp and a snarl. Apologies, stale jokes, and sneers at the propertyless workers followed one another in close succession. The gist of his harangue was as follows:

"In this case I am going to try simply in the closing argument to select a few of the monuments that it seems to me stand out in this case and that point a way to a proper verdict.

"Now, in the first place, a whole lot has been said here as to the nature of the controversy that existed for a number of months before November the 5th, 1916, between two classes of individuals there at Everett. Upon the one side were the people who were living in the city of Everett, who had made their homes there, who had come there for the purpose of carrying out their future destiny in that city. It was their home. Their interests were there. Their families were there. And upon the other side were a class of people who did not claim Everett as their home, who did not come there for the purpose of amalgamating with the citizenship of the city of Everett. They were not coming there because they had work there, nor because they were seeking work there; they were not citizens of Everett, nor were they seeking to become citizens of Everett, and there arose a controversy between the citizens of Everett on the one hand and these people from the four corners of the earth upon the other. The first thing we want to inquire into to find out if we can from the testimony in this case exactly what was the nature of that trouble that existed between them.

Why was it that upon the one hand there was a band of people congregated down here in the city of Seattle from all over the land and making one excursion after another, attempting to break into the city of Everett? Why was it that there were citizens of Everett up there seeking to do only one thing, asking only one thing, that these people keep away from Everett?

"Was it a fight to win the right of free speech on the one hand? Was it a fight on the other hand of a group of individuals who were simply seeking to force the open shop? Or was it a fight of a more serious nature on either hand?

"I grant you that the origin of the trouble arose because a man was seeking to speak upon the streets of Everett and he was stopped. But long before November 5th that original incident was lost sight of and forgotten. The controversy had grown to a magnitude that overshadowed the original incident. It was necessary in order that you might understand the situation with which the people of Everett were confronted that you should be apprised of the nature of the organization to which those people belong, that you should be apprised of the nature of the place in the world that they had attained, and that you should be apprised of the nature of their propaganda that they were seeking to inject into the city of Everett and that locality.

"I want to say right here and now that I have the highest regard for organized labor. Labor has the right to organize. There is not any question about it; there is not any dispute about it. Labor has organized and it has made a manful fight, and all down the pages of history you will find that labor, thru its organization and thru its lawful methods pursued under its organization, has gradually bettered its condition.

"It is not a question, and never has been in this case, as to the right of the labor men to organize; the right of the laboring man to use all of the lawful methods for the purpose of bettering his condition. The question in this case is as to whether any organization, whether it be a labor organization or any other, has the right to use unlawful methods; whether it has the right, because it may have the power, to use unlawful methods.

"Now there were coming into the city of Everett people representing this organization known as the Industrial Workers of the World. What was the propaganda that they were seeking to introduce there? They put upon the stand their chief exponent in this part of the country, to tell you what their purpose was in coming to the city of Everett, and what the doctrines were that they were teaching to the people that congregated there in the city of Everett. Mr. Thompson was upon the stand for about two days, and he delivered to this jury a lecture, which he says was a resume of three lectures that he gave up there in the city of Everett. He was asked whether or not he talked on sabotage and he told you what he had to say about it. He said sabotage was 'a conscious withdrawal of efficiency, a folding of the arms.' But Thompson says it is never the destruction of property, and yet the organization that sends him out to talk on sabotage puts out right along with him the literature that has been adopted by the I. W. W. as a part of their propaganda, defining what sabotage really is and it gives the lie to Mr. Thompson. It may mean working slow; it may mean poor work; it may mean folding of arms; it may mean conscious withdrawal of efficiency. So far sabotage is legal and anyone has a right to use it. But it may mean the spoiling of a finished product, it may mean the destruction of parts of machinery, it is the destruction of property. 'Sabotage is a direct application of the idea that property has no rights that its creators are bound to respect.' It does not say that certain kinds of property has no rights, but that there is no property that has any rights that are bound to be respected. But Thompson says that is not sabotage.

"Sabotage is what? Where is that old song book? Let us see whether it means simply the folding of the arms. (Cooley dived into a mass of pamphlets, but being unable to locate the song book he came up with Elizabeth Gurley Flynn's pamphlet on Sabotage, reading from it as follows:) 'Sabotage itself is not clearly defined. Sabotage is as broad and changing as industry, as flexible as the imagination and passions of humanity.' Why, if it consisted simply of a folding of the arms, if it consisted simply of the withdrawal of efficiency, there would not be much flexibility to it, would there, and the passions of humanity would have nothing to do with it? That language means that sabotage means anything that the imagination can devise and the passions of men adopt, if they had the power to use it and get away with it. Oh, it is not wrong! No matter what form it takes it is not wrong, because they say so in their official publication. 'The tactics used are determined solely by the power of the organization to make good in their use. The question of 'right' and 'wrong' does not concern us.' Put the two together. Legality and illegality, those terms have no meaning to a man of the Industrial Workers of the World. Why? Because there is no law that they are bound to respect except the law that is made by them in their own union hall. It is in the song book, 'Make your laws in the union hall, the rest can go to hell.' That is the class of people that we had to deal with, who were coming there to Everett.

"In Spokane there were twelve hundred convictions upon a valid ordinance, and yet, after they had convicted a hundred of them they didn't stop coming, and two hundred, and two hundred and fifty, and five hundred, and they continued coming there until the city jail of the city of Spokane was filled, until the county jail of Spokane county was filled, until an old deserted school house was filled, and then until an army post jail was filled. A species of sabotage! They weren't willing to accept the verdict of one jury, or ten juries, or of a hundred juries, that they were violating the law. They had made their laws in their union halls and they were going to speak at a certain place, upon a certain street of Spokane; and they were going to compel the citiz-

Charles Ashleigh speaking at the funeral, of Looney, Baran and Gerlot.

ens of Spokane to let them speak when they pleased, where they pleased, and say what they pleased; and they kept it up until after Spokane had the expense of a thousand trials and had upon its hands a thousand defendants it began to think it had better yield and let them speak when they pleased, where they pleased and say what they pleased. And Spokane was licked!

"Is it any wonder that the citizens of Everett said 'If you have no regard for law we will meet you on your own ground; we are not going to be bankrupted; we are not going to be hammered into defeat as they were in Spokane; we are not going to have you sabotage us in that manner by your numbers; we are not going to have your people coming from the Dakotas, from Montana, from Oregon, and from all over the various parts of the state of Washington, and camping down on us until we surrender to you. We are going to keep you out of here.' Now, that may not have been strictly legal, but it was human nature.

"There is not hint anywhere in the argument of either counsel for the defense in this case as to what was ever done in the city of Everett by the I. W. W. that would constitute new methods and new tactics. Do you remember the testimony over a period of time there before Labor Day that they allowed them to speak without interference and a meeting was held there and every time they went up with a chip on their shoulder and were not satisfied when no one interfered with them. When they were there speaking on the corner of Hewitt and Wetmore somebody was going around the city of Everett distributing a nasty stinking chemical in the theater building, into the store buildings, into the business houses, into the automobiles. And the paper in the next issue gloats over it and intimates that the reason the officers did not arrest Feinberg was because they were evidently too busy chasing a cat of malodorous tendencies. When Thompson was upon the stand and was being questioned about sabotage and about cats; he could tell you what a cat was, he got a bit halting in his speech when he was asked what it meant when they said that the claws of the cat had been sharpened, when he was asked what a 'sabcat' meant, but when he was asked as to what a cat of 'malodorous tendencies' was he said he didn't know unless it was a skunk. But by that was meant that the skunk accomplishes sabotage. You never heard of a skunk that did sabotage by simply a withdrawal of efficiency, never!

"Now as to incendiary and phosphorous fires. Fire Chief Terrell tells you that up to the date of September 28th, the date of the first known phosphorous fire in Everett, that up to that time, in all of his experience upon the fire force of the city of Everett, it never had come to his knowledge or observation in any way that a phosphorous fire had ever occurred in the city. It occurred there, known to be a phosphorous fire, and within a period of two months at least two other fires occurred, mysterious, the origin unknown because the fire had progressed to such an extent that no one could tell how it did start."

Mr. Vanderveer: Didn't your detective go to work September 21st?

Mr. Cooley: Yes sir, he did.

"And they would have you believe that the detective was up there setting those fires. That, I know, is an insinuation not supported by any evidence in this case, and the detective wasn't working up there, he was operating down here in the city of Seattle. He was sending his reports to Blain before the Wanderer started out, before the men started out on October 30th, and that goes a good way to explain how it happened how these people were met on these different excursions and were not permitted to come within the city of Everett. They were trying to get into the city of Everett, to use their own judgment, to act on their own initiative, according to instructions that had gone out. And the officers stopped the thing before it started.

"What were they coming to Everett for, these forty-one men who were met? Were they coming to hold a street meeting? Forty-one men, enthused with the enthusiasm of the belief in their grand and glorious doctrine that they are teaching, forty-one men starting out as crusaders to carry the gospel of their organization to the benighted of Everett, forty-one going up there to be martyrs, to be beaten for the cause, and nothing else!

"I have told of the tactics and methods advocated, used and encouraged, by this peculiar, particular organization, so you can judge the character, purpose and intentions of the individuals that were seeking from time to time to force themselves into the city of Everett, in order that you may judge the two hundrd and sixty that left on the Verona on November the 5th.

"But there is another matter you should likewise take into consideration in determining the character of the individuals of that crowd. Regardless of all environment, regardless of the effect of all legislation, regardless of all social conditions, men are born—not all with the same propensities, not all with the same natural ambitions, not all with the same qualifications, and out of the entire mass of humanity there is a certain percentage that were born without any ambition, born without any incentive; they go thru life without any incentive, constantly tired. Now I am not here to say that all the I. W. W.'s are that kind of people. I am not here to say that because a man is a member of the I. W. W. he is a tramp or a hobo. But there is a class that has been recognized in this country ever since the country existed, a class that don't want to work, that would not work if you gave them an opportunity. These are a percentage, I don't know how large, and I say that every one of these people are members of the I. W. W. organization or should be. Why? Well, in the first place, you don't have to show any qualification for any line of work. You don't have to make proof of anything whatever to become a member of that organization. And is there any inducement for a man who has been drifting here and there, walking the ties, counting the mile posts as he walks from one place to another, to join that organization? It gives him a pass upon every freight train that travels the length and breadth of the land. One of the best inducements in the world.

"There is another class of people in this country that are born with criminal instincts implanted in their very natures; they are scattered all over this land and we have them with us and we will always have them with us. There are men who are driven to crime thru misfortune; there are men who commit crime under the influence of environment; but there is a percentage of men who are habitual, natural and instinctive criminals. Now I don't say that because a man is a member of the I. W. W. he is necessarily and instinctively a criminal, but I do say that every habitual, instinctive criminal, who knows that he intends to violate the law upon every opportunity to satisfy his own criminal desire, has every inducement to become a member of that organization.

"There are a few uncontested and undisputed facts in connection with the occurrence at the dock. Jefferson Beard was killed on that dock. No doubt about that! The defendant was on the boat. No question about that! There is no question that the conversation between McRae and the people on the boat occurred substantially in the language that you have heard repeated here by witnesses for the State and for the defense, all agreeing that the conversation preceded the shooting. There is no dispute that McRae turned partially away from the boat and that one of the first three shots fired hit McRae while he was turning. The burden of the whole argument of the defense was that when somebody on the boat saw McRae put his hand on his gun he was justified in shooting. It is not material whether Tracy shot Jefferson Beard or somebody else. It is not material whether Tracy fired a gun or not, provided the evidence in this case satisfies you beyond a reasonable doubt that Tracy was a party to the conspiracy to go up to the city of Everett to violate an ordinance of the city of Everett.

"But have you any doubt that Tracy was seen

on the boat? Hogan saw the window and he saw a man with his face at the window shooting in his direction. Hogan wasn't thinking of the exact angle at which the boat was standing to the dock, but he knows he was standing at such an angle to the boat that he could see a man in a certain place on the boat. And he testified he did see him.

"It wasn't Thomas Tracy that was looking out of that window, it was Martin. It wasn't Thomas Tracy dressed for the occasion, it wasn't Thomas Tracy shaven for a picnic, it wasn't Thomas Tracy wearing a Sunday countenance, it wasn't Thomas Tracy gazing placidly out of a mild blue eye! It was Thomas Tracy, alias Martin, with his face drawn down into a scowl of hatred, with his eyebrows lowering over his eyes, gazing at John Hogan, not only gazing at him thru a window, but gazing at him over a gun! And if there is anything that would impress itself into the memory and recollection of a man it is the remembrance of a face filled with venomous hatred, the eyes shooting daggers at you while he is gazing at you over the muzzle of a gun—and you are not going to forget that!

"Counsel for the defense says this is an important trial, that important questions are involved, that the verdict in this case will have a great deal to do with the ultimate future of the working man and organized labor. I don't think that matters of that kind should enter the minds of the jurors in arriving at a verdict, but if it does, I want to supplement what counsel for the defense has said. I want to say that in my mind a verdict in this case will have much to do with the future success and the future advancement of honest labor in every line and in all organizations. It will have much to do with clarifying the situation insofar as this one organization is concerned. Every organization don't preach the doctrines that are preached by this organization, and if this jury by its verdict does not support that kind of method and that kind of procedure it will aid in purifying an organization that otherwise might do a world of good, but as it stands today, uttering the propaganda that it does, pursuing the tactics that it does it, is a menace not only to society, but is a menace to the welfare of the other labor organizations that believe in pursuing lawful methods, in a lawful manner. This is an important case in that regard.

"I believe that it is a fortune thing that a jury of King County and a jury from the city of Seattle should have been called to try this case. The seed was not planted in Snohomish County! The plot was not hatched in Snohomish County! It was hatched down here in Seattle. The expedition started out from Seattle, not this one alone but many of them. Seattle was the base, the enemy's base, and it was from here that they started. Just down here almost in sight of this court house is the place where we claim the plot was formed, and it has come back here, and we come into court and lay it at your feet. They returned here, they have brought the case here for trial, and we are satisfied. Now we lay it before you and say,—'As citizens of Seattle do justice to the city of Everett and Snohomish County.'"

With these words ringing in their ears the twelve jurors retired for their deliberations, the court having entered an order discharging from further service the two alternate jurors, Efaw and Williams.

Retiring shortly before noon, the jury consulted for nearly twenty-two hours, taking ballot after ballot only to find that there were some who steadfastly refused to agree to any compromise verdict. Then, shortly after nine o'clock on May 5th, two full calendar months after the start of the trial and just six months to the day from the time of the tragedy of the Verona, Foreman James R. Williams announced the result of their deliberations, and the word sped out to the many hundred thousands who had spent an anxious and sleepless night;

"We, the jury, find the defendant, Thomas H. Tracy, NOT GUILTY!"

CHAPTER IX.

SOLIDARITY SCORES A SUCCESS

"I. W. W. Not Guilty!"

In this headline the daily papers of Seattle, Washington, gave the findings of the jury. With an unbroken series of successful prosecutions of Labor to the credit of the Merchants and Manufacturers Association this, the first great victory for the working class on the Pacific Coast, was a bitter pill for the allied employers and open shop interests to swallow.

With Tracy freed and the I. W. W. exonerated, there was nothing for the Snohomish County officials to do but to release the rest of the free speech prisoners. Yet the same contemptible spirit that had marked their actions from the very start of the trouble led them to hold the prisoners for several days and to try to make a few of the men think that there would be a trial of a second prisoner.

Part of the men were released in Seattle and part in Everett. All went at once to the I. W. W. hall upon gaining their freedom, and from there nearly the whole body of released men went to Mount Pleasant cemetery to visit the graves of their dead fellow workers.

Returning to the hall, those who had previously been delegates, or who had fitted themselves for the work while in jail, immediately took out credentials and started on an organizing campaign of the Northwest, with the uniting of the workers in the lumber industry as their main object.

The dearth of workers due to the war, the tremendous advertisement the I. W. W. had received because of the tragedy and the trial, and the spirit of mingled determination and resentment that had grown up in the jail, made the work easy for these volunteer organizers. Members joined by the dozen, then by the score, and finally by the hundreds.

Gus Johnson **Felix Baran** **John Looney**

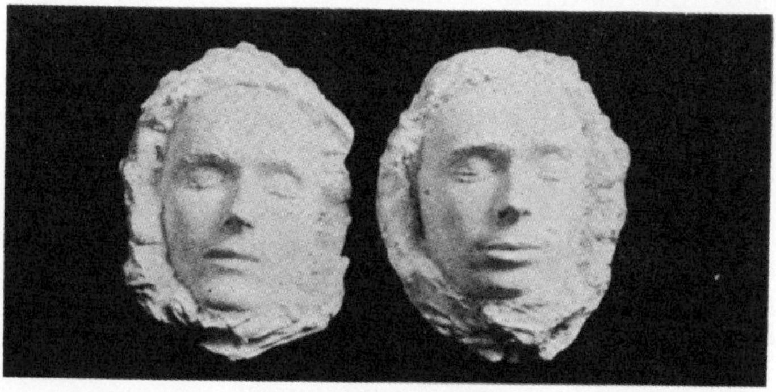

Hugo Gerlot **Abraham Rabinowitz**

Seattle had but two officials under pay on November 5th—Herbert Mahler, secretary of the I. W. W., and J. A. MacDonald, editor of the Industrial Worker. By July 4th, 1917, one year from the time of the loggers' convention at which there were only half a hundred paid up members, the I. W. W. in Seattle had thirty people under pay, working at top speed to take care of the constantly increasing membership, and preparations were under way to launch the greatest lumber strike ever pulled in the history of the industry with the eight hour day as the main demand. That strike in which thousands of men stood out for week after week in the face of persecution of every character, in the face of raids upon their halls and the illegal detention of hundreds of members by city, county, state and federal agents, and in the face of deportations by mobs of lumber trust hirelings, deserves a volume to itself.

This activity in the lumber industry reflected itself in all other lines, particularly so in construction projects all over the Northwest. Demands for litertaure, for speakers, for organizers, flooded the offices of the organization and many opportunities to organize had to be passed by simply because there were not enough men capable of taking up the work.

Part of this growth was of those who had interested themselves in the trial. Many of those who had gone on the witness stand for the defense afterwards took out membership cards in the I. W. W. The women of Everett,—considerably more inclined toward revolutionary ideas than the men there, by the way,—were among the first to ask for a "red card."

Too great praise cannot be given to those who voluntarily gave their services to the defense and thus helped to bring about a verdict of acquittal. Thru the work of Mr. A. L. Carpenter a great deal of valuable information was secured and it was thru his efforts that Deputy Joseph Schofield was brought from Oregon to testify for the defense. For his activity on behalf of organized labor Mr. Carpenter received the rebel's reward—he was discharged from his position as district manager of a large corporation. Scores of Everett citizens gave splendid assistance to the defense, asking only that their names be withheld on account of the Commercial Club blacklist.

All persons directly in the employ of the defense proved their worth. Deserving special mention in their work of investigation were Rev. T. T. Edmunds, W. A. Loomis and John M. Foss. The Reverend Edmunds, being no follower of a "cold statistical Christ" and having more of humanitarianism than theology or current religion in his makeup, was able to gain information where many another investigator might have failed. The expert services of Loomis were of no less value, while the particular merit of the work of John Foss was that he went to Everett immediately after the catastrophe, at a time when chaos still reigned and when the blood-lust of the deputies had not yet completely given way to craven fear, and worked there night and day until a verdict of acquittal for his fellow workers was practically assured. Both as an investigator and as correspondent to the I. W. W. press, C. E. Payne, familiarly known as "Stumpy," proved himself invaluable. Charles Ashleigh handled the publicity for the Everett Prisoners' Defense Committee in an able and efficient manner, while to Herbert Mahler credit is due for the careful and painstaking handling of the large fund raised to fight the case thru the courts.

"Justice" is an expensive luxury in the lumber kingdom. Independent of the large amount of money spent directly by individuals and by branches of the I. W. W. the cost of the verdict of acquittal was $37,835.84. Nearly thirty-eight thousand dollars! Thirty-eight thousand dollars to free innocent workers from the clutches of the law! The victims in jail and the murderers at liberty! But then, the last thing expected of "Justice" is that it be just.

Whence came the fund that, as a token of solidarity, set the free speech prisoners at liberty? In the financial statement of the Everett Prisoners Defense Committee it is set forth in full. Summarized, this report shows that Labor united in the defense of the prisoners, that, while this case was more largely financed directly thru the I. W. W. than any other trial of the organization, there were many and generous contributions from local unions of the American Federation of Labor, from the Workers' Sick and Death Benefit Fund, from various other working class societies and from sources so numerous as to make special mention impossible. But these receipts varied from a dollar bill sent by "A poor Working Stiff" from North Bend, Oregon, to a donation of $3.75 from the Benevolent Society for the Propagating of Cremation at Yonkers, New York.

Hundreds of dollars were raised in Seattle by the I. W. W. thru smokers, dances, theatrical benefits, entertainments and collections by speakers who told the story of Bloody Sunday before societies of every kind and character. The Dreamland Rink meetings, attended in every instance by thousands of people, were the means of bringing hundreds of dollars to the defense. A considerable fund was raised directly within the organization by the sale of embossed leatherette membership card cases issued in memoriam to the martyred dead. In Seattle notable service was rendered by the International Workers' Defense League.

The nature of the case demanded heavy expenditures unlike those required in any of the previous trials in which I. W. W. members were involved. Many of the witnesses were men who had beaten their way from long distances thru storms and snow to be in readiness to testify in behalf of their imprisoned fellow workers, and most of these had to be maintained at a relief station until called upon the stand. The care of the wounded was an added item, and there were many necessary expenditures for the big body of prisoners held as defendants. To each of the men who was released at the end of the six months imprisonment there was given a sum of $10. Owing to the sweeping nature of the conspiracy charges and because of the large number of witnesses endorsed by the State, all of whom re-

May First at Graveside of Gerlot, Baran and Looney.

quired investigation, there was a large sum required for use in taking these necessary legal precautions. Heavy charges were also made for the work of the stenographers who recorded the evidence, this being an item borne by the State in most parts of the country. The totals of these expenditures were as follows:

Counsel fees in full	$8,470.00
Legal investigation	8,955.36
Court stenographers	3,354.30
Miscellaneous legal expense	1,304.20
Office expense	1,942.53
Publicity work	4,830.44
Miscellaneous accounts	8,457.37
Total expenditures	$37,314.20

A balance of $521.64 was sent to the General Headquarters of the I. W. W. and this, with $581.36 which remained in the General Office from the sale of voluntary assessment stamps, was set aside as a fund to be used for the maintenance of HarryGolden, Joseph Ghilezano and Albert Scribner, three of the boys who were seriously injured on the Verona.

The financial report was audited by E. G. Shorrock and Co., certified accountants, and by a committee composed of Harry Feinberg and J. H. Beyer, representing the prisoners, C. H. Rice, representing the Seattle unions of the I. W. W., and General Executive Board member, Richard Brazier, representing the General Headquarters of the I. W. W. The statement made to contributors to the fund concluded with these expressive words:

"On behalf of the defendants, and the Industrial Workers of the World, we take this opportunity to express our grateful appreciation to all contributors, and to all the brave men and women who assisted us so nobly in this great struggle to save seventy-three workingmen from a living death at the hands of the Lumber Trust and the allied commercial bodies of the Pacific Coast.

"It was the solidarity of the working class, and that alone, which brought about this great victory for labor, so let us turn fresh from victory, with determined hearts and unquellable spirit to unflinchingly continue the struggle for the liberation of all prisoners of the class war, remembering always that greatest expression of solidarity, 'An injury to one, is an injury to all.'

"THE EVERETT PRISONERS DEFENSE COMMITTEE.

THOMAS MURPHY,
CHARLES ASHLEIGH,
WM. J. HOUSER,
RICHARD SMITH,
HERBERT MAHLER, Sec'y-Treas."

Seattle, Wash.,
June 12th, 1917.

CHAPTER X.

THE BANKRUPTCY OF "LAW AND ORDER"

The facts in this case speak pretty well for themselves. To draw conclusions at length would be an impertinence. He who runs may read the signs of decay of Capitalism, the crumbling of a social system based upon the slavery and degradation of the vast majority of mankind. And from the lips of the prosecution counsel—the Voice of the State—we have the open and frank acknowledgement of the bankrupcy of law and order, the failure of government as it is now administered.

It is no part of this work to attack The Law. The Law is august, majestic in its impartial findings and the equality of its judgements, always however with due allowance for those subtle distinctions so incomprehensible to the masses which exist between high finance, kleptomania and theft. The Law strips no one of his possessions; under its beneficent reign the rich retain their wealth and the poor keep their poverty. Founded on dogma and moulded by tradition, The Law stands as a mighty monument to Justice. It is ever in this way that we show our respect and reverence for the dead. Being an outgrowth of precedent it gains added sanctity with each fresh proof of antiquity, differing in this regard from automobiles, eggs, women, hats, the six best sellers, and the commoner things of life. Surrounded by mysticism, surcharged with the language of the dead, and sustained by force, who is there would have the temerity to question the sanctity of The Law?

It remained for Attorneys Black and Cooley—and not for the outcast industrial unionists, socialists or anarchists—to charge that The Law is a bankrupt institution, and it was for the citizen-deputies — and not for the despised workers — to prove the truth of the indictment. Truly Society moves in a mysterious way its blunders to reform!

With the true logic of the counting-house Cooley admitted that the mill owners had formed a mob to protect themselves from the rabble, they had pursued illegal methods to prevent the breaking of The Law, they had jailed men in order to preserve Liberty, they had even blacklisted union men in order to give to every man the right to work where, when and for whom he pleased. There is no escaping such logic if one owns property. Of course those who possess no property are the natural enemies of property, and law being based upon property, they are defiers of The Law, and Society being upheld only by observance of The Law, they are the foes of Society. It is not best to kill them in too large numbers for they are useful in doing the work of the world, but they must be kept in fear and trembling of The Law and made to respect it as sacred and invilable, even if we do not. So argued Black and Cooley.

But the whine of Black, the snarl of Cooley, the moody silence of Veitch, alike served as a confession that "law and order" was a failure. The plea of the State was that all law is the creature of property and when the power of the law proves inadequate in its function of protecting the accumulations of wealth the possessors of property are justified in supplementing The Law with such additional physical or brute force as they can muster, or in casting aside The Law altogether, as it suits their convenience. To the workers The Law must remain sacred while to the leisure class Property is the thing to worship, for however much robbery is to be condemned, the proceeds of robbery are always to be respected.

Their further contention was that the streets are for traffic, for maintaining commerce, in other words to aid in the gathering of property and to enhance the property values already cleared. Out of the graciousness of their hearts the business men and employers allow the pedestrians to use the streets incidental to the purchase of goods or to journey to and from their tasks in the factories, mines, mills and workshops. That the streets might be used for social, religious, political or educational purposes does not enter their calculations, their ledgers carry no place for such entries on the profit side. Free speech is tolerated at times provided nothing of importance is said.

Two trials were going on in the court room at the same time; that of Thomas H. Tracy and the I. W. W. before a property-qualified jury, and that of the existing system of law enforcement before the great jury of the working class. And just as surely as was the verdict that of acquittal for Tracy and his union, was there a most decided judgment of Guilty upon "law and order." For Tracy was not freed by the law but by the common sense of the jury who refused to consider him guilty and viewed him as a class rather than as an individual. Under the existing conspiracy laws he might well have been considered technically guilty. But "law and order" technically and otherwise was proven guilty, and the charge that Capitalism is guilty of first degree murder, and a host of other crimes, was clearly proven.

Why? Why all the brutality depicted herein? Why?

The answer is that we are living in an insane social system in which money ranks higher than manhood.

To be more specific the outrages at Everett had their roots in the belief that the men who labor, and especially the migratory and the unskilled element, form an inferior caste or class to those who exploit them. The dominant class viewed any attempt to claim even the same civil rights as an assault upon their supremacy and integrity,—this to them being synonymous with social order and civilization. This is always more evident where a single industry dominates, as evidenced by the occurrences at Ludlow, in the coal district, Mesaba in the iron ore section, and Bisbee where copper is the main product. Everett controlled by the lumber interests clinches the argument.

A community dominated by an industry, impelled by a desire for high profits; or under the spell of fear or passion, whether justified or not, cannot be restrained by law from a summary satisfaction of its desires or a quieting of its apprehensions. Before such a condition the fabric of local government crumbles and lynch law is substituted for the more orderly processes designed to attain the same end. The Everett outrages were no example of the rough and ready justice of primitive communities. The outlaws were in full possession of local government, legislative, judicial, and executive, yet they fell back upon brute force and personal violence and attempted to protect the lumber trust profits by tactics of terrorism.

Insofar as the law can be wielded for their immediate purpose a capitalistic mob, such as these at Everett, will clothe their violence in the form of ostensible legal process, yet often the letter and the spirit of their own class-influenced laws will be ruthlessly thrust aside. They want law and order, efficacious, impartial, august, in the eyes of the general citizenry, but they want exemption of their class from the rule of the law on certain occasions. Strongly would they deny that all law is class law, made, interpreted and administered in behalf of a privileged property-owning class, yet the facts bear out this contention.

The conception of impersonal and impartial legalism has been generally accepted along with traditional moral opinion and the naive belief in the excellence of competitive, individualistic, and unrestrained business. But this historical case has proven, as nothing else could prove, that these bonds are relaxing and the faith and formulas underlying the whole legal establishment are the subject of attack by an increasingly large and uncompromising army of dissenters.

From the developments of the Everett situation one can sense the rising tide of industrial solidarity. It was the unity of the workers that won the great case. It will be the unity of Labor that will win the world for the workers, just as the embryonic democracy of the toilers in its blind groupings has already cracked the shell of the industrial autocracy of the present day.

At present we are at the parting of the ways. There is not sufficient faith in the Law to hold the dying wage system together and there is not a sufficiently clear conception of the solidaric ideal of a new society to bind the rebellious elements to a definite program. So chaos reigns in society and events like those at Everett may be expected to arise until the struggle of the exploited takes on a more constructive form and develops the necessary power to overthrow capitalism and all its attendant institutions.

Industrial unionism is the only hope of the disinherited and dispossessed proletariat. It is the voice of the future. It spells at once Evolution and Revolution. Its assured success means an end to classes and class rule and the rearing of a race of free individuals.

The strength of the workers is in industry. Every worker, man, woman or child, has economic power. The control of industry means the control of the world.

He who strives to bring the workers closer together so that their allied forces in an industrial organization may overthrow the wage system and rear in its place an Industrial Republic in which slavery will be unknown and where joy will form the mainspring of human activity, pays the highest homage to those who, in order that the spirit of Liberty might not perish from the land, gave their lives at Everett, Washington, on Sunday, November 5th, 1917:

FELIX BARAN,
HUGO GERLOT,
GUSTAV JOHNSON,
JOHN LOONEY,
ABRAHAM RABINOWITZ.

FINISH